Doing Research Projects in Marketing, Management and Consumer Research

As interpretive research perspectives become increasingly influential in many fields of social science research, so it becomes more important for inexperienced researchers to become familiar with the philosophical perspectives, data-gathering techniques and analytical methods that derive from interpretive research.

This book draws on these interpretive traditions to illustrate precisely how they can be applied to research projects for first-time researchers in the fields of management, marketing and consumer research. Offering many practical examples drawn from existing studies and suggesting new topics for consideration, this book brings together major themes of interpretive research within a practical guide to researching and writing a research project. Topics covered include:

- choosing the topic;
- planning and writing the academic research report;
- gathering qualitative data for interpretation;
- themes and concepts of interpretive research;
- the major interpretive traditions: semiotics, phenomenology, ethnography; critical discourse analysis, feminism and gender studies; literary theory and narrative analysis.

Suitable both for first-time researchers and those with more experience, this is an ideal guide for anyone undertaking research in this area of study.

Chris Hackley is Senior Lecturer in Marketing at Birmingham Business School, Birmingham University. He has published extensively on the subject of marketing and research.

Doing Research Projects in Marketing, Management and Consumer Research

Chris Hackley

Routledge
Taylor & Francis Group

LONDON AND NEW YORK

First published 2003 by Routledge
2 Park Square, Milton Park, Abingdon, Oxon, OX14 4RN

Simultaneously published in the USA and Canada
by Routledge
270 Madison Ave, New York NY 10016

Routledge is an imprint of the Taylor & Francis Group

Transferred to Digital Printing 2005

© 2003 Chris Hackley

Typeset in Sabon by Wearset Ltd, Boldon, Tyne and Wear

British Library Cataloguing in Publication Data
A catalogue record for this book is available from the British
Library

Library of Congress Cataloging in Publication Data
A Catalog record for this book has been requested

ISBN 0-415-26894-x (hbk)
ISBN 0-415-26895-8 (pbk)

Printed and bound by Antony Rowe Ltd, Eastbourne

Contents

Boxes

Foreword

Obviously, what the world needs is a how-to book that is clearly geared to the interests, talents and skills of the undergraduate or graduate student that covers the introductory material. Now, at last, into the breach strides Chris Hackley with this new text on *Doing Interpretive Research*. Specifically, Chris provides a carefully crafted, masterfully well-written, expertly constructed, wonderfully useful tutorial to guide the student through the process of understanding and applying the various interpretivistic approaches to marketing, management and consumer research. In essence, Chris tells the story of qualitative or post-positivistic research in a reader-friendly way that will endear itself to students even as it prepares them for applications to their own interests and careers. He offers helpful instruction for those eager to adopt approaches likely to lead towards interpretivistic epiphanies, qualitative discoveries and post-positivistic insights. Not so much 'Interpretation For Dummies', I guess, as a pithy compilation of *What You've Always Wanted To Know About Interpretivistic Methods But Were Afraid To Ask*.

In addressing these issues, Chris has shown remarkable breadth of coverage in a way that introduces his audience to the full spectrum of interpretivistic approaches from which to choose – ethnography, depth interviews, semiotics, hermeneutics, phenomenological methods, critical theory, literary analysis, feminist studies, postmodernism and so forth. Each approach receives careful consideration with detailed attention to both its merits and its limitations, to key learning objectives, to important caveats, to practical guidelines, and to one or more inspired illustrations. In short, Chris equips his readers with a toolkit – bordering on an arsenal – for attacking a wide range of questions as timely as they are fascinating.

Some might view the work by Hackley as a bit like a cookbook in an area suffused with postmodern relativism where, most appropriately, 'anything goes' in choosing one's ingredients and recipes. But, if so, it is a gourmet cookbook that prescribes the judicious use of truffles and foie gras in an era when other books on topics related to marketing research are fast-foodish or fad-foolish paeans to the culinary analogues of hot dogs and French fries. Put differently, imbued with a fine sense of interpretivistic inquisitiveness, Chris refuses to condescend to the all-too-prevalent McDonaldization of Methods.

So here it is – a sumptuous feast for the interpretivistically inclined. Dig in, I say, and enjoy it with the appropriate degree of dedicated delectation. For there is much to savour here and much that will enrich our diets as interpretive researchers.

Morris B. Holbrook
Dillard Professor of Marketing
Graduate School of Business
Columbia University

Acknowledgements

This book has evolved from personal experience of teaching and supervising in marketing, management and consumer research. This experience has been connected to the work of international students of marketing, management and consumer studies doing undergraduate, master's and in some cases PhD-level research projects, dissertations or theses. The non-attributed examples of interpretive research applications in this book are adapted from their experiences as student researchers, and mine as supervisor. I thank all the many excellent students I have been privileged to supervise.

While my own students over the years are too many to name I will specifically thank Dr Barry Ardley and his supervisors Mr David Pickton and Professor Peter Baron at De Montfort University, Leicester, UK, for giving permission for me to refer to Dr Ardley's insightful work in the chapter on phenomenological research.

I am grateful to colleagues in the universities in which I have worked over the years for many enlightening discussions on supervision and research methods in marketing and related areas. I owe a particular debt to Dr Marylyn Carrigan, Senior Lecturer and Dissertation Tutor at Birmingham Business School, the University of Birmingham, for conscientiously reading a draft of this book and offering helpful and perceptive suggestions.

Professor Morris Holbrook of Columbia University, New York, has published much definitive work that has pioneered interpretive research in marketing, consumer research and beyond. His unique contribution to the field made him an ideal person to write a foreword for this book. I am grateful for his approachability and kindness in agreeing to do so.

Finally, the book has appeared because of the encouragement and constructive critique of the anonymous reviewers of the original proposal and the enthusiasm of Routledge's Editor, Francesca. Once again, my thanks.

The book is dedicated to Suzanne, Michael, James and Nicholas.

Introduction

Doing research projects in marketing, management and consumer research

This book draws on interpretive traditions of social science research to illustrate how these can be applied to qualitative research projects for first-time researchers in marketing, management and consumer research. It is also useful as a primer for more experienced researchers who are not familiar with the wealth of philosophical perspectives, data-gathering techniques and analytical methods that derive from interpretive research. The book offers many practical examples drawn from recent studies and also suggests many new topics.

Interpretive research perspectives have become highly influential in many fields of social science research, both as ways of developing rigorous constructs for quantitative research studies and as ends in themselves for researchers seeking 'rich descriptions' and qualitative insights. As management and marketing studies have grown in popularity as the subjects of taught university courses, powerful traditions of interpretive research have emerged within these fields. In the USA influential research agenda based on interpretive methods have emerged in the fields of consumer behaviour and advertising, epitomized by work in the *Journal of Consumer Research* and the *Journal of Advertising*. Interpretive approaches deriving from ethnography and literary theory have also appeared as research studies in the *Journal of Marketing Research* and *Journal of Marketing*. The 'interpretive turn' in academic management and marketing research in Europe and the UK has resulted in many new research studies being published in leading journals, such as the *European Journal of Marketing*, the *Journal of Management Studies* and the *British Journal of Management*. There is now a well-established book series, the *Routledge Interpretive Marketing Research* series, which brings together the work of leading US and European writers on diverse interpretive traditions in interpretive marketing research. Published studies include those providing ethnographies of management in differing organizations and in contrasting management functions, those focusing on consumption as a major site of meaning and social identity formation, or on the situated symbolic practices of marketing management and the symbolism of marketing techniques and concepts.

Many others draw on traditions of phenomenology, gender studies, anthropology and critical discourse analysis.

Interpretive approaches have also become increasingly influential in management practice. For example, the field of brand and marketing consultancy employs techniques deriving from ethnography, as evidenced by press coverage in the UK *Sunday Times* Business Section (25 August 2002, section 3, p. 8). The author has found that the world's leading advertising agencies increasingly employ interpretive techniques drawn from anthropology in their pursuit of penetrating consumer insights that they can use to inform the development of marketing and communications strategy.

The intense interest in interpretive concepts, techniques and philosophies that originated in anthropology and qualitative sociology has led many more student researchers in university business schools to adopt interpretive perspectives for their own undergraduate or postgraduate research studies. Many research students have applied interpretive approaches in their PhD research. However, student researchers who wish to find out more about interpretive social research find a vast library of texts that deal with a huge number of methodological variations, many of which are written for readerships already well versed in research practice and philosophy. Relatively few texts are available for first-time student researchers in management fields who are interested in learning more about interpretive perspectives for qualitative research.

This book brings together major themes of interpretive research within a practical guide to researching and writing a research project. It is interdisciplinary in spirit in that it acknowledges the common ground and common interests in the various management and business sub-fields. It treats marketing, management and consumer research as areas that explore aspects of overlapping organizational functions and activities. The first part of the book reflects this as it takes a generic approach and focuses on practical advice for the pragmatic first-time marketing/management student researcher. The later chapters offer sophisticated introductions to important interpretive research traditions and suggest practical hints on how to apply these to produce a successful research project report. The aim is to help the many students and researchers in management fields who wish to see how to apply these concepts in their own research projects.

Chapter 1

Interpretive perspectives and the independent research project

Chapter outline

This chapter explains the scope, perspective and structure of the book. *Doing Research Projects in Marketing, Management and Consumer Research* is aimed at a very broad range of student researchers working in and across management and marketing subject areas. It has a distinctive approach that combines practical hints and insights with new theoretical developments. This approach emphasizes everyday, practical management problems and issues; creative, inductive research designs; and the use of naturally occurring research data sets.

Chapter objectives

After reading this chapter the student will be able to

- appreciate the role of the research project in the student's management education
- understand important distinctions, such as those between exploratory and confirmatory research designs
- be aware of the scope of possible research topics in marketing and management research
- understand the nature and importance of the supervisory relationship

---

Who this book is for

This book is written primarily as a practical guide for students doing a research project for the first time. However, it will also be useful for those with some experience of social research in business and management fields who want to learn more about interpretive theories and methods. Many students on taught business and management courses are not familiar with social science research concepts and terms. The independent research project (also described as a 'thesis' or 'dissertation', depending on different countries' traditions) is an entirely new experience for many students on taught bachelor's or master's degrees. University departments do provide research workshops and dedicated personal academic supervisors, but the research project must, in the end, be completed by the student as an independent researcher. The book focuses on practical advice for pragmatic student researchers but also introduces important developments in research theory that provide the essential intellectual framework for the academic research project.

The book is written so that it can be usefully read from beginning to end but it can also be 'dipped' into for tips on particular topics. Throughout the text there are examples and illustrations drawn from completed student research projects. The author and colleagues have supervised many successful research projects at first degree, master's degree and PhD level. Many of these projects are referred to in order to show new student researchers what kind of work is possible and how it can be accomplished.

This book is aimed at a wide readership of business and management student researchers with a particular interest in marketing-related issues. The book will also be helpful to those studying for research degrees in areas that connect to business, management and consumer studies. Students of combined degrees in social science, arts and humanities whose studies bring them into contact with marketing, consumption and advertising will also find the book a useful resource for planning and writing a research project. The book emphasizes qualitative data-gathering methods and theoretical perspectives that draw on the interpretive social research traditions. This implies a creative and cross-disciplinary, yet theoretically well-founded approach to social research in marketing, management and consumption. It is hoped that student researchers can use the book and the many sources that are cited within it to make their independent research project a more satisfying, rewarding and, perhaps, less stressful experience.

The research project is a daunting task even for the most able student. Even with the guidance of an excellent supervisor it still represents a stepping-off point from taught courses. Students on research degrees of PhD and MPhil can also find that writing their first-year progress report brings them into contact with issues of research philosophy, data-gathering methods and data analysis that they have not encountered in their studies before. The relative lack of research theory in the vocationally orientated curriculum of most business and management degrees means that the student then has a very wide gulf to cross to write a successful (and enjoyable) research dissertation. For many students the very idea of 'research' seems removed from their everyday experience. This sense of research as a special activity distinct from conventional studies can seem particularly strong in business and management courses. Taught courses in this area often derive directly from managerial perspectives and problems. Such problems may not be theoretically complex in themselves but research theories can help to generate insight and understanding and to suggest possible practical solutions.

Students with differing educational backgrounds will have different levels of knowledge of social research concepts. The vocabulary of social research in marketing and management is very different to the vocabulary of conventional texts used in taught courses. This book is written for those with no prior knowledge at all but it is also useful for those with some knowledge of social research who wish to learn more. Almost from the beginning there will be technical terms and concepts that may be new to the reader. Part of the student's task in completing the academic research project is to show that he or she can learn and use new concepts in discussing and evaluating research approaches to generating knowledge. The book introduces these specialist terms gently and places many of them in glossaries at the end of each chapter.

The range of possible project topics in the world of marketing and management

One of the most important aims of this book is to offer ways of researching the everyday, practical activities of management that do not seem irrelevant to or distant from the everyday concerns and activities of managers. The book advocates ways of researching that can be directly relevant to practical issues in these fields. The emphasis is placed on research perspectives that make theoretically informed interpretations of data and theory. While some introductory research methods texts emphasize the construction of questionnaires and the administration, and statistical analysis, of surveys, this text, in contrast, emphasizes the research value of naturally occurring qualitative data such as conversations, interviews and researcher observations. This approach to primary research is broadly labelled the 'interpretive' approach.

The book cannot make the research project a simple task but it does attempt to provide a number of clear signposts for students who want to do an interesting, creative and perhaps cross-disciplinary research project that reflects their own interests and abilities. In the following chapters there will be many examples of specific research projects and possible research projects that can give students ideas for refining their own research topics. The kinds of general topic area that might be researched using this book include, but are not limited to, those listed in Box 1.1 (The list is offered to stimulate the student's own research ideas: the suggested topics are deliberately broad, many overlap and each could be framed in a different way from those implied.)

There is indeed a huge variety of possible topic areas in marketing, management and consumer research. Within these topic areas there are

Box 1.1 Some general topic areas that can be researched using the approaches in this book

- Managerial or critical examinations of consumption and consumer issues with regard to particular product or service categories (e.g. new technology products), industry sectors (e.g. banking, leisure, manufacturing) or market segments (e.g. the 'cognitively' young older consumer, the 'generation X' younger consumer)
- International marketing studies with a particular industry/product focus (e.g. the design and management of international market entry strategies)
- Cross-cultural comparisons of consumer or advertising activities and practices
- Managerial or critical investigation of management activities and processes in specific organizations or settings
- Case study comparisons of business success factors in comparable industry sectors
- Explorations of management techniques in particular settings
- Critical examinations of the social role, organizational implications and human consequences of marketing and management activities and practices
- Localized case study research based on live in-company projects
- Studies of small business growth and development
- Studies of environmental management issues
- Qualitative psychological studies of consumer choice behaviour in particular consumption settings
- Studies that focus on a specific managerial aspect of marketing in a specified product/market such as pricing, promotion, distribution effectiveness
- New product development and innovation processes in a given organization or industry
- The management of, and consumption in, creative industries and the arts
- Creative processes in management practice
- Studies of relationships and control issues in the management of sourcing and supply
- Studies that focus on the human dimension of management such as reward systems, performance appraisal methods, motivation, job choice and satisfaction
- Gender-based studies focusing on a particular context of consumption or management

- Studies of management perceptions of the operational efficiency of specific management systems and processes
- Studies of tourism management in particular national and international settings
- Strategic planning models and practices in higher-level organizational management
- Effectiveness and/or efficiency in organizational marketing management assessed through inter-company or intra-industry comparisons
- Approaches to the management of key accounts or other aspects of 'relationship' management in service sectors
- Intra-organizational studies of communication and information systems framed, for example, as 'internal marketing' studies
- Managerial marketing segmentation practices in specified product industries
- Experiential studies of managing and being managed in organizational settings
- Experiential studies of consumption and its role in identity-construction and social positioning in specified social settings with regard to particular categories of consumption
- Studies that focus on how language is used to construct management identities and managerial authority
- Brand management studies in particular markets or industries
- Marketing communication strategies and practices in specified settings and product/market sectors
- Studies of social exclusion in, and through, marketing activity
- Studies of management failure and organizational dysfunction
- The promotion and nurturing of entrepreneurial behaviour and activities in particular industrial and social settings
- Non-profit and publicly funded managerial activities
- Experiential studies of entrepreneurship in action
- The effective management of technology in organizations
- The social and organizational implications of new technology
- The effects of particular technologies on employee job satisfaction/ on operational effectiveness
- Qualitative studies of service delivery in banking and other financial services, air or sea travel, retailing, and in any aspect of customer care

many variations possible on how the research issue is framed and expressed, which questions will be asked or explored, and which values will be implied. More will be said about how to choose a topic in Chapter 2. However, it is worth pointing out now that new student researchers typically think in terms of big categories when they first think about what to research. They often suggest 'branding', 'car retailing' or 'advertising', or they suggest that they will look at, say, factors affecting demand in personal computer markets. Later they learn that setting out a research project is both more complex and simpler than they realized. It is more complex in the sense that the way the research questions, issue or problem are phrased is crucial for the research design. Putting a research topic in a particular form of words carries implications about the data-gathering techniques and analytical stance of the research. On the other hand, research projects are also far simpler than trying to get to the core of a big category like 'branding'. A good student research project does not try to invent a grand theory but states a simple question that can be investigated in a reasonably systematic and thorough way, given the time and resources available to the student researcher. The research project that is part of a taught higher degree does not have to generate new knowledge. It simply has to demonstrate that the student has acquired certain academic, intellectual and practical skills. If the project is interesting and creative, then so much the better.

Interpretation and the research process

This book emphasizes a research approach that takes a theoretically informed interpretation of primary or secondary sources. Furthermore, it emphasizes an approach to primary research that uses naturally occurring sources of data such as interviews, written (textual) accounts of events and states, and observation (including participant observation) in everyday settings. There are several advantages to this perspective.

First, the kind of *data sets* that are emphasized are particularly suitable for student research projects because they are relatively easy to access and *samples* need not be randomized. Students completing a research project as part of a taught degree very rarely have the time or resources to complete a rigorous quantitative study, even if they have the statistical competence. Questionnaire surveys are time consuming and expensive to administrate, and the return rates are notoriously low. Studies based on experiments, too, are difficult to organize in marketing studies. Unless they form part of a sophisticated and carefully conceived research design, questionnaires or experiments conducted within the tight time-scale of taught programmes rarely generate robust findings.

Interpretive approaches offer a way of researching a given topic in depth and with sophistication without a statistically secure universalization of findings. Given that interpretive approaches usually rely on *qualitative* data (e.g. interviews, observation, focus groups) for their major findings, they are often used in the initial construct formation phase of studies that aim for statistical generalization at some future stage. However, it should be remembered that interpretive studies do not seek generalization of findings as their primary end. Rather, they seek a rich and insightful description of a particular issue, problem or event in its social context.

'Quantitative' and 'qualitative' research approaches

It is, incidentally, important to note that many interpretive studies have a *quantitative* element to data gathering. The categories qualitative and quantitative are not mutually exclusive in research. Most research studies are a mixture of both with an *emphasis* on one or the other. For example, if a research project attempts to build a case analysis of a particular brand a researcher might want to analyse textual material on that brand such as newspaper editorial and Internet chat-room dialogue. In this way the researcher could build a picture of what this brand means to people. Such a study would often make use of a simple quantitative content analysis in which the textual material is categorized according to content criteria. If the brand in question is, say, Ford, the researcher might want to see if text reflects trust in Ford products, reliability, excitement, technological sophistication, or negative qualities such as lack of reliability and so on. A content analysis could investigate which values are more common in texts about Ford. Once the researcher has built up a content analysis then he or she could develop an interpretive discussion on why such values seem predominant in texts that refer to this brand. The research might make use of a relevant theoretical framework, such as Moscovici's social representations theory (Moscovici, 1984) to generate a deeper level of analysis concerning why particular ideas (in this case, about brands) become produced and sustained in everyday conversation and interaction.

In ways such as this, elementary quantitative analysis is often combined with creative interpretation in the same study. In this case, a study of branding could be 'framed' in terms of a theory such as social representations theory.

The academic and educational rationale for the independent research project

A second major reason for emphasizing interpretive approaches is that a research project conducted as part of the requirements of a taught degree is part of the student's broader management education. The aims of the student research project are partly educational and are not simply aimed at generating solutions to, or insights into, management phenomena. Students of management require skills of research design, problem formulation, data gathering, analysis and interpretation that they can draw on in their managerial careers. More pragmatically, management students often use the research project as a 'way in' to an area of work. They can make industry contacts and acquire specialized knowledge of a key area that will be of benefit to potential employers. In recent years the author has supervised student marketing and management projects into WAP communications technology, mobile phone telephony pricing strategies, Internet music distribution, international market entry strategies in the motor industry, interactive advertising planning and many other vocationally motivated projects. Interpretive studies are particularly suitable for exploring areas in which the student does not have prior practical or theoretical knowledge.

Interpretive research theories are sophisticated and can be conceptually complex. Consequently, they are entirely appropriate for advanced studies in marketing and management. Their usefulness for students is that they offer a way of doing an exploratory piece of research utilizing naturally occurring data sets that are analytical and theoretically rich as opposed to being merely descriptive. Intellectually robust research projects based on either qualitative or quantitative analysis share a quality of 'thought-throughness'. They explore coherent questions and offer carefully qualified responses to those questions. Interpretive theory offers a way of giving that quality of thought-throughness to qualitative studies that, in the absence of theory, would lack the intellectual quality demanded by the standards of higher education. Interpretive research often relies on qualitative data but also entails an intellectually critical engagement with that data in order to go beyond mere anecdote or reportage and satisfy the criteria for advanced studies in business and management.

As noted above, 'interpretive' studies seldom seek findings that can be true for all time and in all cases. Rather, they tend to seek insights built on a careful and well-informed reading of a particular issue in a given social and/or organizational context. The great majority of students who study for under- or post-graduate taught degrees in marketing and management will never go on to conduct large-scale quantitative studies. They will, however, need skills of systematic data collection and interpretation that they can utilize in organizational settings. Such skills are integral to the educational outcomes of higher degrees. Students need to learn and apply strategies of investigation in order to examine everyday problems and issues in marketing, management and consumer research in a creative and theoretically informed way that they will find motivating and that will build their knowledge of that area. Interpretive traditions of research offer a valuable resource for such students.

The theoretical basis of interpretive research

The interpretive research perspective rests on a set of assumptions about the nature of human understanding. These assumptions inform the interpretive stance on social research in marketing and management. While this book offers practical advice on how to conduct research projects throughout the range of marketing and management topics, it does have a strong theoretical stance. This stance is informed by the *hermeneutic* tradition of social research.

The 'hermeneutic circle' and interpretive process

The interpretive research perspective draws on hermeneutics. Hermeneutics, the study of interpretation, derives from Biblical exegesis. For Holbrook and O'Shaughnessy (1988, p. 400) the idea of the *hermeneutic circle* is helpful in explaining the interpretive process (see also Thompson *et al.*, 1994).

> In the Hermeneutic Circle, an interpreter's tentative grasp of the whole text guides an initial reading of its parts. The detailed reading, in turn, leads towards a revision of the original overview. This dialogue between reader and text then proceeds through subsequent iterations of a circular process that . . . tends towards its own correction.

Social research can be conceived as the analysis of texts in the sense that research data are crafted into a textual representation of what is being researched. For example, a questionnaire survey generates results that can be represented on paper in words and statistics. The written-down results are a representation of what took place (a questionnaire survey). It is the task of a researcher to interpret the results of the survey, write the results down in a text and then to interpret the results. Similarly, a *depth interview* can be transcribed into a text of a dialogic exchange between researcher and interviewee. The text that results is a representation of what took place (the depth interview). Social research in marketing management is a hermeneutic task in this sense. Text and researcher are engaged in a cycle of re-interpretation and substantiation. The researcher engages with the text to draw meaning from it. The meanings that the researcher reads in the text are then communicated in the research report and substantiated with examples, such as direct quotes from the interview text.

For Holbrook and O'Shaughnessy (1988) different forms of understanding are employed in the physical sciences on the one hand, and the humanities and social sciences on the other. Humans seek meaning and live 'embedded within a shared system of signs based on public language and other symbolic objects' (p. 400). Consequently there is a need for an interpretative social science that does not assume that the physical and the social world are entirely analogous. In other words, they agree that researchers should not necessarily bring the same assumptions to research in the physical and social sciences. They suggest that researchers can acknowledge that the material being researched in each case has different characteristics. The way we might understand and describe the activity of a tree and its cells reflects a different kind of reality to the way we might understand an idea or an emotion. The behaviour of managers and consumers is self-constructed in a way that the behaviour of cells is not.

Thompson *et al.* (1994) discuss the ways in which the idea of the hermeneutic circle is used in consumer research. Holbrook and O'Shaughnessy (1988) invoked it to discuss what they see as the culturally situated character of scientific knowledge (p. 433). In other words, they use the hermeneutic circle to articulate their view that there is not a science or method that can stand outside history beyond interpretation. The hermeneutic circle is often invoked in consumer research in the context of qualitative data interpretation (Thompson *et al.*, 1994, p. 433, citing Hirschman, 1990, and Thompson *et al.* 1989, 1990). Thompson *et al.* (1994) suggest that a third use of the hermeneutic circle is to refer to 'a general model of the process by which understandings are formed' (p. 433). They see it (p. 433, citing Benhabib, 1992, and Faulconer and Williams, 1985, as support) as a model that offers insights into the nature of human understanding:

> Personal understandings are always situated within a network of culturally shared knowledge, beliefs, ideals and taken-for-granted assumptions about the nature of social life.

Human understanding, then, is necessarily mediated by social context. It cannot be objective in any pure or absolute sense. We make sense of our everyday experience by deploying strategies of interpretation. These strategies can take many forms but are drawn from the cultural and social context of which we are part. Hermeneutic research seeks to elicit insights into the 'unspoken' background of socially shared meanings by which a person interprets his/her experiences (Thompson *et al.*, 1994, p. 432).

Hermeneutics, then, is the field of study that broadly informs the interpretive research perspective. The latter chapters of this book will introduce a number of differing theoretical traditions that fall under the interpretive/hermeneutic category. However, the category 'interpretive' research is also used as a general label in theoretically informed qualitative studies (e.g. in Szmigin and Carrigan, 2001).

Non-quantitative and exploratory research projects

A little more should be said here about quantification in social research. Many texts demonstrate relatively simple statistical tests that can be usefully used in small-scale research projects, such as T-tests, Chi-squared tests, Wilcoxon and other tests of statistical significance. There is unquestionable value in this approach, particularly since basic statistical and numerical understanding is indispensable for students aspiring to a managerial career. However, there is also a strong case for developing intellectually rigorous research designs that do not employ statistical tests. This book can be used in conjunction with books that teach these quantitative methods; it is itself devoted entirely to qualitative data-gathering methods and associated theories of data analysis.

There are many possible reasons why a research project may not require a substantial quantitative element (see Box 1.2). It was noted above that qualitative research is often conducted in the early stages of research projects to generate constructs and hypotheses that can eventually be measured in a quantitative study. However, not all qualitative research implies the possibility or the desirability of measurement. Interpretive traditions offer means of making sense of qualitative data as an end in itself. At undergraduate and master's level students may well wish simply to embark on an investigation of a chosen area, problem or issue. As their knowledge develops they may wish to formulate a more specific research objective but this may not require measurement. If a student wishes to investigate a topic of which they have little prior knowledge, then an *exploratory* research design based mainly on qualitative data is the most appropriate.

Many topics that fire students' interest have arisen from their own observations and experience of marketing and management and therefore

---

Box 1.2 Reasons for not moving to a quantitative phase in a research project

Pragmatic reasons
- Lack of adequate statistical competence
- Lack of time and/or resources to conduct a sampling exercise on the necessary scale
- Poor survey response rates

Theoretical reasons
- Exploratory research design for a novel or under-researched topic that lacks well-established theoretical frameworks
- Theory-driven research objectives
- The philosophical stance of the researcher

may not fall neatly into existing theoretical categories or frameworks. In such cases an 'exploratory' research design is often appropriate. A qualitative approach can preserve the student's sense of original investigation and, therefore, motivation remains high. Even if the topic is one that has rarely been researched an experienced supervisor can usually suggest appropriate areas for literature review. 'Exploring' a topic implies that the student researcher does not take preconceived ideas into his or her research project. Rather, the researcher has found an area and a set of questions that are interesting and important and seeks to find out more about them. The aim is not to confirm a *hypothesis* or to prove or disprove a theory but, simply, to find out more so that what we do know can be developed and elaborated, and perhaps placed into initial categories. Exploratory studies are precursors to theory. Creative investigation generates ideas and speculative theories and explanations. Exploratory studies can be fertile sources of ideas for student researchers. Most importantly, they can help students develop a researcher's caste of mind and learn the skills of systematic investigation (see Box 1.3).

Interpretive projects and 'cross-disciplinarity'

Another important reason for conducting an interpretive project is that many students who come into postgraduate marketing, management and consumer studies from social science and humanities backgrounds, have useful knowledge they can draw upon to give their research a sense of coherence with their previous education. They may have a theoretically informed idea of their own particular 'take' on a marketing/management topic. Students of literature, for example, have a range of interpretive strategies that they can bring to their understanding of texts in marketing.

Box 1.3 Reasons for conducting an exploratory research project to satisfy taught degree criteria

- To develop research skills based on qualitative data-gathering techniques and non-random sampling approaches
- To advance personal knowledge of a chosen area of marketing management
- To engage with personal experience and interests and to connect with practical management issues and practices
- To develop knowledge and skills relevant to a chosen career area
- To investigate under-researched and cross-disciplinary topics
- To utilize previous knowledge in the arts, literature or social sciences

'Cross-disciplinarity' occurs where researchers combine features from disparate research traditions, in other words they work 'across' disciplines.

Reader response theory, for example, has been used to understand how consumers 'read' and respond to advertising (Scott, 1994b). Reader response theory is typically used in literary studies but it has been suggested by researchers that there is a powerful analogy between reading a work of art or literature and 'reading' other kinds of texts, such as an advertisement. Developing this analogy through reader response theory Scott (1994b) generated new insights into the way consumers understand, and respond to, advertising. Similarly, graduates of political and social science will also have studied theories that they can bring to bear on their research projects. There is a growing interest in politics from marketing researchers. Political parties and individual candidates use many marketing techniques to promote ideas, get candidates elected and to garner votes. Within social sciences such as psychology and cultural studies the importance of marketed consumption is increasingly acknowledged in research and teaching. 'You are what you consume' and, from a sociological point of view, much can be learned about society, power and relationships by studying consumption practices. From a managerial point of view, many social scientists work in consumer psychology to learn what motivates and excites consumers so that advertising agencies and manufacturers can respond accordingly. Within organizations, organizational and occupational psychologists are interested in how managers manage their organization's activities, especially its contact with consumers. In all of these cases it is clear that management and marketing topics and issues are accessible to a wide range of research perspectives and disciplines. While business education tends to be driven by practical management problems, it is also part of the broader intellectual tradition of the social and cultural sciences. The approaches taken in research projects should rightly reflect the breadth and variety of approaches in social research methods.

Interpretive approaches, then, can frame research projects in a theoretically informed way that satisfies the requirements of higher educational programmes. Interpretive work is not inferior to or less rigorous than quantitative research. It is particularly apt for 'exploratory' studies that do not seek to confirm a hypothesis but consist in open investigation of a broadly conceived topic. Of course, quantitative studies can be exploratory and are not always attempts to confirm hypotheses. The researcher conducting exploratory factor analysis, for example, is making an informed interpretation of data just as the qualitative researcher does in an exploratory project. Each approach also entails a thorough evaluation of the topic area and the available literature, systematic data gathering and informed interpretation of data. The differences between exploratory interpretive research and exploratory quantitative research lie in the data-gathering techniques and the theoretical assumptions behind the interpretation of data.

What are academics looking for? The skills that a research project demonstrates

The approach taken in this book is to try to deal with practical questions at the beginning so that any student researcher can use the book to help with their project whatever kind of research design they are using. One of the most pressing practical questions that concerns students who have not done any research before is 'What are my supervisors looking for?' The answer is not simple or straightforward, but it can be explained in part by reference to the kinds of skills that academics feel can be learned, and also demonstrated, through the independent research project.

The independent research project conducted as part of a taught academic course is a demanding, essential and often exciting part of a student's higher education. It is a means of teaching, learning and also assessment. The supervisor teaches research skills in discussions with the student, and there are also usually research methods classes to attend in support of the research project. The student learns and practices skills in conducting the research, and the written academic research project report itself is the means of assessing higher level educational attainment. The skills needed to research and write a successful academic research project are both practical and intellectual. While the assessment of the research report itself is largely based on academic and intellectual standards, these standards imply many practical skills. The practical skills involved in conducting and writing a research report include gathering and organizing data, planning time and scheduling work, selecting appropriate information, negotiating and other interpersonal skills. An intellectually persuasive research report will imply high attainment in many or all of these practical skills.

There are many social and communication skills required in doing research (see Box 1.4). For example, the supervisory relationship must be maintained by keeping in contact and maintaining goodwill. The student must be able to communicate his or her research ideas clearly, and he or she must also be able to listen to the supervisor's advice and act on it. The student's own life must be managed to sustain personal motivation and to plan for the required time and resources that the research project will demand. If practising managers or other academics are asked to give time for interviews then this access must be negotiated. If interviews, group discussions or other qualitative data-gathering approaches are to be conducted then these require social, communication and interpersonal skills too. The need for the student researcher to demonstrate complex sets of skills such as these explains why the independent research project is so important in the overall assessment of taught bachelor's and master's degrees. The independent research project is not just an outcome: it is a process.

Box 1.4 Examples of some of the interdependent skills required to successfully complete academic research projects in management and marketing

Intellectual skills
- Critical reading, understanding, evaluating ideas
- Integrating new learning with existing knowledge
- Skills of logical inference: drawing on evidence and reasoning to construct persuasive arguments
- Selecting and summarizing relevant points from appropriate information sources
- Drawing logical connections between differing research studies

Communication skills
- Communicating research ideas clearly, verbally and in writing
- Writing the research report in a succinct and lucid academic style
- Listening to and acting on advice from supervisors or others
- Skills of editing and sub-editing prose to create a clear and persuasive report structure

Interpersonal skills
- Negotiating access for research interviews or other data gathering
- Managing the supervisor, negotiating goals, gaining agreement on topics
- Handling qualitative data-gathering sessions with sensitivity and professional competence

Practical/emotional skills
- Time management: sustaining motivation to meet deadlines
- Breaking down activities into sub-goals for scheduling and prioritizing
- Reflecting and learning from experience: modifying views in the light of new knowledge
- Interviewing and other primary research skills

The skills listed above are interdependent: one is often implied in another. For example, reviewing or changing existing beliefs in the light of new knowledge is an intellectual quality. It is also a feature of emotional maturity that one is able to do this. Adept negotiation skills and self-motivation are also qualities which reflect emotional maturity, as well as demonstrating management skills. Although there is considerable blurring between skills it is useful to set out a number of them in this way because it can show students why they will not be judged on the outcome alone. It does not matter if the research has not produced a striking or novel business solution or a new theoretical advance. Carrying out and producing the research project report is itself an achievement that demonstrates advanced intellectual, personal and managerial skills. The research report is the tangible outcome but implicit in this tangible outcome are many intangible qualities.

Independence and the research project

The independent project also demands a degree of maturity because academics will not be well disposed towards a student who does not demonstrate sufficient independence. Some students do ask constantly for reassurance and for ever more explicit direction, forgetting that the independence of the research project is a central part of its educational value. However, it is just as bad not to contact the supervisor enough. Academic supervisors have different views on contact. Some insist on regular meetings throughout the research process. Others want only an initial meeting to establish the topic and research design. Then, once the student researcher has conducted the work and written up a full draft, they will agree to read it and offer comments and advice prior to final submission. It is important for the student researcher to meet with the supervising academic to get a feel for his or her personal style in order to judge the degree of contact required. Of course, this will also depend to some extent on the needs of the student researcher and the nature of the project undertaken.

What academic supervisors want

Many first-time student researchers feel that they have to embark on the project without knowing what the academic supervisor wants. Broadly, what academics want to see in such work is maturity, evidence of reading and good-quality written work that reflects a good quality of thinking. Academics like to see research reports that are carefully written and clearly structured. They like clear, grammatically correct writing. It is important to proof-read the draft so that the text is not strewn with typographical and grammatical errors. The research report should satisfy the narrative conventions specified by the particular university department in structure and style. It should, of course, be entirely the student's own work. It should develop ideas logically and clearly and link them together within a broader theme. The very best research reports have an element of novelty in that they develop ideas creatively or with an unexpected line of discussion.

Overall, the best answer to the question 'What are academics looking for in a research project?' is one that evolves during the course of the research process. As a student begins to understand the process of researching and writing, he or she will also gain increased understanding about what academics expect and hope for. Reading academic research papers in the journals is especially important for getting a sense of the writing style and tone required. Academics will not expect students studying for bachelor's or master's degrees to produce research that is worthy of publication in an academic journal. Academics themselves know from their own efforts to publish their work how difficult this is. They will give credit for work that reflects earnest work and genuine efforts to learn, and which demonstrates qualities appropriate to the level of education of the student.

Plagiarism: how to avoid the charge

Most university research project guides have a section on *plagiarism*, warning of dire consequences for the student if the work submitted is found to have plagiarized any other work. The growth in Internet-based businesses selling pre-written essays and dissertations has created a sense that this is now a 'problem', so universities are increasingly sensitive to the issue. The independent research project must be entirely the student's own work. It is vitally important that the criterion of 'independence' is satisfied. However, it is also true that few ideas are truly original and research projects in particular are substantially a review of existing ideas. This is why there is often confusion over what, exactly, constitutes plagiarism.

Plagiarized work is research or other writing that is reproduced in a project report as if it is the author's own words when in fact it has been copied from another source. Many students, especially those working in a second language and trying to understand a new educational culture, find it difficult to distinguish plagiarism from legitimate paraphrasing. The *literature review* component of the research project report describes, summarizes and evaluates the published work of writers in a field. It can seem odd, and even presumptuous, to reword this work. However, the research project is not merely an extended paraphrase of the work of established researchers. It is the student researcher's discussion and views on this previously published work. The distinction between copying or plagiarizing and legitimate quoting and paraphrasing is difficult to grasp for some students, but it is a crucial one.

Literature reviewing demonstrates important academic skills. If a student researcher can summarize a particular piece of research or theory succinctly it demonstrates that he or she has read and understood the work. This kind of engagement with the published research of eminent academics is an important part of the Western university tradition.

Students sometimes feel that is presumptuous for a student researcher to summarize, criticize and/or paraphrase a study conducted by a published researcher. On the contrary, it is considered that this demonstrates a mature intellectual engagement with the work. This is a higher order intellectual skill: it demands that the student can read and understand the research and also that he or she has the linguistic skill to articulate that understanding without relying excessively on the quoted words of the original author. It is most important that this is demonstrated through a balance of direct quotes, paraphrases and summaries.

All written or graphic material that is reproduced unchanged from a source should be accompanied by the author and page citation (e.g. Smith, 2003, p. 4); written material should be placed within quote marks. Footnotes may be used where appropriate. A paraphrase of a short section of work should also normally have the original author cited. The student researcher's own text may be summarizing or discussing another author's published research, but if it is not using that author's published words then quote marks are not needed. The concept of plagiarism is a mark of Western higher education in some ways since it implies that student researchers can engage with intellectual work as equals to the original authors. This is why plagiarism is considered so important an issue by universities. The plagiarist fails to demonstrate one of the most important groups of intellectual skills that the independent research project is designed to assess: the skills of reading, understanding, critiquing and discussing the published work of established researchers.

School students of literature are often asked by the teacher to describe, criticize or discuss a particular piece of poetry or prose. Many direct quotes are useful for this purpose but there can be no mistake that the discussion must make use of the student's own original ideas and words. The student's considered views on the piece of work are being sought and their ability to demonstrate their understanding by articulating those views will be assessed by the teacher. Similarly, the independent research project requires students to engage with published research studies in an active and critical way so that the original author's words are reinterpreted by the student researcher. This is what strictures against plagiarism are designed to encourage. Plagiarism is a serious charge and, where proven, can prevent graduation, so student researchers should make every effort to ensure that they cannot be accused of it by carefully citing every source that they have used.

Standards of scholarship

The independent research project conducted in a higher education context is a test of a student's scholarship. Scholarship consists in assimilating different sources of information into a new piece of written work. The standards required are high. Not only do research project reports in the UK and the USA have to be clearly structured with a well-defined problem or issue, logically ordered and written in appropriate and grammatically correct English, they also have to satisfy standards of good scholarship. 'Good' scholarship is not easy to define. It has many dimensions.

For academics, scholarship is their craft and it is evident in published articles in well-established academic journals. In an important sense scholarship is an aspect of rhetoric because the best 'scholarship' consists in the highest quality of argument. 'Argument' in this sense does not carry its everyday meaning of acrimonious or antagonistic disputes. In academic work 'argument' is a general term that refers to all kinds of scholarship conducted in written form. All written academic work is an 'argument' in the very broad sense that it is written to persuade. The writer wants the reader to be persuaded that the arguments and positions taken in the work are plausible and that they can be logically inferred from the evidence that is presented. Even where a student researcher has conducted a literature review on the current state of reward management research for a human resources management project, he or she is still constructing an argument. The interpretation of research literature is not final or beyond dispute. The student researcher must state their views of that literature and try to support them with appropriate citations or direct quotes. In a broad sense, even a discussion must 'argue' in favour of its points of view. While the tone of academic writing is normally moderate and emotionally detached, the writer must still persuade the reader that the points of view that are offered are well founded and logically coherent.

Carrigan (2003) refers to a typology of the characteristics of scholarship in Jankowicz (1991). The characteristics include careful use of evidence to support arguments, care and accuracy in the identification of information sources, and thoroughness in the coverage of the subject matter. 'Thoroughness' implies that arguments and points of discussion are well balanced. This in turn implies that alternative points of view are acknowledged and evaluated. A further characteristic is integrity in the use of data and the formation of arguments and points of discussion. The reader must believe that the work has intellectual integrity. In other words, the reader must feel that the work and arguments presented represent a sincere attempt on the part of the writer to investigate and report a topic whatever the findings may be.

For most academics, 'scholarship' also implies that the subject of the research project is placed in the context of previously published studies in academic journals or research texts. The literature review is, then, a very important part of establishing the scholarly credibility of the work. In this section (discussed at greater length in Chapter 3) the student researcher discusses previously published research that is relevant to the project topic. It also draws on previous work to establish problems and issues, analytical concepts and theoretical frameworks that will be used in the study itself. In the case of novel or cross-disciplinary topics it can be difficult to find previously published work in precisely that area. In such cases the student researcher should review studies that address issues and areas that are in some way relevant to or related to the specific focus of the research study. He or she must build an argument to justify the chosen approach in terms of what previous research appeared to neglect. At undergraduate or master's level the student researcher does not need to identify a clear 'gap' in previous research to the same degree required of a PhD. He or she would, however, need to review a selection of high-quality work that showed that their topic of study is logically related to a number of previously published research areas.

For example, one research student wanted to do a study on the rebranding of a country as a tourism destination. She had to look at a variety of literature to offer a broad discussion on relevant research. Useful published research was found in public relations and corporate communications research, in tourism management, in human geography research and in published work on brand management. She also found helpful sources in the tourism management literature. There will be times when a student researcher finds the kind of published study or studies that fit(s) their research topic exactly and locate(s) it within a defined field of work. In many other cases student researchers will need to demonstrate their skills of scholarship by integrating published research from a variety of areas in order to give their study an appropriate literature context.

How to get the most out of this book

It was mentioned earlier that this book has been written so that it can be read from beginning to end, but it can also be used as a reference text to learn more about particular aspects of the research project process, about data-gathering approaches and about particular theoretical perspectives. For example, students on postgraduate degrees who have already completed an undergraduate research project and know what topic they want to research, might wish to go straight to Chapter 2. Chapter 2 discusses problems and issues related to crafting the initial research proposal. The matter of choosing a topic and crafting the research problem or issue to be investigated is critical in designing and planning a viable research project. Many pitfalls can be avoided by paying sufficient attention to just this initial stage. Success or failure in the research project is often determined right at the beginning. The choice of topic and title is, perhaps, the most important element of the whole project. If a topic is thought-through and a title carefully crafted in view of the resources and time available, then there is every chance of the project being successful. Many student researchers find that, with no experience of research, this is the part that confuses them the most because they cannot envision what the process entails.

Chapter 3 aims to help with this problem. It discusses the document – the research report, thesis or dissertation – that must be produced. This is particularly useful for getting a sense of the whole research project process. The chapter reviews the issues in 'writing up' the project and offers suggested chapter headings for research project reports. It suggests chapter headings for projects that use newly gathered data (primary data) and also for projects that are based on existing, publicly available research articles and market data (secondary data). All this information is extremely useful for new research students. Many texts on research methods do not go into much detail on the practical issues involved in successfully conceiving of, and completing, a research project. They tend to dwell on the technicalities of data-gathering methods and analytical procedures. New student researchers can gain confidence from reviewing the whole research project process in terms of the final product.

Many students embark on their research project without understanding what it is they must produce at the end. They can subsequently find that their research loses direction. For example, some research students acquire more and more data and more and more copies of relevant research papers, but they have little idea of how to organize all this information and write up their project. It is very useful for research students to have some idea of what they must produce from the beginning of the process. This helps a lot with research planning and time management. It is also helpful to know the pitfalls and problems in advance. Finally, if a research student knows what their whole research will look like in outline when it is finished, they are less likely to make unwise decisions during the process. They can, in other words, use their scarce time more efficiently. Chapters 2 and 3 are written to help with just this problem.

Chapter 4 begins to establish the techniques for gathering data, if primary data will form part of the research project. The chapter does not seek to set out the basis of each method in detail but focuses on practical hints on how to use these data-gathering methods successfully. Research projects that use primary data have to discuss and justify their chosen data-gathering 'method'. This is an important part of supporting the findings or insights that the research generates. Students doing their first research project may have never had to justify their arguments to this degree before. Essays completed as part of taught courses cite academic sources but do not have to support their claims in the same way as independent research projects. Essays are substantially reviews of previously published work. While the academic research project report does indeed have to have a critical literature review, it must also go beyond this. Bachelor's and master's projects do not have to generate new knowledge or theory, but they do need to be able to support their conclusions and arguments carefully. A clear rationale for choosing a particular data-gathering method is therefore very important.

Students who know what they want to research, know how to write a research project proposal and have a working knowledge of data-gathering techniques may feel that they want to develop more sophisticated analyses of their data. For these students Chapters 5 to 10 will be particularly useful since they outline particular traditions of research theory that have been used in recent high-level studies and can be adapted for the student research project. Chapter 5 introduces more of the conceptual vocabulary of interpretive research in order to set the scene for the treatment of particular interpretive research traditions that follows in the remaining chapters. Interpretive research approaches share many common themes and priorities and overlapping techniques. However, each approach is also distinctive in important ways. The student researcher can survey the information on each to decide which particular interpretive approach, or combination of approaches, is most suitable for their research project.

Chapters 6 to 10 introduce traditions such as phenomenology/existentialism, semiotics, literary theory, postmodernism, critical discourse analysis, critical theory, ethnography and others, which have much to offer the novice researcher. They can be drawn on selectively to develop more sophisticated analysis and discussions that go beyond a naïve description of qualitative data. As the interpretive theoretical perspectives become increasingly important in framing qualitative data gathering and analysis in both managerial academic settings, this book can be used as a primer for marketing, management and consumer research specialists who want to learn more about particular interpretive traditions.

For most student researchers, the task of deciding on what topic to research is the major hurdle at the very beginning of the research project process. The following chapter deals with the problems and possibilities of this important issue.

Glossary

Confirmatory research design When a theory seeks to explain and predict certain events in the world (such as consumer behaviour in response to an advertising campaign) researchers might seek confirmation that its predictions hold in specific circumstances. They would, then, design a 'confirmatory' research study. This would normally be a research design that employed quantitative methods to test a hypothesis in a 'positivistic' research approach.

Data set The primary research material gathered by the researcher.

Depth interview A long interview that explores an aspect of the world of the interviewee's experience.

Exploratory An exploratory research design seeks insight and understanding, it does not seek to confirm generalizable facts.

Hermeneutics The study of the theory of interpretation. Hermeneutics derives from approaches to Biblical interpretation or exegesis.

Hypothesis A hypothesis is a statement of fact about the world that can be tested by observation. Hypotheses are often phrased in terms of cause and effect such as 'If x, then y'. Hypothesis testing research usually applies statistical tests to quantitative data sets. An interpretive research design, in contrast, would normally have a broader, less specific research problem or issue as its main organizing principle.

Interpretive research 'Interpretive' refers to a broad and diverse category of research traditions that emphasize the use of qualitative data in exploratory and creative research designs. It is assumed that the theoretically informed interpretation of research data to generate rich descriptions of everyday events and issues is a legitimate and fruitful social scientific approach.

Literature review An extended discussion of previously published academic work that is relevant to the research topics under investigation. The literature review sets the context for the research project and identifies issues, research gaps and analytical concepts that may be used in the project.

Plagiarism Use of another's work without proper acknowledgement.

Qualitative 'Qualitative' data sets are made up of non-numerical material such as transcripts or audio-recordings of interviews, field notes of researcher observations, records of conversations, and any kinds of social text such as books, newspapers and advertisements.

Quantitative 'Quantitative' data sets are, as you would expect, numerical. In business and management questionnaire surveys are often used to gather data that can be quantified. Statistical analysis is then performed on the data.

Sample Researchers cannot collect all the primary material that could possibly be relevant to their study. They must be content with a partial sample of all the relevant material. There must be a criterion for selecting the sample so that the data gathering is systematic and the data set collected is the best one given the research objectives of the study.

Chapter 2

Choosing the topic

Chapter outline

This chapter focuses on the choice of research topic because this important decision must be considered in the light of its implications for research project method, scope and structure. The choice of topic, and most importantly the way it is phrased, has major implications for the success of the project. This chapter aims to help student researchers to think through their research project ideas and to judge whether a particular research problem, question or issue can make a viable project.

> ### Chapter objectives
>
> After reading this chapter students will be able to
>
> - understand the importance of the choice of research topic
> - understand the importance of how the research topic is crafted and expressed
> - appreciate the need for thinking through the research idea in terms of the implications for research design

The range of research topic choices in management and marketing

As Box 1.1 in the previous chapter suggests, the choice of possible topics for a research project in marketing, management and consumer research is very wide indeed. There are many social phenomena that can be researched from one or all of these perspectives. The scope of such studies may be broader than many student researchers realize. Marketing, for example, is a functional area of organizational management but it can also be conceived as a pervasive presence in citizens' lives in developed and developing economies. Successful marketing may be indispensable to organizations but the institutions, activities and values of marketing are hugely influential beyond the organizations they serve.

In many industrialized and post-industrial economies marketing activity is often seen as a source of social problems, as well as a means of generating wealth. In underdeveloped countries the lack of a marketing infrastructure is considered a painful absence and a major barrier to the creation of wealth and the reduction of poverty. Marketing is a management field: practically every organization engages with markets at some level, in some way, even if the terms of engagement may often be far from the familiar world of consumer goods transactions. People are employed to 'manage' this engagement and to manage all other organizational activities and relationships. Marketing management is not just about big organizations, executive managers and consumer goods markets. It is, crucially, about consumers and consumption in every context, since all marketing activity is premised on assumptions about the nature, needs and social practices of consumers.

'Management' itself is a broad and amorphous category encompassing all manner of directing, coping, co-ordinating, strategizing, organizing, resourcing, allocating, investigating and making judgements, from the executive pomp of major global corporations to the humble local store, small business or charity. Management goes on with vast resources and armies of subordinates, and it also goes on with no resources and no subordinates in small business. The management experience is vast and varied and its engagement with markets and consumers offers a fertile source of research topics.

The world of consumption is a vast arena of symbolic human practice that is rich in research possibilities from many perspectives. The analogy is a powerful one: we can be said to 'consume' not only perishable items such as food, drink and fuel, but also clothes, motor cars, theme parks, service encounters, even the sheets we sleep on are 'consumption' items in this sense. Any aspect of consumer experience is valid material for researchers in marketing since it all contributes towards a greater understanding of the end of marketing activity: consumption. It has been suggested that consumption has become the primary symbolic human activity in developed economies. This may take the consumption metaphor too far for some tastes, but it can hardly be doubted that marketing actively seeks to transfer meaningful values and norms from their origins in non-consumption social life to the products and practices of marketing. Hence as consumers we are encouraged to realize our aspirations, wishes and fantasies of fulfilment through our consumption of marketed brands, products, services and lifestyles. The scope of possible topics and questions for a research project in the marketing area is, therefore, indeed very broad.

The student's preferred research topic might evolve from a particular industry issue or problem, or it might entail a more personal issue perhaps deriving from experiences as an employee, a consumer or a researcher. We all experience marketing activity as consumers and form ideas of how this activity might be managed. For example, we queue in shops and banks (service delivery quality), we buy products that we like (customer loyalty and relationship marketing) and products we dislike or products that were delivered poorly (relationship recovery, marketing operations). We take part in social rituals of consumption when we go out to restaurants, to see a show in a theatre or cinema, or to watch a football match. We read newspapers, eat advertised chocolate snacks, drive branded cars and wear branded goods. As consumers our practices of consumption might generate ideas for research projects. Our experiences of being 'managed' either as consumers or as employees might also generate ideas.

The project topic may evolve from an interest in *functional* managerial issues, for example the student might be interested in examining how service quality might be improved in a particular industry context, say banking or restaurants. It may be that the student simply has an interest in an area and wants to learn how things happen, for example how advertising strategy is developed in an advertising agency. There may be a particular question that interests the student, such as how tourism destinations are influenced by the service quality of travel agents and their staff, or how tourism operator brands influence the Internet purchase of 'packaged' holidays.

The case for 'exploratory' research

The range of possible topics is indeed broad but the way that the research topic or question is crafted is of great importance. At undergraduate or master's level, research projects do not normally need to have a hypothesis. Exploratory studies rather than hypothesis testing studies are often more suited to the student researcher. For example, the research question deriving from a *functional* or managerial interest can usefully be cast as a broad exploration. Say the research question is looking at the influence of travel agency staff on consumer choice of tourism destinations. An exploratory research design builds fewer assumptions into the research question and makes it less likely that the inexperienced student researcher will find the project speeding down a 'dead end'. In other words, if a research question implies that there is a relationship between two variables (in this case, travel agency staff attitudes and consumer destination choice) then the research may discover late in the study that the relationship does not hold. Tourism destinations may not be influenced by travel agency staff at all. The staff may be influential in the choice of tour operator or airline, but the destination choice may be more influenced by other factors.

Too specific a research question, for example, one that postulates a direct causal relationship between variables, may be searching for a causal relationship that isn't there. A functionally driven research question (i.e. one to do with managerial efficiency or effectiveness) might presuppose a link or causal relationship, say, between sales promotional activity and sales, or between celebrity endorsement and brand equity. It might proceed from essentialist categories such as 'quality' or 'strategy' or 'brand equity' that are not necessarily useful in describing or explaining organizational action in practice. An exploratory research design gives the student researcher the flexibility to adapt the research to new knowledge.

There may also be an assumption implied in the research question that the student with little or no experience of a particular industry can solve problems that practical people encounter every day. 'Managerial' research projects are particularly prone to this fault: seeking to improve marketing or management processes may be a laudable aim for a student research project, but is it realistic? If experienced people have been tackling a particular problem every day of their working lives, how likely is it that a student project can find the best way for direct entry into the Chinese motor car market for a Western car manufacturer or solve an industrial relations issue in the coal mining industry? Functional research projects may well provide new insights into problem solutions or new ways of conceiving of the problem, but it is important for the intellectual quality and practical credibility of such projects that they are framed modestly as explorations seeking insights and understanding, rather than making grand and hollow claims about solutions.

If the research project topic is too ambitious or unrealistic in its aims the research is going to get sidetracked into arguments that are needed simply to defend the basic assumptions. This is a sure way to stifle research creativity. It also takes the fun out of research if you can't change your mind and explore something unexpected but interesting that emerged from the investigation. Furthermore, it is a poor research ethos that forces researchers to ignore issues that arise because they don't fit into the *a priori* categories that were built into the research question. For all these reasons, first-time student researchers often find that broad, exploratory research questions or issues are the safest and most appropriate.

The 'working' title and topic

A 'working' title is statement of a research question, issue or area that is phrased broadly so that it can be made more specific at a later stage. It is useful in exploratory research that research questions have some flexibility. If a person starts out by, say, researching branding in a particular product market and then, mid-way through the project, decides that communication is central to the issue, it would be an intellectually flawed exercise if they could not adapt their research to take in a change of emphasis from branding to brand communication. Research projects should not have to perform logical somersaults to defend the coherence of the question. This would be a little like setting out on a world back-packing trip with a bad map, then insisting that the map is right – therefore this mud patch on the left must be Copacabana Beach.

Research questions should initially be couched in exploratory terms even if the original interest from which they evolve is one of a functionalist, managerial, normative nature. 'How can this work better' is a natural question to ask for people attracted to marketing studies through a managerialist vein of thinking. In most cases an intellectually honest investigation will reveal the assumptions built into the question and hence lead into an exploration of the preconditions for the problem. In any case, in marketing and other management fields, people working in that field feel that they already know how things could work better. They feel that the hard part is trying to implement the necessary changes. Self-evidently, in most cases, since implementation of managerial practices and solutions is difficult, the problem itself is not as simple as it may appear to the naïve researcher. A project entitled 'Resolving customer dissatisfaction in service encounters in the motor car hire industry' is quite likely to generate some useful insights into customer experiences in that context, but it cannot do as it claims and 'solve' the problem, because it is a complex and continuing issue of management. Research questions should be realistic about the limitations of research.

The project proposal

Deciding on the topic area and the importance of wordcraft

The choice of topic must be motivating for the student otherwise the research experience will be a chore. It helps greatly if the topic is also motivating for the supervisor so a degree of negotiation is most helpful. The supervisor can help the research student to clarify issues and assumptions involved in the topic idea. The supervisor can also get a feel for whether the topic falls within his or her range of interest and expertise. Wherever possible research dissertations should not be a mere chore for the supervisor because where they are this is quickly sensed by the student and a key element of the motivational framework for doing the dissertation is flawed. This may be out of the hands of both student and supervisor if the faculty administration dictates the issue.

The process begins with a research proposal that represents the initial ideas on how the project will unfold. As mentioned above, in the initial stages of the project a 'working' title may be sufficient. For example, a project entitled 'The relationship between advertising and sales in the notebook segment of the UK computer retailing sector' would be rather too specific. This would be a somewhat over-ambitious project that reveals a naïve understanding of the complexity of the issues involved. Such a project would need to be radically modified at a later stage, when the student researcher realized that they could not satisfactorily establish the stated relationship. However, if the same project proposal is worded in more general terms as, say, 'An exploration of advertising strategy in the note-book segment of the UK computer retailing sector', then there is scope for the precise aims of the project to be re-appraised later in the light of the information that is gathered and the understanding that is developed. An over-ambitious, sweeping project proposal can risk setting the student up for failure. A more modest, carefully qualified proposal is usually wiser. Proposals must be interesting and they must have a point or a question that will structure and drive the research. However, this can be phrased broadly because the project may then reach its full potential in an evolutionary way.

The need to choose a topic and stick to it

Doing the research project entails acquiring knowledge that is new to the student researcher. This new knowledge then, obviously, changes and informs the way the problem or issue is conceived. However, there must be a definite topic area and a general perspective that cannot be changed. It is unsettling for students and worrying for the supervisor if students change their minds about the topic they want to research half-way through the process. Research projects that are part of taught degrees are often con-ducted in a tight time-scale and with limited resources. Supervisors are often responsible for large numbers of students. Therefore, a radical change of topic mid-way through the process can present special dif-ficulties. There are some circumstances when this might be possible, but in most cases it is much wiser to create a project proposal that can be clearly related to the project report that is eventually written. As with every aspect of the research project, any difficulties can be worked out with sensible discussion and negotiation.

Another reason why the topic area should not be changed once it has been decided is that many institutions require a research proposal to be submitted as a first stage in the process. This proposal will form the basis for the project and the student must produce work that is clearly con-nected to the proposal. Before writing the proposal students should take time and trouble to explore different topics, different research designs and different problem formulations. This is why academics always try to encourage students to begin thinking about their research project long before it is time to submit (advice that is, unfortunately, seldom heeded). Then, when the student has decided on a topic proposal in discussion with their supervisor, they need to stick to it. The precise way the topic is con-ceived, though, can and should subtly change as the research progresses.

For example, a student might decide to investigate comparative advertising strategies for motor cars in the UK and China. As they progress in gathering data they might decide to focus on a particular brand or class of car. They might also refine their project to focus on a specific market segment. They could even change the emphasis of analysis from a broad concern with 'advertising strategy' to some aspect of creative execution, such as the portrayal of speed in motor car ads, or the representation of masculinity that is produced through the visual imagery of the ads. They might be let down by brand managers in the car industry who had previously agreed to grant an interview but who now do not have time. In this case they might seek alternative interviewees, perhaps from the advertising agencies themselves. All this can change the emphasis of the research question and the consequent analysis and discussion. But the important thing is that, however the emphasis of the project may change, the broad topic, scope and aims do not. That is why a broad, exploratory working title for the project proposal is often, pragmatically, the best starting point.

Writing the proposal

Different universities ask for slightly different things in their project proposal. They all, however, have the same general purpose. Proposals are designed to get the students to think carefully about their research project and to begin to think through and plan how they are going to complete it on time and to an acceptable standard. Many institutions try to get students to think about their proposal quite early in the year even though the project often does not have to be submitted until the very end of the course. Academic staff often find that a high proportion of students leave serious project work until rather late in the year, leading to a panic when submission time is near. The project is itself a major learning experience for students and it is unreasonable to expect that they can plan the entire process in detail in advance. However, if students take the proposal seriously it can save a lot of stress later. The things that are normally required in the research project proposal are listed in Box 2.1.

Box 2.1 Research project proposal checklist

1 Topic area and working title
2 Major research questions/issues/problems to be investigated
3 Areas of literature (topics, academic journals, article titles) relevant to the review
4 Methods of data gathering (for empirical projects)
5 Research activities/time-line for research

The importance of reading the academic literature

One of the best ways to prepare a proposal is by reading the academic research on the topic the student is thinking about researching. This will mean taking the trouble to use the databases of academic literature that are usually available in most university libraries such as 'Proquest', 'Emerald', 'ABI-inform', 'EBSCO' and ATHENS. University library staff are the experts in 'literature searching' and they are usually only too happy to advise students doing research projects. Reading the academic literature has several benefits. First, students begin to understand the academic style of writing, including the use of conventions such as *Harvard referencing* and the use of appendices. Second, acquiring a good understanding of the published research in relevant areas is a major part of the project process. It can be especially useful for students to see how academics develop their own research because they choose to copy or adapt the approaches they read about.

For example, the author studied for a taught MSc in Marketing some years ago. He was particularly interested in marketing and corporate communications, both to external and internal audiences. The research project he produced grew out of some reading on 'mission statements'. A group of researchers had collected many examples of published mission statements and had then analysed their content using a simple content analytic framework. The author extended this work by collecting more mission statements from a particular industry sector (higher education) from the organizations' published reports, web sites and other communications. He adapted the previously used frameworks by adding a few categories. The study was published (Hackley, 1998) with some theoretical development that had not been present in the original project.

Originality of research

In the above case, as in many examples of research, researchers can extend existing research studies, though usually on a smaller scale than the published study. Student researchers are sometimes worried about the originality of their work if they adapt or extend a previously published research study. Adapting previously published research studies should not be confused with plagiarism. It is not only entirely legitimate: it is an extremely useful way of carrying out a first research project without 're-inventing the wheel'. Student research projects must be original in the sense that they must be the student's own work. They do not have to be original in the sense of being an entirely new, never-before-thought-of idea. Indeed, no research falls into this category. Every individual researcher researching in good faith from their own particular perspective will produce original work in the sense that it is their own 'take' on a given topic.

Most academic published research is linked with or extends previous published work in various ways. Conceptual papers, that is, published research that does not draw on primary data sets, review previously published research to draw attention to theoretical anomalies or gaps and to suggest new lines of discussion or investigation. Empirical research papers that do use primary data sets often reproduce previously used research designs and use them on new sets of data to test the findings. Such papers also often explore old data with new theory, or explore old research problems with a new angle or concept. 'Originality' in academic research consists in the particular arguments, style and combination of ideas employed. Originality in student research projects does *not* mean never-before-imagined ideas or findings. Reading published research and drawing ideas, examples and ways of working from it is absolutely the best way for student researchers to form their own ideas about the kinds of research possible and the appropriate academic style of research writing.

'Deductive' and 'inductive' research designs

The terms 'deductive' and 'inductive' are often used in research theory. *Inductive* means reasoning from the general to the particular. For example, if something seems true in many varied circumstances, it may also be true in specific circumstances. *Deductive* means reasoning from the particular to the general. If a causal relationship or link seems to be implied by a particular theory or case example, it might be true in many cases. A deductive research design might test to see if this relationship or link did obtain in more general circumstances. Generally, a deductive research design would test a theory, link or relationship that has been suggested, claimed or postulated by a particular theory. The findings would support or modify the theory, or perhaps cast doubt on its assumptions.

In social research inductive designs would normally be exploratory. Strictly, inductive research looks at many cases in order to induce general patterns or relationships. However, major research studies can go through both inductive and deductive phases. If, say, a hundred sales people are interviewed about their motivation, a researcher might be able to induce a general proposition about sales person motivation that seems to be true for a large number of the interviewees. The researcher might feel that this proposition has not been considered in the previous research and theory on sales force motivation. Perhaps a large number of interviewees mention that having a boss with good communication skills is very important for their motivation. The researcher could then use a deductive research design to 'test' this proposition on an even larger number of cases, perhaps by means of a questionnaire. The finding would then provide material for reflection and modification of a theory of sales person motivation.

This kind of inductive–deductive research design is very common in post-doctoral business research. It is particularly characteristic of a style of research that is often loosely labelled *positivist* research. In business research applications the label positivist often implies that researchers are trying to discover simple and direct causal relationships, such as a relationship between sales manager communication style and sales force motivation. The kind of research described above takes time, resources and statistical expertise. It also requires researchers to be very familiar with specialized research methods. Researchers need to have an in-depth understanding of a specialized body of theory. These are compelling practical reasons for *not* doing this kind of research study in an undergraduate or master's research project. However, the illustration does show how inductive and deductive research phases can contribute to understanding a particular research problem.

Given the emphasis of this book it should be noted that many academic and business researchers who work in interpretive traditions feel that this research style, also called the *hypothetico-deductive* approach, has a limited range of useful application. It tends to work best where there is already robust theory that can make strong predictions. Some interpretive researchers have argued that there are few examples of this kind of theory in the management and marketing area. Some have also argued that this kind of theorizing is not necessarily appropriate for a wide range of problems and issues in social research in management and marketing.

The concepts deductive and inductive are not only used in the context of research design. They can be applied to reasoning and thinking styles. In this sense deductive and inductive are not mutually exclusive ideas. Arguing and analysing necessarily draw on both inductive and deductive thinking in the process of reasoning about a particular problem or issue. For example, if I go out of the house three days in a row and get wet because it is raining, I might take an umbrella on the fourth day. I have induced a hypothesis: 'If I leave the house without an umbrella I will get wet.' Therefore I carry an umbrella to prevent getting wet when I leave the house. However, if I decide to test this hypothesis deductively when I go on summer holiday to southern Italy, I will find that my hypothesis does not hold true in that situation. I could carry my umbrella around in Rome for weeks in the summer and never get wet, unless I fell into one of the fountains. In our daily life we use deductive and inductive thinking to understand the world and to make predictions. If we relied exclusively on one or the other thinking style we would not manage very well at all. Many large-scale research designs, as in the illustration above, move from inductive to deductive and back again as theories are refined and developed. It is therefore rather a simplification to say that a research design is either inductive or deductive. Research is always both.

The student–supervisor relationship

One other matter deserves mention before we move to the next section. The student researcher's success depends a lot on their supervisor. It is always wise, and simple good manners, for students to attend meetings when requested, listen to the advice offered, and meet deadlines when asked to do so. It is very unwise to fail to contact the supervisor for months on end, then to demand advice and guidance by tomorrow. In the great majority of cases supervisors sincerely want their research students to do well and many will go an extra mile or two to help. However, students must be aware that it is a two-way street. 'Independent' research project means exactly that. Students must work independently but under the guidance of the supervisor. Too much contact, or too little, can have a negative effect. In almost every case a little consideration and goodwill on both sides solves any problems.

Many university departments set out procedures for making contact with supervisors. Some allow a good deal of flexibility. Some supervisors prefer regular meetings and updates. Others expect their students to go away and work independently once a careful initial discussion has set out just what their topic is to be and how they should go about researching it. Supervisors of this inclination would usually want to review only one draft before submission. Both supervisors and students have differing needs and preferred ways of working: the main rule is that friendly and courteous consideration on both sides can make the process more satisfying for both parties.

Supervisors have a wide range of knowledge and expertise but their most important attribute for the student researchers is their experience of judging, evaluating and designing research projects. In many cases it is not necessary that a supervisor be a specialist in a given sub-area of marketing or management for he or she to be able to give useful advice and to judge the success of a research project at undergraduate or master's level. Academics are often required to read and judge a wide range of papers in their work as reviewers for academic journals, research funding bodies and PhD proposals and theses. Student researchers should be aware that experienced academics have read, and in many cases written, a great many research papers and have developed strong research skills that enable them to help students research a wide range of topics.

'Empirical' and 'conceptual' research projects

The chapter will now discuss another important distinction, briefly mentioned earlier, in the kinds of project that can be undertaken as part of taught degrees. Some research projects at taught degree level in management and marketing are based mainly on existing sources of information such as academic papers, published economic data and/or internal company records. Such projects are often termed 'conceptual' projects to distinguish them from projects that make use of original information that is gathered by the research student. Projects that generate original data are often called 'empirical' projects. The section below will elaborate on the issues and problems of each kind of project. It will then return to important issues of what topic to research given the special demands of these two categories of research.

Empirical projects

Marketing, management and consumer research projects in higher education can be either predominantly empirical, conceptual, or they can include elements of each. *Empirical* knowledge derives from experience and empirical research projects utilize first-hand experience of primary data sets from, for example, interviews, survey data or observation. The primary data is placed in the context of available literature (in the literature review) and is then analysed for insights or findings. An empirical project report will represent the student's own systematic investigation into the topic. It will include a critical review of relevant research literature, perhaps including important practitioner literature (trade press, industry reports) and published market studies too. The general findings from the review are then evaluated in the light of the student's first-hand experience of the particular topic area, that is, their interpretation of the empirical data that has been gathered.

The amount of primary data in the empirical project can vary greatly. In research projects that are part of taught courses, data sampling may be based on very small samples for practical reasons. Qualitative data-gathering techniques use sampling approaches that are not required to provide a basis for statistically significant generalization. Data can be based on *convenience samples* and need not be *randomized*. Primary data can be used to enhance a primarily conceptual project or it can be used as the major basis of argument for a project. One MSc student project the author has supervised used three focus groups, another used four interviews. The amount of primary data that is useful depends on the research question. It is also important for student researchers to remember that even if small samples are representative of larger groups, that is, if they share the major characteristics of the larger groups, findings are still limited to the immediate research context and should be expressed cautiously in view of this. It is an important inductive principle of research that even if a particular fact or relationship between variables is true in millions of cases, we cannot know for sure if it will be true in the next case we examine.

Many projects combine elements of both conceptual and empirical approaches. One way of combining the two approaches is to focus on the literature review while carrying out a limited number of short interviews to get important practitioner or consumer perspectives on the topic. These perspectives can then be acknowledged and used in the discussion. Many projects in marketing and management that investigate a live problem do so by reviewing relevant literature on research and practice and then comparing the major findings with first-hand interviews with practitioners. In this way an empirical component can be added to a mainly conceptual research project. Conducting interviews with practising managers also has the added benefit of sharpening students' research interviewing skills and filling out their knowledge of the area. It can also be a useful exercise in getting contacts in an industry that might offer employment prospects after graduation.

'Conceptual' projects

Conceptual projects with no first-hand data are also acceptable at this level. These projects are not based on primary data but use mainly existing published sources of information. Conceptual projects consist of an extended critical review of available research literature around a particular set of research issues, questions or problems. Students who survey academic literature will see that many published research papers in marketing, management and consumer research are like this. They report no empirical findings and have no data as such, but they explore issues or problems related to research. Many are simply a critical review of previously published literature that explores the state of knowledge in a particular area. Such a review would normally try to spot gaps or neglected areas or issues on previous research in order to make suggestions about how future research might contribute to greater understanding. Other conceptual papers are more intellectually complex in that they develop sophisticated themes related to research philosophy and methods and about the scope of research in that field. Some conceptual papers offer historical analyses of particular traditions of research to show how it has developed and what influences have shaped that development.

The 'conceptual model'

Conceptual projects can induce a *conceptual model* from the literature review. A *model* in management and marketing research is a representation of an event or process that illustrates something important about that event or process. Placing some related ideas in a conceptual model can be quite a powerful textual device for making particular points or summarizing particular relationships. Models in basic management and marketing text books are often, simply, related concepts placed in boxes with arrows showing the direction of causation or the flow of decision-making. In advertising research, for example, there are hierarchy-of-effects models of advertising effects; in marketing there are models of sales cycles and new product diffusion; in management there are models of employee motivation and decision-making. The model in the conceptual student project will be drawn from a synthesis of findings from the literature and will suggest possible implications of this synthesis for management practice or for future research.

For example, one of the author's MBA students once wrote a project on advertising ethics by first reviewing literature on the topic. She then developed a taxonomy or list of ethical problems that can arise with particular advertisements. These included mis-description, overt use of negative social stereotypes, sexually provocative imagery and so on. The researcher found that, while countries tend to have their own regulatory systems for advertising, individual advertisements often seem to succeed in by-passing these criteria with subtle use of symbolic texts and imagery. She then induced a conceptual model of criteria for evaluating the ethical status of particular advertisements. This conceptual model included the major criteria that could be used to judge an individual advertisement's ethical status. The research report applied the conceptual model by giving several examples of advertisements and judging their ethical status by applying the content criteria in the conceptual model.

Another of the author's students was interested in the ways advertisers seem to target the insecurities of young women. The project was framed as a study in 'social fear'. The concept of social fear was intended to express the appeal of advertising that targets young women to sell products that exploit their fear of being unattractive or being rejected by a group. Products such as treatments for fresh breath, products to get rid of body hair and to prevent spots came into this category. She conducted an extensive literature review that addressed issues such as theories of advertising effects and ethical issues in advertising. She then collected a selection of print advertisements and creatively induced from them a typology of social fear in advertising. The typology of social fear was the conceptual model in the research project.

Other conceptual projects do not develop a conceptual model as such but, rather, develop abstract ideas and themes. One project explored the claims that research in marketing often makes to being a kind of science. The student wrote a reflexive, first-person research project expressing his bewilderment at the conflicting views in marketing. He discussed the various ideas he had been exposed to on his taught MSc in the light of his own career aspirations in marketing. A reflexive and relatively unstructured research project only reads as a credible piece of work if it is well written and well informed. This project was based on many articles published in marketing research journals that discuss research theory and relevance in marketing. It evaluated articles that claim marketing to be a science, and articles that pour scorn on that presumption. It reflected on the implications this lack of academic consensus has on the education of aspiring marketing professionals. It did so in a lively and well-informed written style.

Conceptual projects that draw on many published articles and challenge conventional wisdom and practice in the field are a pleasure to read from an academic's point of view, at least if he or she is sympathetic to that view. To make such a project credible the student must demonstrate that he or she has read and thought about a large number of high-level academic papers and, moreover, understood them. Another MSc student wrote a conceptual project that entailed a critical appraisal of the literature on the sub-field of political marketing. Again, to make this piece of work credible as a research project she had to show that she was familiar with much of the current and recent literature and ideas in that field. The writing style had to be mature and elegant and the themes developed had to demonstrate a good working understanding of research in the field.

It is wise for any student researcher considering a conceptual project to discuss it carefully with the supervisor. Projects that criticize conventional wisdom and practice need careful handling. Critical projects fit best with critically inclined supervisors. Some supervisors prefer student researchers to limit the scope of their research to exploring smaller-scale questions rather than critiquing fundamental aspects of the field as a whole.

More issues on the wording of the project title and topic

We have already discussed the importance of topic choice in general terms. What follows is a more focused discussion on some of the specific problems that can be solved at an early stage if this part of the process is done carefully. Many students get stuck at this first stage of the process because there are simply so many choices. Even more confusing is the way these various topics choices can be expressed. As the research project report is a written text, the wording is all-important. Potential research topics can be expressed in different ways which have vastly differing implications for research design and analysis. Putting the research problem or issue into words is often the most difficult and the most important part of the whole exercise. If the project is clearly defined and achievable then the rest of the process should fall into place.

There are many traps to avoid when deciding on a project title and topic. For example, it is very important not to choose a topic merely because it seems interesting. It must also be one that can be researched easily in the available time and with the available resources. 'The impact of US Government economic policy on the level of marketing activity' might sound impressive but how would you go about studying such a broad question? Perhaps narrowing it down to a particular industry sector (motor manufacturing) and a specific aspect of Government policy (monetary policy) might help but this remains a huge question for a 10–20,000 word research project that has to be completed within one or two semesters. Even if one case study of one organization was conducted, attributing marketing activity in the firm to US Government policy would not be easy. There could be other causes, such as shifts in consumer demand, competitor activity or internal marketing initiatives that might equally influence the level of marketing activity. And what would constitute a good measure of marketing activity? Many research projects that initially sound good to the first-time researcher come apart at the seams under more careful examination. It is essential that the research title and topic are picked apart, criticized and thought through at the very beginning. The cost of not thinking carefully enough about the title at the beginning could be a research project that runs aground when it is too late to start again.

It is important that a project is interesting to the student because that is where the motivation for seeing it through will come from. It is also important to think of practicalities such as can the topic be researched? Is the information available? Is there time? Can the topic be reasonably researched in a short report conducted over a few months? Box 2.2 lists some of the major issues to consider in choosing the project topic and title.

Getting access to data or to interviewees

Accessibility to information and/or interviews is a major consideration. Students must be sure that they can get access to interviews or other information in organizations before they build that data into their research question. Getting access to interviews or other company data cannot be presumed upon. Organizations are busy, complex places. Promised data

---

Box 2.2 Checklist for choosing a project topic

- Is the topic interesting to you?
- Does the research problem make sense to people when you explain it to them? Is it clearly and succinctly expressed?
- Does your supervisor feel that it is appropriate? Does it fall within the required subject domain? Is it sufficiently important/interesting?
- Can you say how you would investigate it? In other words, is it do-able?
- Is enough relevant published research-based literature available to support a substantial critical literature review?
- Does the topic depend on access to confidential or sensitive information?

may not, in the end, be provided. Interviewees may cancel at the last minute, or move jobs. Students often send letters asking for interviews and wait many weeks for any response. It is good practice to follow up the letter with a phone call or email within a week. It is also important to address the enquiry to a named person who has responsibility for the area of interest.

If the student's approach is considerate then practising managers often enjoy giving interviews. For the student, the experience of conducting interviews with practitioners is usually very positive. In most cases students doing research projects find that practitioners are extremely friendly, helpful and constructive and the help they provide can be a most rewarding part of the research process for the student. It can also be so for the interviewee. However, be prepared to interview a different person to the one you had approached initially, and possibly at a different time. Also, be prepared to travel to the interviewee's office at a time of their choosing. For students, the principle should be that obtaining interviews is very valuable, since they can add the practitioner's perspective to your research. Just don't make your whole research project plan dependent on access to a specific interview or particular piece of company data, in case it doesn't happen.

Many students have privileged access to particular kinds of data and it can be wise to exploit this. For example, students studying in foreign countries can often pick a topic for a comparative study that draws on cross-cultural issues because of their expertise in two (or more) languages and their knowledge of two cultures. The author has often encouraged students to conduct comparative studies of management, consumer or marketing practices in the UK and their own home country. In this way students can make use of their special knowledge of two cultures.

For example, one Japanese student collected magazine advertisements for particular brands of car from Japanese magazines and compared these to the advertisements for the same car in UK magazines. She used a semiotic analysis (discussed later in the book) to draw out the different cultural codes that domestic readers might use to understand the meanings within the ads. She also used the analysis to infer the differing domestic and foreign positioning and segmentation strategies that manufacturers were trying to deploy. This master's project was later used as the basis for a (successful) PhD proposal. In other examples, a Malaysian student studied advertising management in Malaysian advertising agencies and compared this to literature on the process in US and UK agencies. He drew on his experience and contacts in the Malaysian advertising industry. A Chinese student did a case study of brand communications strategy in the fast-food sector in Beijing, again using US and UK literature as a basis for comparison. She had previously worked for a major advertising agency in Beijing and was able to ask friends at the agency for useful material. Another

Chinese student explored the Chinese motor car market as a potential market for UK and US motor car manufacturers. In each case students were able to exploit their special contacts and knowledge to enhance their research project.

Dealing with a scarcity of published research

Access to primary data is not the only potential difficulty in conceiving of a research topic. Both empirical and conceptual projects must have a substantial literature review as their basis. If the chosen topic is novel or new there may not be very much literature in publication that deals with that precise topic. For example, research into the marketing effectiveness of new media topics such as interactivity and Internet communications can fall into this category. Even if the student researcher finds some useful sources, this field is changing so quickly that the few books and articles that are in print quickly fall out of date. This makes it difficult to ground the project in an adequate literature review. One solution to this problem is to investigate a new or novel topic as a subcategory of an old one.

For example, a student who wishes to do a project on interactive media would, at the time of writing, find relatively little authoritative published academic research that could be the basis of the project literature review. Instead, the novel topic could be presented as a subcategory of a well-established one, for example by calling the project 'The role of interactive media on media strategy decisions in advertising'. There is plenty of available academic literature, text books and practitioner articles on media strategy in general advertising. By locating a new topic within a well-established one the student can be sure to find plenty of existing published work on which to base a thorough literature review.

'What', 'why' and 'how' questions

We have already emphasized the importance of the choice of words in expressing the project proposal and title. Of particular importance is the kind of question that is implied in a research proposal. Different kinds of question imply different methods and analytical approaches. Students new to research are often unaware of the implications different kinds of question have for their whole project.

'What' questions

For example, many topics entail 'what' questions. A common way of crafting a research question in marketing is to ask 'What is the connection or link between x and y?' Very often this will be cast in terms of the possible impact of a marketing variable in a particular managerial intervention.

This could be a question of causation such as 'What is the impact of celebrity endorsement on sales of a brand of sports shoes in the UK?' or 'What is the effect of a 10% price reduction on consumers' perceptions of the quality of brand X?' Such questions, while legitimate research topics, carry assumptions that dictate the character of the research to be conducted. First, such questions assume that the categories contained in them ('celebrity endorsement', 'brand') are unquestionably appropriate to the circumstances. Defining the terms in no way avoids this problem because the categories, however defined, set the terms of researcher engagement with the topic. As a result there will inevitably be an element of logical circularity to a project in which an essential category is taken for granted.

To put this in another way, the first question assumes that 'celebrity endorsement' has an impact on sports shoe sales. In social research in marketing, management and anything else, you can always find what you think you are looking for. If you assume that 'celebrity endorsement' is what drives sales in the sports shoe market then that is what you will 'find'. But there could be other ways of conceiving of this relation. Perhaps the brand exposure is the important thing and the celebrity component is incidental. Perhaps celebrity endorsement is the wrong phrase to use: members of the public know very well that celebrities often 'endorse' products that they don't use. Perhaps the celebrity association with the brand is the important thing and not the endorsement as such. Clearly such questions of conceptual clarity and causal relations in marketing can and should be discussed in the research project report. However, in marketing research in particular, it is all too often the case that they are not. Marketing research projects do need to offer a balanced justification of their assumptions in order to satisfy broader intellectual criteria.

It is useful to be aware, also, that in many cases the academic assessing or second marking the research report may not be inclined to accept that certain concepts and relations can be taken for granted. In the above case it would be wise for the student to pose a broader research question exploring the nature of demand for sports shoes in the UK (or other) market so that, should any causal relation become evident during the course of the research, it can be reported in an appropriate context. Alternatively the research proposal could explore the *role* and *nature* of celebrity endorsement promotion in a national sports shoe market. That way, the research findings are not presupposed in the research question.

It is an important part of the ethical and the intellectual integrity of management research that conventional or given categories, phrases and relations are inverted and questioned and their use critically examined in local contexts. As mentioned above, marketing research has a record of perpetuating essential concepts in self-confirming research exercises. For example, research that investigates the role of the 'marketing mix' in particular product markets legitimizes the 'marketing mix' as an important and useful category of management activity. One may argue that the 'marketing mix' is just that: important and useful. But research that accepts given categories and the relations implicit with their use is likely to lack a spirit of creativity and critique. A research project is an opportunity to explore creatively an issue or area and thereby intellectually develop and enrich the researcher. As an intellectual exercise a research dissertation should be an exercise in challenging assumptions and picking apart native categories. An inexperienced researcher should not feel bound to decide what they are going to find before they start looking. So the topic chosen can be framed initially as a working title exploring, investigating or examining an issue, problem or relationship. If the topic is cast in this way the issue is left open. The topic may change emphasis or direction depending on what the researcher finds. Initial categories (such as 'celebrity endorsement' or 'marketing mix') should be established by critical inquiry and not simply asserted by definition.

'Why' and 'how' questions

'Why' questions, as well as 'what' questions, can be inappropriately phrased in a way that implicitly supplies the answer. For example, the research question 'Why does marketing orientation offer sustained competitive advantage for commercial organizations?' is clearly a question that has answered itself. Incidentally, this is a question that, even phrased in an exploratory style, is probably beyond the scope of a student project unless they can get access to senior executives of several organizations. 'How' questions also need to be used with caution. The question 'How do encyclopaedia sales people maximize their effectiveness in sales interviews?' assumes that direct selling is an important sales channel for encyclopaedias. How many encyclopaedias are sold by direct sales these days? A student researching this project would find out half-way through the process that encyclopaedias are rarely sold this way these days so there would be a shortage of available research sources. It would be more useful to the student who is interested in this area to investigate either, a) encyclopaedia sales and distribution in a given market, or b) sales interview styles in any context. In general it is a useful practice for first-time student researchers to pose open questions so that they are not caught out later by the presuppositions implied in particular kinds of question.

We tend to phrase social research questions in terms of 'what', 'why' and 'how' when we first embark on an independent study project. Students new to research cannot be expected to know that they set traps for themselves in phrasing questions in this way since they presuppose particular ways of knowing and understanding. It is far from unusual for a student to do a conscientious research project investigating such a question only to be told at the end that they were not awarded a better mark because their research question was too narrow or was otherwise inappropriate to the subject. 'What', 'why' and 'how' imply that there is a 'what', a 'why' or a 'how'. In social research there may be highly complex relations between an event and its consequences or antecedents. At undergraduate or master's level, an open investigation into a topic tends to be a wiser exercise for the student. It is also a more creative exercise to conduct an open investigation that is not stunted by the need to defend the assumptions implied in the question.

The choice of research topic, then, is a particularly important aspect of research planning. Considerable thought must be given to the way the topic title and research proposal is drafted. Getting this right and thinking it through can save a great deal of stress later in the process. The next chapter discusses the outcome of the research project process, the project report, also called the dissertation or thesis. It is particularly important for student researchers to understand that a written document, a text, is the goal of their efforts. If student researchers appreciate the likely structure, tone and style of this text at the beginning of the process it can make research design and planning much easier.

Glossary

Conceptual project   Project that does not make great use of primary data but, rather, develops a conceptual analysis from a synthesis of published research and existing available data.

Convenience sampling   A method of choosing a data sample based on convenience, such as when academic researchers in psychology or management use their own students as research respondents or participants.

Deductive   Normally refers to reasoning that proceeds from the particular to the general. If a fact or relationship between variables seems to hold in one case it might hold in all cases.

Empirical research project   Research that generates new data.

Functional   In this chapter 'functional' refers to research projects that seek to address a functional area of business such as accounting, operations, marketing, service or manufacturing from a managerial problem-solving point of view. 'Functional' has a different meaning in sociology and cultural anthropology, often described in terms of a biological metaphor that emphasizes the systemic interdependence of parts.

Harvard referencing   The style of referencing used in this book. It entails citing references in the text with author and year. The full reference is placed in the references section in alphabetical order at the end of the document.

Hypothetico-deductive   A style of research that derives a hypothesis from a body of theory, tests it empirically and uses the findings to inform or modify the theory.

Inductive   Reasoning that moves from the general to the particular. For example, if a causal relationship seems to hold in many cases it might be tested to see if it holds in more cases.

Positivism   In social research the term usually refers to a set of assumptions about reality and knowledge that have some similarity to the precepts of a branch of philosophy of knowledge called 'logical positivism' (Ayer, 1936). In management research 'positivist' often refers to research that assumes that the social world can be treated as materially real in the same way as the physical world.

Randomized   Randomized data is collected according to a principle of random sampling, that is, no element of human judgement is involved in the selection of data and each unit of data should have an equal chance of selection.

Chapter 3

'Writing up' the research project

Chapter outline

This chapter discusses each part of the research project in order to give students a rounded view of the whole document they must eventually produce. Having this view will help with research planning and time management. It will also help students' confidence to know how the various parts of the research project fit into the whole. Some common problems and difficulties can be anticipated and tackled in advance. The chapter suggests research project chapter headings for both conceptual and empirical projects.

Chapter objectives

After reading this chapter students will be able to

- see both the parts and the whole of the research project writing-up process
- plan the research knowing what kind of text must be produced
- anticipate some of the common difficulties and opportunities in research writing
- set out with confidence on the research process

'Writing up' and the research process

'Writing up' is often considered to be the final stage in the research project. However, it is strongly advised that students think carefully about the written document that they must produce right from the beginning of the project process. By doing this students form an idea of the whole picture of a research project before they embark on it. In contrast, many first-time student researchers begin the project without appreciating the nature of the desired end-result. They attempt each stage without knowing why it is important and how it fits into the whole. This can result in poor planning and loss of direction. Academics are very familiar with student research projects that are flawed because they are poorly structured. If students have a holistic idea of what kind of text they must produce then the process can be much less stressful and more successful.

The common idea of 'writing up' research implies that the research process is separate from the writing process, and also that 'writing up' somehow requires less attention than the research. Neither is true. Research is constructed through writing. Research cannot be communicated unless a narrative is constructed to tell the research story. Therefore, it makes perfect sense to consider the narrative conventions of research as part of research design. This does not imply that there is one right way to write research projects. People plan and write their research in different ways. The process of writing, and the style in which the researcher writes, can differ widely.

Some student researchers gather data and literature over time and then write up a draft of the whole project. Others prefer to do their literature search first and write up the project chapter by chapter. If the project is deductive in style, the literature review will come first in the research process as well as appearing early in the research project report. If, on the other hand, the research is inductive in style (see previous chapter for discussion on deductive–inductive research designs) there will be an initial literature review followed by a phase of data collection, followed by another more closely focused literature review. The research report will, however, be written up in the same sequence as for the deductive research project, with the literature review early in the sequence of chapters. This is because research writing does not always have to accurately represent the process of research. Indeed, it would be impossible to do this. A research study that takes several months and entails false starts and blind alleys would not make easy reading if it were described in every detail. The sequence of actual research activities depends to a large extent on personal preference (and on the preferred style of the supervisor) and upon the nature of the project. The report itself need not necessarily reflect this sequence of activities. It is more important for a research report to satisfy some of the accepted narrative conventions of research in that field. In other words, it must look like a research report (or thesis, or dissertation) in order for readers to accept that it is one.

Students conducting a research project have to construct their research question, to read widely around that topic, to choose a suitable method of inquiry, and to reflect on their own assumptions as they attempt to make sense of their question and of the answers. Many university and business school faculties have their own conventions for style, tone and structure of such projects, typeface and references style, contents and chapter headings. Many academic supervisors have individual preferences in such matters. It is wise for students to make sure they understand exactly what conventions they are expected to observe in their research project. However, there are principles of good practice that apply to every research project. Research reports need to have certain things, like literature reviews, research objectives, findings, references and so on. They need to be presented in an appropriate sequence. The report also has to be written in an appropriate style or 'tone'. The next section will develop some themes on this most important aspect of research writing.

The academic writing 'tone'

The 'tone' of a piece of writing refers to what it conveys through, for example, its grammatical conventions and vocabulary. Tone can be generally formal, informal, conversational, authoritative, amusing, serious, technical and so on. It is difficult to define tone since it is a matter of interpretation. The best way to address the issue for research writing is to say that the tone must seem to the reader to be appropriate for a research text.

The appropriate writing tone is often identified with the standards of 'good' scholarship referred to in Chapter 1. Academic writing styles can sometimes seem obscure and pretentious to readers more familiar with newspapers or popular novels. Academic papers are often strewn with the technical jargon of social science. Sentences are long and often carry multiple subclauses as academic writers build in contingencies to everything they want to say. It is important to recognize that, while some writers are obscure because their thoughts are not clear, much academic writing uses technical terms and stylistic conventions because they have become part of the accepted way of writing in that field. It is an important part of the student researcher's task to begin to understand the purpose of this style and to write in a way that is somewhat like it.

Some of the stylistic conventions are easy to grasp. For example, many research papers are written in the 'third person', as when the authors refer to themselves as 'the authors' instead of simply saying 'I'. This convention can rhetorically produce a sense of detachment or objectivity. It makes the research writing sound more rigorous. It is often a good idea for student researchers to adopt this convention although it is not always required. Many interpretive traditions of research adopt the first person grammar and use 'I' when referring to the author. Different academics have different preferences. If in doubt it is a good idea to write in the third person because that is the traditional approach.

Writing in the third person, while a somewhat stilted prose style, can help to encourage a disciplined approach to writing up the work as a piece of systematic research rather than as a personal story. Again, while writing in a disciplined and conventional style is usually advisable for student researchers it is not the only way. Published researchers have attempted to challenge this convention and have written very personalized accounts of their research. Holbrook (1995) has even devised an interpretive method of research he calls 'Subjective Personal Introspection' that has been used in various published interpretive consumer research studies (e.g. Shankar, 2000). Brown (e.g. 1995) has produced some of the most vivid, and funniest, pieces of writing in academic marketing using an exclusively personalized style. Marketing authors have used poetry and lyricism to shed new insights on marketing as a Romantic endeavour (e.g. Brown *et al.*, 1998, and in consumer research, Sherry and Schouten, 2002). It is probably fair to say that you have to be a very experienced and creative scholar, and a confident writer, to produce a credible research report in as frankly a subjective vein as these authors. For most student researchers, writing in the third person is the 'safer' option.

Another important aspect of writing tone concerns the way 'arguments' or points of view are constructed and assertions made. As also mentioned in Chapter 1, the entire research report is an argument, in a rhetorical sense. The research project process can be seen as a test to see whether the student can develop or explore points of view of some complexity drawing on a variety of sources. In the research report he or she must show that they can sustain this for eight, ten, twelve or twenty thousand words, depending on the requirements of their department. This is not easy, which is why the research project is considered to be the most advanced part of any academic course of study. The report will attest to the student researcher's standard of scholarship. For academics, a high standard of scholarship is difficult to define, but they know it when they see it. It consists in plausible, clearly expressed, thorough and well-supported intellectual work.

Making claims and supporting arguments

Credible research writing depends on not making incredible claims. The acquisition of more knowledge usually makes people less extravagant in their claims, therefore more modestly styled prose suggests to the reader that the author has more knowledge. The stance of the true researcher is that one knows little or nothing. Knowledge progresses in very small stages, if it can be said to progress at all. Academics working in a particular field know a lot, but this knowledge shows them how much more there is to know. This does not mean that one has to write only about topics that can be reduced to tiny subtopics. Neither does it mean that research writing should be excessively cautious in making assertions of any kind. There is plenty of scope for creative exploration in ideas, as long as the writer is frank about what is speculation and what is a more substantive claim. Assertions, claims or suggestions should be carefully and logically supported with reasoning or evidence.

Any assertion in a research report (such as 'Management researchers still understand relatively little about motivation in the workplace') needs to be supported very carefully with references to published authorities, to other sources or by careful reasoning. Inadequately supported assertions are probably the most common reason for losing marks in a research project report. The examiner will not normally judge the student researcher's writing on whether or not what they write about is true. Much of social science is speculative and can only be judged on its coherence or its logical connection to other bodies of theory or evidence. The examiner is, however, looking for a good quality of argument and discussion. This implies that authors should show that they are aware that their point of view is not the only one that may be right. Authors of research reports should show that they are aware of a number of possible points of view. There is a lot of published research literature on employee motivation so the above assertion would, at least, need to be placed in a context of a careful review of a good range of that literature in order for the examiner to accept that the writer has sufficiently supported the claim.

So, before embarking on the research report, remember to read as many academic research papers as possible to grasp the academic style and to become familiar with a range of research in the field of interest. Second, remember that academics who have devoted their entire career to researching a specific topic often feel that, while they know a lot, they still know much less than they'd like to. Consequently the last thing they want to read is a piece of student research from a writer who thinks they've cracked the whole problem in a semester. Popular business and management texts tend to use grammatical conventions which imply that they offer solutions: 'Managing quality better in financial services'; 'Relationship Marketing, the new paradigm for business success'; 'Emotional Intelligence: the key to effective management'. These are not, to my knowledge, the titles of real books, though they could be; I've made them up. They employ grammatical styles that are very (too) common in this field. Students should be aware that a research project should not make too much use of the popular, consulting style of writing that is seen in many teaching texts. Write in a style that shows caution towards assertions, supports points with careful reasoning and evidence from literature and research, and show awareness that there may be alternative points of view that have not occurred to you, the researcher.

The project report structure

At this stage it will be useful for student researchers to have an insight into what they must produce at the end of the research process. In the end, academic research into social topics such as management and marketing is a textual enterprise: that is, the researcher is engaged in producing a text to be read (and judged) by others. Knowing how the various written components will fit together is extremely useful in planning the research, and writing, process.

Each kind of project (empirical and conceptual) has similar requirements that it must follow in order to satisfy the intellectual standards of higher degrees. The chapter headings in Boxes 3.1 and 3.2 are offered as flexible guides to the broad content of an independent research project.

Whether a research project is mainly empirical or mainly conceptual the student researcher still needs to demonstrate an informed point of view in a carefully developed and structured piece of written work. It is not enough to simply summarize a series of articles or book chapters and pass this off as a conceptual project. In both styles of project there must be a problem/issue formulation, a set of criteria for selecting relevant literature and a way of evaluating or discussing the theories and findings in that

---

Box 3.1 A suggested *empirical* research project chapter order

Project Title: must be clear and carefully phrased

Abstract: 100–150 words summarizing the project aims and main findings

Contents page
Chapter 1: Including the introduction; overview of research issue/problem; research objectives; major theoretical assumptions; outline of the project as a whole
Chapter 2: Critical literature review; locating the issue/problem within relevant published research; identifying key concepts and issues
Chapter 3: Method: offering an explanation and justification of the particular approach chosen; referring to published authorities to back up the chosen approach; explaining why the chosen approach was most appropriate in the circumstances
Chapter 4: Empirical research report; reporting findings from primary research
Chapter 5: Synthesis of literature review with empirical findings; discussion of major issues
Chapter 6: Concluding comments and recommendations

References: Harvard method, full reference for every authority cited in the dissertation

Appendices: may include additional graphs or data that would have interrupted the flow of the text, such as interview transcripts

Box 3.2 A suggested *conceptual* research project chapter order

Project Title: must be clear and carefully phrased

Abstract: 100–150 words summarizing the project aims and main findings

Contents page
Chapter 1: Introduction: overview of research issue/problem; project objectives (e.g. to review current developments in a particular field); outline of the project
Chapter 2: Extended critical literature review; locating the issue/problem within relevant published research, identifying key concepts and issues
Chapter 3: Conceptual model; inducing the major features or findings from the literature, or developing main arguments regarding future research or practice
Chapter 4: Applying the conceptual model to a set of case examples
Chapter 5: Synthesis and discussion
Chapter 6: Concluding comments and implications

References: Harvard method, full reference for every authority cited in the dissertation

Appendices: may include additional graphs or data that would have interrupted the flow of the text

literature. The findings of the empirical project, or the conceptual model/findings of the conceptual project, will form the basis for the analysis/discussion, so in both there must be a clear point of view that can be developed logically.

The particular structure chosen for the project can vary but every project will contain, in whatever form, the elements of these suggested structures. That is, the project must contain a clear research problem, issue or question that the supervisor has agreed is appropriate. It must contain a careful, substantial and critical review and evaluation of relevant research papers and other published sources. Finally, it must contain a careful assimilation of major findings that discusses the needs of future research and/or the implications for current and future practice. The following sections will discuss in more detail the particular problems and issues arising at each stage in these suggested project structures.

The abstract and chapter one

The abstract and chapter one can often be written last of all. That is because with exploratory research one does not know how the story will turn out until the end. Hence the abstract and chapter one could change many times before the final write-up. This is to some extent a matter of personal preference. Some researchers prefer to gather data, think about the issues, make notes and reflections, draft some sections and collect relevant research articles until the last moment then write a first draft of the project report in one go. Others prefer to start at the beginning and write a chapter at a time in sequence. The abstract will summarize the whole project in about 150–200 words. Chapter one will explain in more detail what the project is about, what its main aims and subject matter are. It will also set the background context and explain why the topic is of interest.

The chapter can begin with a problem statement about what issues the research will seek to address. It can then set out some background to set the report issues within a broader context of a particular industry, a particular tradition of literature or a specific problem. It will need to set out three or four major research objectives. Finally, the chapter can outline the whole project report, indicating what each chapter deals with, how the research was conducted and briefly summarizing the major findings and/or conclusions. This gives the reader a good idea of what to expect and, more importantly, shows that the report is the result of a carefully structured, well thought-through and systematic piece of scholarly research (see Box 3.3).

Project research objectives

It is important to remember that repeating the aims, objectives and themes of the research in the abstract, in chapter one and in the final chapter, is not only appropriate but necessary. It is necessary by convention and also

---

Box 3.3 Chapter one suggested content

Abstract: 150–200 words that describe topic, problem, methodological standpoint and main findings.
Introduction: statement of the research problem or issue, reasons why it is important and/or interesting
Background: setting the context with regard to particular industry or research issues
Main research objectives
Major method(s) or philosophical/conceptual standpoint
Brief outline of the chapter themes that follow

to remind the reader that what is being written is structured according to a consistent set of questions or themes. The objectives would usually be set out in chapter one, returned to at several stages during the report, and finally restated in the concluding comments. In this way the writer clearly signals to the reader that the research was well conceived and systematic. In general it is a good idea in research writing to make it easy for the reader to see to why particular points and sections are relevant to the main theme. A degree of necessary repetition can help in this aim.

Research aims and objectives are very important, though it should be remembered that they need not be complex. It is not necessary to produce an original contribution to knowledge in a taught master's or undergraduate degree course. For this level of research project objectives can be quite simple and straightforward. They are important because they indicate that the researcher had a focus for the research and that this focus is the basis for the narrative structure of the report. A report must tell a story of a piece of research. A story must have a plot that develops through a beginning, a middle and an end. A research report that drifts along without a point of focus will give the reader the impression that the researcher never quite thought through what it was they wanted to find out. The research objectives also provide an internal measure of the success of the research. If the final chapter can say to what extent the objectives were achieved then the report is likely to be well structured.

As mentioned in the previous chapter, the research report is not a temporally linear representation of the research process. That is to say, the report is not the same thing as a research diary and does not necessarily describe the precise order of events. In exploratory research the objectives may be crafted in final form at the end of the research process because they, like the broad research question, will be modified during the research. Some research objectives, such as 'To critically review the existing state of theory from a selection of leading journals' need not change during the process. This is a broad and straightforward objective for a conceptual project. Other, more specific objectives might well evolve and change in emphasis, although they will have been present in some form from the beginning.

For example, a research project might set out 'To find success factors in entrepreneurial marketing'. The researcher might find that this objective was too broad. Research interviews with marketing entrepreneurs might well generate interesting findings regarding the origins of the entrepreneurial mentality but these insights may be personal, rooted in the entrepreneur's particular biography and experience. The phrase 'success factors' implies that 'factors' are the same for every entrepreneur in every entrepreneurial situation. Furthermore, entrepreneurial activity is conducted in many different industries and takes differing forms. To be entrepreneurial within a health service implies different behaviours, outcomes and priorities to being entrepreneurial in, say, a television production company or a small retail business. Hence the broad objective could be refined to accommodate the specific research context and priorities.

Many research objectives are very simple. For example, the student researcher might wish to use words such as investigate, explore, evaluate or examine a particular area or problem. He or she might wish to investigate relationships between events or variables or to explore a particular problem. Modestly phrased objectives often pave the way for the most sophisticated research because they imply that the student researcher understands the complexity of the issue or problem that is under investigation.

Reflexive writing and the achievement of research objectives

Interpretive research reporting traditions often adopt a *reflexive* stance. *Reflexivity* in research means being aware of being aware. In research writing it implies open and transparent acknowledgement of all the circumstances of the research context, including the personal reflections of the researcher. Many models of scientific inquiry that are based on physical science have no place for reflexivity. They are written to rhetorically produce a set of findings that are independent of author and of method: they are written to be universal, and anonymous. Interpretive research traditions, in contrast, give a voice to the researcher. In student research work, in particular, it is important to show that there is awareness of limitations of method, of sample, of ways in which the findings were influenced by the assumptions, beliefs and research style of the researcher.

In a reflexive research project it is quite appropriate for the researcher to comment on how the research project evolved. There is no need to pretend that it all went without a hitch. Indeed, the examiner will normally want to see that the student researcher has developed his or her research skills and subject understanding through reflecting critically on how the project was conceived and carried out.

It may be appropriate to refer to the refinement of research objectives in response to the researcher's developing understanding. The change in objectives should be made clear and the reasons for this change explained. In interpretive research designs, then, the recrafting of research objectives is a legitimate part of the research process. In strictly 'positivist' research that seeks to support or reject a specific hypothesis, changing the research objectives would not be in keeping with the research ethos. It would be a form of 'cheating', although a careful reading of the research would soon reveal the inconsistencies in the story. In interpretive research the integrity of the research process is the important thing and this includes being sensitive to flaws in the original problem formulation and research objectives. It also entails being sensitive to unexpected insights emerging from the research. In a creative research design such unexpected insights can be accommodated within the project and these changes can be openly discussed.

'Critical' thinking and the literature review

Whatever research topic is decided upon it is essential to locate it in an appropriate body of literature. The research project should seem to have evolved out of a careful consideration of previous research in similar related areas. Some research projects (conceptual projects) consist mainly of an extended review of literature. Other, managerially oriented projects, may be based around a particular industry problem. For an academic research project, solving a managerial problem is not enough. The problem, and the means of solving it, must be set within a context of previous and recent research. This entails reviewing a cross-section of published academic journal articles relevant to the research topic. The literature review must be 'critical' in order to satisfy a major criterion of higher academic accomplishment.

Examiners of research projects often regard evidence of 'critical' thinking as a necessary condition satisfying the higher educational objectives of the research project. However, what academics mean by 'critical' thinking, research and writing is often far from clear. The word 'critical' is often used in managerial writing as a synonym for 'important' (as in, for example, 'marketing is a critical business function'). Many academics feel that 'critical' thinking is the same as intellectually 'rigorous' thinking. These terms imply that in research writing differing theories and perspectives have not simply been accepted at face value by the researcher. Rather, the critical or rigorous researcher has compared them to each other and evaluated each theory or perspective in terms of their apparent qualities and shortcomings. Work that does this well demonstrates a deeper level of understanding and a more penetrating quality of intellect than work which takes a passive position towards theories and merely accepts them uncritically. In other words, the literature review that merely repeats the views of several authors on a topic is not 'critical'. Research writing that is 'critical' demonstrates a higher level of intellectual accomplishment than this.

'Levels' of critical thinking are outlined in Box 3.4 to try to illustrate this point more clearly. Box 3.4 is offered to help students understand this idea of 'critical' analysis so that they can incorporate it into their work.

Level I: Uncritical thinking

Uncritical thinking is exemplified by referencing a theoretical or conceptual model (such as E. Jerome McCarthy and the four Ps of the Marketing

Box 3.4 A suggested schema of levels of critical thinking

Level 1: Uncritical thinking: uncritically accepting the assumptions built into concepts, theories and axioms

Level 2: Problem-based critique: focusing on the possible 'usefulness' or 'effectiveness' of a given concept or model for solving a practical managerial problem

Level 3: Critical engagement with the epistemological assumptions of normative (problem-solving) models

Level 4: Sociological critique: opening up the political dimension of marketing and management discourse to question which interests might be served by particular representational conventions

Mix) and applying the concepts of Ps to a marketing management issue. This may be appropriate in work of a managerial problem-solving vein. The conceptual coherence or practical usefulness of the framework used is not a major consideration in such work. Coherence and potential usefulness are taken for granted and such research seeks to investigate its topic within the assumptions set by the chosen model. This kind of research may be managerially or practically useful if it is set within a defined management problem. The difficulty is that such work may not necessarily satisfy the educational demands of an academic project since it uncritically accepts the assumptions that are implied by the model. Such assumptions might include the following:

a   that the marketing mix cake-baking analogy is indeed analogous to practical marketing management;

b   that the framework is internally coherent so that logical inferences can be made from it;

c   that it generates insights that have practical utility to marketing professionals;

d   that it has universal applicability to any marketing context;

e   that the mix elements are decisive in market success;

f   that marketing managers have strategic control over all mix elements.

The marketing mix framework might be defended against these criticisms, but research projects that fail to acknowledge fundamental criticisms of the constructs and conceptual frameworks used are usually confined to the uncritical level of analysis.

Level 2: Problem-based critique

Thinking at this level entails analysing the usefulness of the theory in terms of how it might deepen insight into a particular issue. It therefore goes beyond the uncritical thinking described in level 1 above. There are two particularly pertinent questions:

1   Does the conceptual model/theoretical knowledge add to or go beyond experiential, 'common-sense' understanding?
2   Does the theoretical model fit well with the situation under investigation?

If the answer to either of these questions is negative, a third question is begged: what other theoretical framework would be useful? The onus is on students to explore a range of theoretical work with application to the particular problem. So, to extend the example, if the student researcher were to apply the marketing mix framework to a particular marketing management problem or issue, they would need to begin with an extensive evaluation of the mix in their critical literature review. The review would have to address criticisms of the practical usefulness and managerial relevance of the framework, discussing weaknesses, strengths and the implicit (and explicit) assumptions that are built into it. The review would seek to move towards a frank appraisal of the mix framework as a basis for managerial problem solving. It would also acknowledge that other frameworks may offer different but equally useful insights.

Level 3: Critical engagement

An example of this level of thinking is Brownlie and Saren's (1992) critique of the Four Ps, in which they engage critically with the logical assumptions underlying the Four Ps. Critical thinking of this kind addresses the internal logic of a theoretical framework or construct. Such reviews may engage with epistemological (philosophy of knowledge) and ontological (assumptions about the nature of reality in social research) issues.

Again taking the example of the marketing 'mix', the review might question the social scientific basis for the model. What grounds are there for this framework? What evidence is there that it is a practically useful or intellectually viable way of categorizing certain managerial marketing activities? This level of thinking is an advance on level 2 because it not only focuses on managerial problem solving, but also begins to evaluate concepts and frameworks in social scientific terms. The marketing mix is, arguably, a framework that evolved from a business consulting perspective and was popularized in marketing management text books. Does this make it an appropriate basis for intellectually rigorous work in an academic context?

Level 3 thinking begins to engage with the difficult philosophical question of how it is possible to 'know' anything at all. This should be not too daunting to advanced students: many primary schools find it useful to teach philosophy to very young children. The aim is not to resolve philosophical questions but to acknowledge them in order to improve the quality of thinking. Many marketing academics argue that marketing has a body of theory that is *normative*, that is, it is designed to assist practical action. This, they suggest, gives it a special character that cannot be evaluated in traditional social scientific terms. Others argue that this may be all right for consulting but that academic marketing and management research cannot claim to be a special kind of knowledge set apart from the rest of social science.

Level 4: Sociological critique

The phrase 'sociological critique' is used here to emphasize a particular mentality in social research. This mentality questions the 'ordinary' and the 'obvious' in social life on the grounds that what is ordinary or obvious seems so by virtue of a profoundly complex process. This very fundamental level of critique asks what alternative ways the situation under investigation could be represented. It asks this on the grounds that every way of describing something suppresses other alternatives and carries certain assumptions and interests. This level of thinking and writing may go beyond the typical marketing or management project. It may cut across into other disciplines in its breadth of perspective and conceptual scope. Many marketing and consumer research projects engage with their subject matter in this way and ask how the consumption of goods in specific social contexts helps consumers to construct a sense of meaning and identity. In the same way managerial projects can ask how managers acquire their sense of meaning by drawing on available discourses (ways of describing) available to their community. Managerial work and consumption need not be seen as 'fixed' or 'given' but can be seen as dynamic processes in which people impose meaning on to their activities through the language and social practices they employ. So, for example, a managerial project would not only ask how effective the marketing mix is in a particular problem-solving context. Rather, it would ask what managers accomplish by using the language of popular managerial marketing to rationalize and justify their actions.

More on the 'academic' style of writing

The use of references

The use of references can seem a cumbersome device but it is essential to academic writing. If a general assertion is made ('Research in marketing has neglected the role of internal communications in organizational marketing effectiveness') there needs to be a citation of published work that supports this assertion. If a student researcher makes any assertion that they want accepted as a statement of fact there does need to be this support from credible published work. The published work should, preferably, come from refereed academic journals of good standing (see the Appendix). As a general rule, the more references the better, provided they are relevant to the point being supported.

It is important to note that citing previously published work does not detract from the originality or freshness of the current research. Citing references does not mean that you can't think of your own ideas. It signals to the reader that your work is based on a sound understanding of the area. It also signals that you understand how your research is thematically linked with previous research. If a passage in the research report is discussing a particular theme or issue that has been previously researched, citing that previously published research indicates that the student researcher has done a suitable review of published work in that area and understands how it is similar to and/or different from the current research project. It is a mark of good scholarship to master a fluid style of referencing so that citations are woven elegantly into the text.

All works cited by author and date (Smith, 1995) in the text of the research report should be listed in full in alphabetical order by author at the end of the report. This is known as the Harvard method of reference citation, as used in this book. The term 'bibliography' is sometimes used to indicate all work read as part of the research even if it is not cited in the research report. However, viewed negatively, a bibliography can be seen as a list of books that the student didn't quite get around to reading. All works listed in the references must have been cited in the report text.

Theories and models

We have already mentioned the idea of the conceptual 'model' as a representation of a process or event. Many academic papers talk extensively of 'theories' and 'models'. These terms can sometime be used as synonyms in social scientific research. Each term refers to or implies a form of explanation for a process or event. 'Models' in management and marketing are often a researcher's idea of how a process might work, such as a consumer decision-making process, a management information system or a marketing sales cycle. There are models of how attitudes are formed, of human motivation, models of quality management processes, models of consumer behaviour and so on and so forth. Many social researchers working in marketing and management research are concerned with creating models either made up of words, boxes and arrows, of numbers and formulae, or all three. Models can be highly speculative, consisting of little more than a few words linked by arrows and put in a highlighted text box. Others are hugely detailed and based on extensive empirical research. Models try to show what elements are important in a process. They also try to show the relationship between elements.

A theory is, strictly speaking, quite different from a model although one is invariably implied in the other. That is to say that a model implies a given theoretical stance and a theoretical stance, or its components, can often be reduced to a model. Theories, like models, are attempts to explain or understand the social world. We all acquire rudimentary theories from our everyday experience. We develop theories of which kinds of people can be trusted, theories of which behaviours are socially acceptable in particular contexts (smiling and being polite) and which are not (getting drunk and being sick over soft furnishings). Our rudimentary social theories are learned from experience but our empirical evidence is clearly very narrow – since we only have the perspective of one individual – so we must continually re-adjust and modify our theories. Social researchers often try to develop theories that are more robust and detailed. They try to draw on a much wider range of evidence, such as the experience of many people rather than that of just one. They also try to develop theories that are important for more than one person and which address matters of much wider significance.

Writers in the business field sometimes refer to 'theory' as counterpoint to organizational 'practice'. This meaning is often pejorative, as when books promoting consulting solutions claim that they are practical rather than theoretical. Another use of the idea of theory refers to speculative, as opposed to factual, discussion and thinking. 'All very well in theory' is a common complaint levelled by organizational managers at business school texts and teaching. 'In theory' it is easy to find solutions to business problems. In practice most solutions have been tried before and failed for some reason. Student researchers need to disentangle the rhetorical use of the word 'theory' as a device of persuasion from its more substantive use as a form of carefully grounded explanation.

It is important for student researchers to understand just what a theory or model is trying to accomplish so that he or she can engage critically with its assumptions and claims. No model or theory is perfect and there are various grounds for criticism. For example, a theory might be criticized for being unrealistic in its main assumptions. Theories in economics are often criticized for lack of realism but they are more important for the predictions they yield than for the extent to which they reflect real life. Theories may also be criticized for missing important details. For example, linear theories of advertising effects may be economical ways of discussing the effects of advertising but they are often criticized for being very partial explanations. That is, they reduce a complex process to one so simple that it ignores important aspects of the process it purports to describe. Again, this may not matter. Economy of explanation is of value in a theory. If a theory is succinct and elegantly expresses particular relationships or processes in a way that can be clearly conveyed, it is likely to become a popular theory in spite of its shortcomings.

Theories may be criticized on the grounds that their internal logic is flawed, or indeed that the research on which they were based is itself methodologically flawed. Theories are the basis of academic work and student researchers need to begin to understand this in order to write a plausible critical literature review. It is important to remember that all models and theories are kinds of explanation. They are not literal, they are figurative because they are representations in words, diagrams and/or numbers of processes and events that are conducted in physical space. They should be seen as extended metaphors based on creative interpretations of events and processes. Different models and theories may be good for certain kinds of insight and less good for others. It is not necessarily a case of right, wrong, better, best in theoretical analysis. The comparison of models and theories needs to be qualitative and specific. Theories, like curates' eggs, can be good in parts. A critical literature review is always better if the student writing it understands the theories being discussed. Consequently the quality of the review is a good measure of the student researcher's theoretical understanding.

Research 'method' and empirical projects

'Method' is important in social scientific research (and business and management research draws on many social science research traditions for its foundations) because it distinguishes research from opinion, hearsay or intuition. The presence of a method in a research project implies that what has been investigated has been done so systematically, carefully and from a theoretically informed intellectual basis. The 'method' is central to the narrative structure of the research story. It gives the research project shape and structure. It signifies that the project has engaged with *epistemological* issues (that is, issues of what kind of knowledge can be generated) to offer insight into a particular area. In this way the 'method' section shows the examiners that the project has, at least, reached levels 2 or 3 of critical thinking in its intellectual standards.

A 'method' suggests that the research was systematic, that it proceeded according to rules and satisfied some of the criteria of social scientific knowledge. Which criteria are best is a matter of acute controversy within research communities. But the novice researcher does not need to deal in depth with philosophy of science controversies. If a research project at master's or undergraduate level demonstrates the ability to apply a given methodological perspective and to show some awareness of its limitations and weaknesses, a major outcome of the research process will have been satisfied. There must be a carefully referenced explanation and justification of the particular approach chosen. The author must explain why the chosen approach was most appropriate in the circumstances. Much of the later parts of this book will explore different ways to approach this important part of the research project, particularly focusing on data collection and interpretive analysis.

The 'method' section will explain which data-gathering approach was taken and why. It will then explain how the data were analysed. For example, many research projects in management at master's degree level use qualitative 'depth interviews' to supplement their investigation with expert knowledge from practitioners. These can be used in a simple 'she said that, he said this' descriptive account of interviewees' views. Indeed, this is quite common in management research projects that use qualitative methods. However, alternative methodological standpoints can be used to place the findings on a more rigorous basis and to generate insights that are theoretically informed and not (merely) descriptive.

The competent use of a method, any method, is most important in student research projects that use empirical data. Social research is an enterprise that attempts to produce and/or communicate ideas, truths and insights that are not normally publicly known through everyday 'common sense' understanding. The use of some kind of methodological and/or theoretical perspective is what makes social research a distinctive way of trying to discover, generate, communicate or test new knowledge. Methods are never perfect or infallible. But in a sense they are all social researchers have.

Specialist methodology texts can sometimes describe their approach in such detail that the generation of knowledge and findings appears mechanistic. Data go in one end of the method machine, the researcher cranks a handle and findings drop out of the other end. In this book there is no such assumption. In this book it is assumed that 'methods' are bound up with the researcher's stance, the theoretical frame and analytical positions used. Method does not stand apart from the research process. Methods are rhetorical devices to persuade readers of the intellectual competence of the researcher and the 'true-ness', or at least the plausibility, of the research. They are important but interpretive research does not invoke research methods mechanistically. Methods are seen as a necessary part of the interpretive process.

Triangulation and relativism

One important concept in using methods is *triangulation*. Triangulation is a common term in qualitative research. It is a nautical metaphor that refers to verification of research findings by reference to more than one source. If a researcher looks at something in more than one way, say by getting two assistants to verify the categorization of some data, then that is a form of triangulation. Using a method of triangulation can mean that findings are more persuasive to readers. However, the concept of triangulation is not always helpful in interpretive research.

The use of triangulation can imply that there is only one version of social truth and, furthermore, that it is available to the researcher, rather like the view that obtains in much 'positivist' research. Interpretive research often proceeds on a *relativist* basis in the sense that it acknowledges the legitimacy and reality of differing perspectives on social phenomena. For many interpretive researchers attempting to triangulate findings merely imitates deductive, positivist research practices. Rather, many interpretive researchers seek to offer a plausible and coherent interpretation of findings that is well supported by the data. They do not seek to triangulate findings because they acknowledge that there are many possible interpretations of any research scenario or social event. However, interpretive researchers still need to persuade the reader that their interpretation of findings is plausible and credible.

It should be acknowledged that management and marketing student research projects are rarely sophisticated in their method. To take one example, a student researcher was interested in how advertising agencies evaluate the success of their advertising campaigns. She reviewed many research publications in advertising that deal with that area but are not overtly theoretical (such as, for example, Kover *et al.*, 1995). She felt that she needed empirical data to develop her understanding and extend her analysis. After many phone calls and letters she found a London agency that was willing to help with interviews with account team staff. In this way the project took on a much more topical and practical tone and she was able to evaluate the published work against the views of the practitioners.

The approach was not deeply theoretical in that there was no particular well-developed interpretive standpoint. In the 'method' section she discussed the depth interview as a data-gathering instrument, evaluating its advantages and disadvantages, strengths and limitations and discussing some alternative ways of analysing interview data. She then advanced one particular approach (a thematic analysis) that, while not a theoretically informed method as such, served her purpose and fitted with the aims of the project. The approach was also consistent with the tradition of much of the published work in the area. The researcher worked alone so she could not triangulate her interpretation of her interview data. However, she was able to understand the theory of advertising evaluation much more deeply by listening to people who are faced with that practical problem every day. The research project report was driven by a practical issue of importance to many organizations and also to academic researchers. It was not a theoretical work as such but the researcher was able to show that her work was careful, systematic and well grounded in published literature.

Presenting the findings, the discussion and the conclusions

After the section on research method the empirical project will report the major findings. 'Findings' are the results or insights that the researcher feels emerged from the primary data. They may consist of themes, patterns, consistencies or other insights that seem to be evident in the data. In qualitative research the findings are supported by many direct quotes and examples from the data. Transparency is important in qualitative and interpretive research: the reader must be able to see why the author made the interpretation of data that they made. If there are many direct quotes and the interview or other material is reproduced in the appendices then the reader can make his or her own judgement on the quality of the interpretation.

After the findings are reported they must be discussed. The 'discussion' or 'analysis' section evaluates primary data findings in the light of the concepts and issues from the earlier literature review. It addresses questions such as these: Does the primary research yield findings that are consistent with the literature on that topic? Does it appear that there are shortcomings, gaps or limitations in the literature? The discussion or analysis chapter is, in several ways, the most important of your report, since it is your chance to pull together the various strands of your research and to say what you really think, based on all the evidence you have gathered. It should demonstrate the researcher's understanding of the method(s) used and the kind of knowledge or insight that has resulted. It should critically evaluate findings and analyse them for logical consistency and coherence with literature-based theories. It should demonstrate that the researcher has the intellectual ability to integrate primary findings with theoretical knowledge.

Finally, the research report will have a short section of 'concluding comments' re-iterating the research story. What did you do, why was it important, and what did you find? Again, there is some repetition involved here as the story of the research project is briefly rehearsed once again. To what extent did the research concur with previous research? To what extent were the research objectives fulfilled? What were the weaker points of your research and what did you feel worked well? You can conclude by (modestly) suggesting what implications your work might have for future practice and/or future research. The appendix and detailed (Harvard method) references sections complete your research report.

In Chapter 4 we will develop the theme of empirical research by discussing several popular and effective methods of collecting qualitative data.

Glossary

'Datum' and 'data'   The research material that the researcher gathers and analyses is the data. Strictly speaking 'datum' is the singular and 'data' the plural, although the word data is often used as a collective noun for a single group of material when 'data set' would be grammatically accurate.

Empirical   Deriving from experience. In management research an empirical research project will include data gathered by the researcher. A *conceptual* research project will not, relying instead on existing published sources.

Epistemology   Epistemology is the philosophical study of knowledge. It addresses such questions as how can we know what we know, what kind of knowledge can we know, and what, indeed, is knowledge.

Method   Every research project employs a systematic or theoretically informed method of investigation. In social science 'method' usually refers to the technique of gathering data and also to the assumptions underpinning the interpretation of data. Very often in social science method and interpretive framework are implied in each other. Note that 'methodology' is the study of methods.

Normative   A 'norm' is a rule that does, or should, govern a pattern of behaviour: normative work in management and business writing and research seeks to develop norms or rules for doing management and business.

Primary data   Original data, obtained first-hand by the researcher.

Reflexivity   The experience of being aware of being aware, in other words the ability to reflect on one's own experience. It is important in a research context because researcher reflexivity gives interpretive research reporting a special character of frankness, self-criticality and self-awareness. In particular, it allows the researcher to be aware of and acknowledge the influence he or she has on the research process.

Secondary data   Existing material that has already been produced for another reason.

Triangulation   This is a nautical metaphor that refers to checking a position from an alternative standpoint. For example, if a researcher feels that a particular finding emerges from data he or she can check that finding by seeking an alternative source.

Chapter 4

Gathering qualitative data for interpretation

Chapter outline

This chapter offers practical advice on a range of qualitative data-gathering techniques. Since analytical standpoints are often implied in particular data-gathering methods, the chapter also begins to introduce some of the themes of research theory that will preoccupy much of the rest of the book. Indeed, data-collection methods are intrinsically theoretical in that they carry assumptions about what qualifies as 'good' data and also about how that data might be 'read' and understood.

Chapter objectives

After reading this chapter students will be able to

- use various differing techniques of data gathering
- understand some of the theoretical implications that are associated with particular data-gathering techniques
- appreciate some of the major difficulties of data gathering
- understand the influence of the researcher in qualitative data gathering and interpretation

---

Introduction: interpretation, data and theory

As was mentioned in the previous chapter, in many cases student research projects do not need to gather primary empirical data. The rules of many university business schools allow that a research report based entirely on secondary sources (a 'conceptual' project) is legitimate. However, there are few projects that are entirely empirical or conceptual. Most combine elements of each. It is important also to note that whatever the sources of the research project, all research entails interpretation. When the student researcher is interpreting the literature or other secondary sources such as market data or published reports, he or she is applying his or her own knowledge, experience and world-view to interpreting, and understanding, those texts. The meaning and significance of published research studies is not necessarily obvious or beyond debate. Readers' interpretation of texts is informed by explicit or implicit assumptions and reading strategies. If primary data have been gathered then, similarly, they must be interpreted by the researcher. Interpretation is a necessary part of research.

Interpretation may be conducted at a common-sense or experiential level. In the common-sense mode of interpretation the researcher takes his or her assumptions for granted and assumes that the reader will hold the very same assumptions. Researchers can sometimes get away with this if they are conducting research on a problem-based managerial issue with which the research supervisor is familiar. However, this approach carries risks. For example, there may be implicit assumptions in the research report that the supervisor or second marker of the report questions. Another, more problematic difficulty is that a common-sense interpretation is unlikely to satisfy fully the intellectual standards required by most university business schools. Academic research projects normally need findings or insights to be justified in terms of a given theoretical stance. Framing a project with a given theoretical perspective makes certain assumptions clear. It means that the work can be judged for coherence in its own terms.

Management is a field of academic study that feeds off the everyday activities of practical people in organizational or consumption settings. Many practising managers feel that 'theory' is only for academics. In this book a different view is taken. A theory, as mentioned in the previous chapter, is just a form of explanation or discussion that attempts to improve on 'common sense' or taken-for-granted assumptions. Theorizing qualitative social research means discussing it in a theoretically informed way that deepens insights and makes the implicit, explicit. It does not imply that student researchers have to try to formulate generalized propositions about the world as a whole. There is a world of difference between formulating a finished theory and discussing research issues and data theoretically. Student researchers are engaged in the latter activity and may well find that it is more intuitive than they thought.

The following data-gathering techniques should, rightly, be used in an appropriate context of interpretive theory. Much more will be said about interpretation in the subsequent chapters of this book. Interpretation takes place according to assumptions: referring to interpretive theory is not overly abstract, obscure or irrelevant. It simply means that the researcher has a theory that can explain and justify their interpretation.

Multi-method approaches

The data-gathering techniques outlined in this chapter are not mutually exclusive: they can be used in combinations or as the main method for a research project (for a variety of approaches, see also Carson *et al.*, 2001, Easterby-Smith *et al.*, 1991, Gummeson, 2000). Many of the research traditions introduced later in the book are often used in combination with a number of data-gathering approaches. *Ethnography*, for example, is noted for its use of depth interviews, field notes and other, informal data sources. *Phenomenological/existentialist* research studies can also use a variety of qualitative data-gathering approaches in combination, particularly the depth interview. Other studies framed simply as interpretive research use combinations of one-to-one interviews and focus groups (as in Szmigin and Carrigan, 2001).

It is important to remember that data-gathering techniques are not theoretically neutral: they carry implicit assumptions about the nature of the material being studied and also about the form of analysis that may be appropriate. In addition, the particular ways that specified data-gathering methods and analytical traditions are applied by researchers are subject to variation. The following is intended to assist student researchers in practical issues of data-gathering, but care must be taken to check that the chosen technique is appropriate to the desired theoretical stance.

Data gathering and student research projects

Student researchers often use empirical data-gathering techniques in a relatively informal way to gather additional useful knowledge and understanding that may add to the project report. For example, many students carry out a literature review of an area with respect to a particular management problem or issue. They may use ad hoc interviews with practitioners for material that will enrich their general understanding and can be used to develop lines of discussion in the report. This relatively informal approach to data gathering can adopt any of several data-gathering techniques. Empirical data gathering can proceed alongside secondary research in this sense as part of a broad process of exploration. The sequence of research activities does not preclude data gathering at any stage in an exploratory project.

For students working in this way the generation of insights and knowledge can appear to be relatively ad hoc. It is quite appropriate to use a small-scale questionnaire survey and/or some interviews to deepen general understanding of different issues. On the other hand, a student researcher may wish to conduct a more theoretically informed and empirically extensive study in, say, an ethnographic style. The student researcher may use a variety of data-gathering techniques including interviews, naturalistic observation, textual analysis and perhaps research diaries. The decision of whether to use multi-method data gathering normally depends upon practical constraints of time, availability of and access to data sources, and the research skills of the student, as well as on the aims and theoretical framework of the research project. In student research projects conducted as part of taught courses, ad hoc methods of data gathering used to supplement critical literature reviews can be as legitimate as more theoretically driven data-gathering approaches. The important thing is how the data are used to enrich the analysis and discussion of a particular set of research questions.

'Interpretive', 'quantitative' and 'qualitative' research approaches

Before the data-gathering techniques are outlined, it is necessary to mention some important issues. One concerns the distinction between the categories 'qualitative' and 'interpretive'. The two terms are often used interchangeably. However, they can imply different things. Some research looks at qualitative data to dig out truths that might be tested to see if they can, in principle, be *universalized*, or tested to see if they are universally true. This kind of research is often conducted as a precursor to a quantitative statistical study. Other qualitative research studies are cast as exploratory or as creative interpretations of the data as an end in themselves. This kind of qualitative research is more properly called 'interpretive' research because insights are based on the interpretation of qualitative data and are supported by reasoning, evidence and theory. Generalizations of the reduced kind that can be easily measured are not sought. This distinction is important because interpretive research acknowledges that data collection is itself a theoretically informed activity and does not stand apart from the interpretive process.

'Qualitative' and 'quantitative' research categories are not mutually exclusive. A great deal of quantitative research has a qualitative component. As mentioned above, qualitative work (such as interviews or group discussions) can stimulate the researcher to think of 'constructs' that can then be measured in a quantitative study.

To return to an earlier example, a researcher might interview sales people to see what particular factors seem to influence their effectiveness. If many sales people seem to talk about their motivation in terms of the personal qualities of their manager, then the research might generate a scale with which to measure the motivational ability of sales managers. He or she could then conduct a larger study to see if there is any statistical correlation between sales managers' motivational ability as measured by the scale and the sense of motivation felt by their sales force.

Significantly, such a study assumes that *nomothetic* (statistically generalized) findings can be useful. This term is often contrasted with *idiographic* research. The researcher seeking nomothetic insights would try to isolate the decisive motivational skill of the sales manager with the intention of making generalized points about all sales managers and their sales forces. The researcher seeking idiographic insights would, in contrast, conduct a depth interview with a few sales managers in order to establish how their approaches to sales management evolve out of their life history and experience.

The study outlined above used 'raw' data (interview transcripts) to generate the initial construct. However, the way that data is understood as 'raw' carries important theoretical assumptions. The researcher organized, conducted, transcribed and read the interviews as if the things sales people said gave a clue to an underlying reality: the factors that influence sales person motivation. A datum itself is assumed to be interesting for what it suggests about the underlying reality. Interviews or other forms of data gathering are said to generate research material that is in a pre-analytic state, not 'cooked', but 'raw'.

However, it is quite evident from the above example that the researcher had a clear idea about what he or she intended to find before any data were collected. In this sense the research presupposed its own findings. For interpretive researchers, data gathering never generates 'raw' research material because the researcher always brings a set of assumptions about the nature of reality and the character of research 'findings' to the data, gathering process.

So, for interpretive researchers, to say that a study is qualitative does not imply that it is simple or straightforward. Much qualitative research does assume that there is an underlying reality made up of causal relations between factors. In other words, qualitative studies can be conducted according to assumptions categorized in management research as 'positivist'. Interpretive researchers, in contrast, use qualitative data to generate insight into the ways in which social reality is constructed by people in interaction with others. The reality lies in the language and meanings of research participants (such as interviewees), not in assumed causal relations which can be implied from qualitative data.

Plenty of research that is predominantly qualitative has a quantitative component. For example, if a student is analysing media texts, such as magazines, to establish how representations of men and masculinity may have changed over twenty years, a quantitatively based content analytic scheme could be useful to narrow down the data set. It would be impractical to analyse every part of every magazine. The researcher may also wish to show that the data set was not chosen idiosyncratically but has some element of objectivity to it. Therefore, the researcher might separate out every piece of text that represents men or masculinity, then take every second piece to subject to analysis. They could also build up a content analytic framework and count how many incidents of masculine representation occur in each magazine. Such quantitative analysis may, or may not, provide a useful basis for subsequent analysis and discussion.

Data-gathering approaches and issues

Sampling, or 'How many interviews is enough?'

Data gathering for interpretive research need not be random, but it does need to be systematic and/or theoretically informed. The word 'interpretive' implies that data are not used to try to set findings beyond dispute or to generalize findings across time and social context. An interpretation is necessarily one of many possible interpretations. In interpretive research the researcher seeks to arrive at insights for which he or she will offer as much evidence and reasoning as possible. They do this in order to make their reasoning transparent and to try to make their interpretation persuasive. Given all this, the selection of data for analysis must be purposive rather than randomized. What is important is to understand why particular data sets were chosen given the aims of the research. It is also important to qualify findings carefully so that they are grounded within the social context that is being researched.

Sampling issues are often resolved by necessity. In qualitative research sampling is often based on purposive or convenience criteria. This means that the sampling decision is driven by pragmatic considerations of convenience or suitability for the particular problem or issue being studied. First-time researchers might ask ten people for an interview and find that three agree. That, then, has to be the sample. You can't force people to agree to be interviewed, just as you can't make people fill in and return postal questionnaires. Quantitative researchers and qualitative researchers alike invariably find that they are making the best of imperfect samples. If you can show that you have a realistic and well-informed awareness of the limitations, as well as the advantages of your sample, your research can be credible and competent.

It is difficult to provide a satisfactory answer to the question 'how much data shall I collect?' The answer is always unsatisfactory because it is always the same: 'it depends'. It depends on the objectives of the research. It depends on the nature of the subject matter, the kind of data that is sought, and the quality of the data that is obtained. It also depends on pragmatic consideration such as time-scale and costs. In the end, two maxims are worth remembering. For student researchers, any primary data is often better than none at all, and second, few marks are awarded for the amount of data collected. The important thing is how well the researcher uses the data they have.

The sample should, therefore, be decided on grounds of a) pragmatism,

b) representativeness and c) quality of insights generated. Pragmatism dictates that student researchers cannot wait months for organizations to reply to their letters requesting interviews or field access. It is, incidentally, a good idea for students requesting research access to find out the name of a person responsible and direct communications to that person. An initial letter followed up with an email or phone call will be enough to determine whether the person has the time or inclination to grant access or interview time. Organizational staff are busy people and some receive many such requests. Student researchers should accept this and thank the people for their time even if the response is negative. If there are positive responses, the technique of data gathering may dictate the amount of data to be gathered. Depth interviews are very time-consuming. A one-hour interview can generate many thousands of words of dialogue. If the student researcher is to transcribe the interview to place in the report appendix, this will prove a very lengthy task even for a good typist. In general, the data sample should, on pragmatic grounds, be manageable yet useful.

In qualitative research in general it is more important for a sample to be representative of a larger group than for it to be random. Randomizing a sample is almost an impossible task even for accomplished researchers. Students doing a project as part of a taught degree need to make sure that whoever they access for data, the insights generated will be relevant to the broader issues in their research question. Simply, if you are exploring advertising effects on young people with regard to alcohol advertising, find some young people who watch TV to do your focus groups. A degree of careful thought and preparation can save time in this respect. Some researchers conduct *pilot* data-gathering sessions to be thorough. These can be very useful in refining the questions you want to ask and practising your qualitative research skills. A pilot interview or focus group also ensures that the people you are targeting for your data sample have something to say that is relevant and interesting to your research.

Quality of data is often difficult to ascertain before it is gathered. However, some sources are self-evidently more interesting and authoritative than others. If a request for an interview is read by a chief executive who agrees to grant it, then take him or her up on that. What he or she says will be useful in the discussion because of its pertinence, and the experience of interviewing and making contact will be useful even if the person may not fall directly into the original sampling frame. Quality of data also depends on the rapport that the researcher can establish with the interviewee.

Research interviews

Conducting research interviews can be useful whatever kind of research design is used. Even in a project that is problem based rather than theo-

Box 4.1 Research interviewing checklist

- Establish the aims of the interview
- Reassure correspondent regarding ethics and confidentiality
- Decide on a formal or informal interview setting
- Decide on a structured, semi-structured or unstructured interview agenda
- Decide whether to audio record the interview and/or to take notes
- Decide whether to take a mainly active or passive interview stance
- Conduct a careful de-brief

retical, interviews with practitioners can give a valuable insight into practical issues. This practical insight can then be used in discussion as a counterpoint to the more theoretically informed perspective of the literature review. In such circumstances the technicalities of the interview process are not as important as the quality of the insights generated. In more theoretically informed research projects the technicalities of the 'depth' interview become more important. There are some general rules of interviewing that it is useful to remember (see Box 4.1).

As a general rule, the most relaxed interviewees give researchers the best quality data. Some researchers are able to strike a rapport with their interviewees so that in the interview situation they become candid and expansive. Few of us don't like talking about our lives, especially if we can do so to a neutral person in a safe and confidential situation. Relaxing interviewees and learning to ask just the right kinds of question at the right time is an art that takes time to develop. Some tips can help the novice interviewer. First, be well prepared. Think through what you want to know beforehand. Prepare a list of questions you can ask if the interviewee 'dries up'. At the beginning, introduce yourself, thank the person for agreeing to the interview and explain just what it is that interests you. Reassure the interviewee that the whole process is entirely non-judgemental and confidential. Explain to them that they can end the interview at any time.

Then, make sure that you are both comfortable. Preferably, find a room without distractions such as noise. Reiterate your aims and briefly go over the interview. The ideal interview is one in which the interviewee understands what the researcher is interested in and speaks unprompted on that topic. In such circumstances the interviewer can take a mainly passive stance. If you are audio-recording the interview, and it is highly recommended that you do, make sure that you have asked the person if this is OK with them beforehand. Ensure that your audio-recording equipment has batteries in it, that you have blank tapes and that the microphone is placed unobtrusively but so that it picks up the interviewee's voice. It is highly frustrating to obtain an interview with a leading practitioner, interview them for an hour and a half, then find that your microphone didn't pick up their voice clearly.

Some researchers will have a good idea of just what they want to know. Others will simply want to hear the interviewee's perspective on particular matters. In either case the fewer questions the researcher asks the better the quality of data. The interview is about that person, the interviewee, not you, the researcher. Research interviewers should be well prepared with questions to ask. But once the interviewee gets going the researcher should use probing questions and comments simply to redirect the interviewee back on to the research agenda without interrupting their flow. If the interviewee raises an important or interesting issue the researcher may want them to elaborate on it. In that case they may ask a supplementary question to probe the issue such as 'could you please elaborate on that answer? Are there other issues that you feel are relevant?' In some circumstances interviewers take a more active stance by probing certain points to achieve greater depth and quality of reflection. However, this tactic can make the interviewee ill at ease and consequently make the data less natural and spontaneous.

A relatively passive style of interviewing does mean that a digressive interviewee may stray onto topics that are not directly relevant. But digression can be used to the interviewer's advantage. The interviewee may be relaxed and expansive and could raise novel or unexpectedly candid issues and insights. If the digression becomes too tiresome the interviewee should never betray boredom or irritation but should gently redirect the topic of conversation.

It is important to remember that being interviewed can be a difficult experience. Many interviewees will feel that there are things they are expected to say, points of view they are expected to hold. For example, practising managers who are being interviewed by students doing an academic research project may imply that their everyday work is more theoretically informed than it actually is. This is not dishonest: we all moderate our conversational responses according to social expectations. It is just trying to be helpful. However, a careful research interviewer will try to anticipate and deflect expectations based on conversational conventions in order to improve the integrity of the data that is generated.

It is a good idea to maintain eye contact, stay interested and give interviewees the space to speak freely. In many research projects the early interviews will be the longest as the researcher finds out what the major issues are. In later interviews the researcher might have a much better informed idea of the topic and may well know what the major issues are so that they ask about these more directly. Interviewers can make notes while the interview takes place as well as audio-recording the interview. These notes can also be written immediately afterwards if the researcher feels that writing would distract the interviewee. The notes might consist of reflections on the manner, voice, intonation, metaphors or any other feature of the interview.

A questionnaire-style interview agenda is rarely necessary in a research interview. This is because the value of the research interview lies, in part, in its potential for spontaneity within the interview interaction. If the interviewer seeks to control what is said by imposing their own prewritten agenda of questions and assumptions then the interviewee's insights, thoughts and reflections might be modified to a considerable extent. The trick of qualitative interviewing is to empower the interviewee while retaining control over the broad agenda. As a researcher, you cannot know this person's job, their life, their problems at work. If you really want to understand their experience as a marketing and management worker in a given context, give them the silence to speak.

The process of interpretation of interview data

Afterwards, it is a good idea to transcribe the full interview onto typed pages. This is, of course, a highly labour-intensive task. If a research interview takes one hour, it can take far longer than this to transcribe it. The advantage is that the researcher has a full record of the discussion that he or she can refer to when arguing a particular point in the research report. The full transcription can be placed in the appendices of the research report so that the reader can see for themselves exactly what was said and make their own judgement on the researcher's interpretation. If full transcription seems too daunting, making notes from the audio-recording is the next best thing. This way direct quotes can, at least, be used to support any point of discussion in the report, even if the full transcript will not be available for the reader to peruse. While you are not attempting to prove that your interpretation of qualitative data is the only possible interpretation, it is important to argue persuasively in favour of one interpretation over alternatives. The presence of actual data in the appendix in the form of a complete transcript is, rhetorically, far more powerful than the occasional quote. If many interviews were conducted it is only necessary to provide complete transcripts of three or four interviews at most. The presence of a typed transcript says a great deal about the conscientiousness and academic professionalism of the researcher.

A further important advantage of transcribing interviews is that interviews are seldom easy to interpret on one or two hearings. In order to understand what the major themes are of a given interview, it can be necessary to hear, reflect on and reread the transcript many times. This is because what is taken for granted in conversation can be the most revealing, but only if it is heard so often that it ceases to be familiar. This may sound odd, but it is an important principle of interpretive research traditions that the everyday, the normal, the taken-for-granted, hides a complex social web of assumptions, codes and obscured, or forgotten, motives. In important respects interpretive research seeks to reveal how the 'normal' is produced. This does not imply that research data generated from interviews are in some way 'biased' or even plain dishonest. The interpretive researcher takes an innocent position towards what they are told: researchers do not try to second guess 'the truth'. What they do is to try to understand where the interviewee is 'coming from' by placing their comments in the broader context of the research topic.

So, it is an important part of interview research for the interviewer to try to see the world through the eyes of the person being interviewed. The researcher/interviewer must not take a judgemental position. Neither should they assume that what is told to them differs, in some way, from reality because it is just a personal view. 'Bias' is not an issue here because the notion of bias implies that there is one truth. Interpretive research interviews seek the interviewee's truth. The personal view is the thing that is of value in research interviewing.

Interpretation of data will be discussed at much greater length later. For the present purpose, we have discussed practical issues in gathering data through research interviews. Another popular method of gathering qualitative data is the 'focus group'.

Focus/discussion groups

It should be noted that the term 'focus group' has a fairly specific meaning in some contexts of marketing research. In this book the term is used in a general sense to refer to research data that are gathered from a group of people simultaneously and interactively. That is, the group of people is in the same space at the same time and they can communicate with each other as well as with the researcher. The focus of discussion may be broad or narrow: the motive for the research may be exploratory, developmental, strategic or tactical (see Box 4.2).

Focus/discussion groups are regularly convened in marketing and advertising research to explore particular questions and issues. The composition of the group must be *representative* of the whole population of interest. This means that it must consist of the same kinds of people as the wider population of interest in terms of age, sex, class or other significant variables. With this form of research sampling is invariably purposive and convenient rather than random or systematic. If, for example, a marketing agency is investigating voter attitudes to local government policies, then clearly the group convened must be local residents of voting age. It would be useful to get a cross-section of ages in this case, but since older people

> **Box 4.2 Focus/discussion group principles**
>
> - Focus groups are useful for exploring topics and generating ideas. They are not usually appropriate for testing concepts prior to going to market
> - Group discussions can be audio-recorded or video-taped and transcribed
> - Group convenors (researchers) stimulate, guide and record the discussion
> - Group convenors should take care to intervene gently if one or two people are monopolizing the discussion. They should actively solicit views from quieter members
> - Group convenors should be clear about the aims of the discussion and the purpose of the research. They should reassure the group of the confidentiality and non-judgemental character of the research
> - Groups cannot be random but need to be representative of a larger population

are generally more politically aware than younger people the groups may well reflect this age imbalance. If a student researcher is investigating advertising ethics, then it can be useful to convene a focus group to discuss responses to particular advertisements. While focus group findings cannot be statistically generalized, they might well express a view that prevails more widely across that particular category of people, provided the group was representative of the larger population of interest.

Focus group discussions are regularly audio-recorded and/or video-taped in industrial market research settings. The researchers then replay these discussions to assess which views expressed might reflect more general positions, or which views seem to express a general insight in a particularly succinct or telling way. Contrary to popular myth, the focus group is not an appropriate way to test ideas. Brand logos, advertisements, new product concepts, product packaging and even political ideas have all been put to the focus group test by less than rigorous market research agencies. The fact is that since focus groups are not randomized they cannot generate views or opinions that can be generalized across larger populations, hence they are not appropriate for *testing* ideas or concepts. The value of the focus group lies in its ability to generate telling insights and novel ideas at an exploratory stage of a marketing, management or consumer research issue. Focus groups offer stimulating material that can contribute to strategy discussions. The 'voice of the consumer' can then be heard in company meetings. In research projects the focus group can offer stimulating perspectives for further discussion and analysis in the research report.

Researchers need to follow some simple rules to get the best-quality data. A focus group should ideally be comfortably seated with no noise or other distractions. The researcher needs good social skills to make the group feel at ease and to reassure members of the confidentiality and non-judgemental character of the process. The researcher also needs to have the confidence to gently intervene if discussions are being monopolized by one or two speakers, by asking quieter members of the group their view. The purpose of the research should be clearly communicated to the group. There have been cases of student researchers losing control of the theme of discussion so that the data was not useful for the project. It is important that the researcher/focus group convenor stimulates and guides the discussion. It can be useful to have stimulus material in the form of storyboards, pictures, role-plays or other stimuli. With focus group discussions, it is often the case that once the discussion gets going little intervention is needed from the researcher. The early stage of the group process is important.

Student researchers seldom need to video-tape focus group discussion, but audio-recording is always a good idea so that what has been said can be carefully examined afterwards. As with individual interviews, the task of interpreting the data is not straightforward. The transcript, or audio-recording, often needs to be read/listened to many times so that the major themes or insights become apparent. At the time of the focus group the researcher's attention is on many things so he or she cannot form insightful interpretations immediately.

The number of groups to convene depends on the topic and the nature of the research design. A research student of the author recently wanted to investigate the influence of alcohol advertising to teenagers in the UK. She convened four focus groups at three further education colleges in the West Midlands. Each group lasted about half an hour and she used bottles of branded alcoholic drinks to remind the groups of the topic. The groups went very well, all the students had much to say about the role of alcohol, and alcohol advertising, in their social lives. The researcher followed a methodological scheme she had seen in published research literature (Ritson and Elliott, 1999) and developed a perspective that reproduced a small-scale but more closely focused version of this and other similar previous research. The focus group discussions were audio-recorded, fully transcribed and placed in the appendix of the research report.

Textual research

Interpretive research traditions are well suited to textual research in which social texts of all kinds are subject to analysis. The foregoing data-gathering techniques of research interviews and focus groups have a textual character in that they generate data that are converted to textual form in transcription. Other forms of text can include advertisements, emails, in-company records and documents, historical records, newspapers, television and radio and magazines. In interpretive research a text is often defined as 'anything that can be described', that is, anything that can be rendered into words or text. These different forms of textual representation have authors, objects and motives, and they imply positions and theories. They are, therefore, excellent research material.

One research project that used textual analysis has already been mentioned. This was the author's MSc project that used published organizational mission statements as the main source of data. The author found a previous study that had conducted content analysis of published mission statements in the private sector. He then collected more examples of mission statements from the public and educational sector and adapted the content analytic framework used in previous research. Another research student conducted a content analysis of a series of advertisements in a selection of UK magazines to explore the changing representation of men and masculinity.

Content analysis can be used on any kinds of text. It is a crude technique in some ways because the theoretical assumptions underlying content categories may not be specified. It can, however, form the basis for a more careful subsequent interpretation. The technique is quantitative in that it entails counting the number of incidents of particular content in a given data set. For example, in the mission statement research mentioned above (Hackley, 1998) the content analytic framework was based on research that showed many mission statements to have similar features of content. Many made reference to the ethics of the company; many referred to the products or services that the company produced; many also referred to stakeholders in the company such as shareholders, customers or employees. These and other features of content were ticked off as each mission statement was looked at.

In this way a quantitative basis for interpretation was generated. The researcher could say that so many per cent of mission statements in a given data set displayed specific content features. The interpretation of these features is a separate matter: why they were there, what they were intended to accomplish, what motives they implied, how effective they seemed to be are all matters of interpretive judgement beyond content analysis. Similarly, the content analysis of magazine advertisements could not, in itself, explain why or in what ways gendered representations in advertisements were (or were not) changing over time. The content analysis could, however, provide a basis for further reasoning and informed interpretation.

Content analyses of textual data can be expressed simply as percentages, or more colourfully as bar charts, pie charts or histograms. One researcher examining changing representations of women in UK magazine advertisements generated graphical representations of the data that clearly showed marked changes in the number of advertisements that showed women as independent of, or as socially dependent on and subservient to, men. While such analyses can be stimulating and revealing, they clearly depend on a way of categorizing textual data than cannot be agreed on by everyone. Whether or not an advertisement portrays a woman in a subservient role to men can be a matter of opinion.

There are two ways to deal with this subjectivity in content analysis. One is to make the content categories clear to the reader and to reproduce the advertisements in question in the report appendices. In this way transparency of interpretation can be achieved so that the researcher can argue in favour of their preferred interpretation of text. The reader can then decide for themselves whether the researcher's position seems plausible to them. A second technique is to test content analytic categories to see if another person would make the same interpretation. In this way the researcher can offer evidence as to the *inter-subjective reliability* of their content analytic categories. This can never be an entirely satisfactory approach since the researcher cannot test their categories with every kind of person. It is, however, rhetorically powerful to show that the researcher's position is not purely a matter of subjective opinion but has been supported by another researcher.

Thematic analysis

A variation on content analysis is thematic analysis. This can come in many forms and can be theoretically informed by differing research philosophies. Put simply, thematic analysis means reading through texts to see if major themes seem to emerge. These major themes may be too abstract to express in terms of content analytic categories. For example, one postgraduate marketing student decided to do a research project on the representation of war in post-September 11th US newspapers. Her literature review drew on work in political marketing and critical work on rhetoric in marketing communications. She decided that there were several major rhetorical themes that categorized newspaper coverage of US politicians' speeches on the terrorist threat. These could be expressed in different ways but nonetheless were repeated in their general form in many reported speeches. Thematic analysis provides a way of making sense of data. Major themes can then be used to structure the findings and discussion sections of the research report.

Naturalistic observation

Observation is a research technique that is often implicit in data-gathering approaches. If we go to a company to interview a manager we observe the manner and style of personnel, we watch the way managers and subordinates interact, we note the quality of the furniture, how good the restaurant is, we notice whether people seem happy, relaxed, aggressive, defensive or whatever. We form implicit and intuitive judgements from this observation. Observation is something that we cannot fail to do as people: we are all expert observers. It makes perfect sense to utilize this social skill as researchers. When we go shopping, or go to a restaurant, to the cinema or to a nightclub, we observe others and their behaviour in that environment. In commercial contexts we are acting as consumer researchers, forming judgements about the provision of a service or the competence of an organization that will inform our own future consumer behaviour and that of others with whom we share our experiences and reflections.

Informal observation is, then, an integral part of interpretive research. Our observations provide the social context that informs our judgements. More formal uses of observation in social research include 'action research' and 'participant' or 'non-participant' observation. Each of these techniques involves the researcher in the process that is being studied. For example, many researchers in the *ethnographic* tradition spend lengthy periods in the company or industry that they are researching. In some cases they take part in the activities by fulfilling a role in the process. During and after their working day they will make *field notes* that record their observations and impressions. Later they will use these field notes as data from which they will compile their research report.

Formal observation research can sometimes take the form of intervening in a social situation to see what results. Some social psychology students once watched from a window over their street as one of their group said 'hello' to passers-by he had never met before. The observers were watching to count how many of the passers-by returned the 'hello' to the person they did not know. Their topic was social convention in greeting rituals.

Researcher/observers who are not seeking to intervene in a social situation should normally try to be as unobtrusive as possible. If they have been granted access to an organization to shadow an employee or to watch management processes, they should at all times consider the ethical issues of confidentiality and discretion. It is a privilege to be granted research access to a company. It is inappropriate in reporting such research to report anything that may embarrass the participant. Speakers in reported dialogue should be anonymous in the research report. The company itself should not be named or recognizable unless by agreement.

Research diaries

Research diaries can be useful if the researcher is seeking an *experiential* perspective from the research participant. Their disadvantage is that they can generate vast amounts of data than can be difficult to interpret. Their advantage is that they offer an intimate channel into some aspect of an individual's experience, provided that people can be relied upon to fill in the diary conscientiously. If, say, a researcher can persuade a senior executive of a firm to keep a diary during a hostile takeover, this would clearly offer a very different research perspective than any other form of data gathering. It is equally clear that such data would need to be handled very sensitively and discretely by the researcher. Diaries can be kept over varying periods of time. They can be written at any time of the day, or at specific times. They can be detailed and analytical or general and personal. It all depends on the researcher's aims and interests.

The interpretation of diary data takes some skill on the part of the researcher. Comments in a diary can be fragmented and difficult to group into thematic categories. As with all qualitative data analysis, the most penetrating analyses result from having a well-informed interpretive perspective. This will give the researcher the theoretical background to generate supported insights from the data.

Researchers themselves can also keep research diaries. These would be supplemental to field notes and would assist in reflexive analysis of the research process. Research diaries can be useful for recording particular events and times so that the chronology of events can be recorded for later reference. Particular impressions can also be revealing in the light of information received later, so recording them carefully as the research unfolds can be useful.

Questionnaire surveys: when not to use them

Surveys are probably the most common data-gathering instrument in business research. There are many texts that advise on question design and survey analysis. In this section we will discuss more general matters of when a survey questionnaire might be appropriate for a student research project, and when it might not be appropriate. Unfortunately, it is not uncommon for the survey to be used as the default data-gathering method for any given business and management research problem. But the questionnaire survey is a very precise research instrument. It answers exactly the question that was asked. This highly specified response tends to be most useful when the research question, the survey design and the analytical approach have been very carefully thought through indeed. In most cases master's and undergraduate student researchers are doing research as part of their learning process. Only in a relatively small number of cases are questionnaire surveys appropriate as the main data-gathering method in an empirical research project at this level of research. Sometimes the research supervisor will advise students to conduct a survey because it makes sense in the broader context of research the supervisor is conducting.

There are practical reasons why surveys are not always the best data-gathering approach for student researchers. A good survey will need careful designing based on a thorough understanding of the research problem or issue. This implies that the survey comes quite late in the research process when the researcher's subject knowledge is already well advanced. Research projects that are conducted as part of taught courses may not allow sufficient time. Second, they can be expensive. Administration costs can be high with postage, telephone calls, photocopying and/or researcher time. Finally, response rates to surveys are notoriously low. This can make analysis highly problematic to all but those with the most advanced, and creative, statistical skills.

Surveys can sometimes be useful as sources of supplementary data. Just as interviews can be useful for adding a practitioner perspective to a project based mainly on secondary research, so too can a simple survey be a useful supplementary basis for discussion. For example, the researcher might wish to ascertain how many managers in an industry have a professional or academic management qualification. This could be useful supplementary information for a project that investigates the professionalization of management in a given context. The most effective questionnaire surveys are succinct, direct and simple. Surveys that attempt to measure attitudes by using scaled questions need to be carefully located in the long-established attitude research literature.

Concluding comments

This chapter has discussed some of the most popular forms of qualitative data-gathering technique. The chapter has taken a mainly practical perspective and has pointed out particular difficulties and advantages of the various techniques. In keeping with the theme of the book as a whole, the chapter has taken the view that data-gathering techniques are implicitly theoretical in the sense that they carry assumptions about the nature of their subject of study and the kinds of analysis that are useful and appropriate. However, while the chapter raised certain important issues on the process of interpretation and introduced some of the interpretive research vocabulary, it did not deal in detail with specific theoretical traditions. Before the book engages with specific traditions in Chapters 6–10, we will look further at the research implications of the interpretive stance.

Glossary

Ethnographic *Ethnography* is a research technique made popular in anthropology. It entails trying to understand research participants from their own perspective with reference to their own cultural values and symbolic practices. Anthropologists have often lived for up to 2 years with the group they are researching. Management researchers tend to use quasi-ethnographic studies based on much shorter data-gathering periods.

Experiential The *experiential* perspective has evolved from humanistic psychology and phenomenological philosophy. It values the experience of the research participant and often seeks to empower research participants by facilitating constructive reflection and informed reasoning.

Field notes Term from anthropology referring to notes, observations, reflections, details and questions written down by the researcher during their period of 'field' research. Management researchers conducting ethnographic research in host organizations would usually make use of field notes.

Idiographic Research approaches that do not seek universal generalizations but, rather, seek insight into a subject's experience by taking into account all their biographical detail.

Inter-subjective reliability Reliability refers to research approaches that generate the same findings in different cases; inter-subjective means agreed upon by two or more people, so inter-subjective reliability means that an interpretation has been agreed upon by the subjective evaluation of two or more people.

Nomothetic Nomothetic research seeks truths that are universal and can be statistically significant.

Pilot studies A pilot data-gathering exercise is conducted prior to the main study. A pilot interview or focus group can be useful to ensure that the sample and interview agenda are right, and also to practise interviewing or other qualitative research skills.

Representative   Interpretive researchers seek samples that are not statistically random but are analogous to the larger research population in significant respects.

Universalized   Research that is often categorized as 'positivist' or 'realist' seeks nomothetic insights that are universally true and can be formulated into hypotheses for testing across very large populations.

Chapter 5

Major themes and concepts of interpretive research

Chapter outline

The interpretive research stance was introduced at the beginning of the book. The subsequent chapters offered practical suggestions for developing and writing a research project. Now it is time to discuss general interpretive research concepts and themes in more detail prior to developing specific interpretive research analytical perspectives.

Chapter objectives

After reading this chapter students will be able to

- appreciate what is meant by the 'interconnectedness' of interpretive traditions as part of the unity of social scientific research
- understand more of the technical vocabulary of interpretive social research
- understand better the role theoretical perspective plays in framing a research project

---

Philosophy of social science and the interpretive stance

Social science attempts to understand aspects of the social world in terms of broader theoretical schemes, and interpretive traditions have their role to play in this endeavour. Writing in the *Journal of Consumer Research* in 1988, Holbrook and O'Shaughnessy agree that 'all knowledge and all science depends on interpretation' (p. 398). Foxall (1995) has expressed a similar view in pointing out that no single model of science can capture the interrelation of different assumptions that act together in scientific research (p. 8). In its broadest sense 'science' refers to the search for a kind of knowledge that can be made public. However flawed our attempts, if we are trying to make sense of the world in ways which, potentially, could reach beyond our personal experience in their implications, we are engaging in activity that connects to science.

This chapter is based on a very straightforward *epistemological* principle. *Epistemology* refers to what can be known: it is the philosophical study of knowledge and is concerned with questions such as what it is possible to know and how it is possible to know it. The epistemological position taken in this book is that what we take to be knowledge is mediated by human interpretation. In most interpretive research traditions it is further assumed that human understanding is not something we acquire alone. We derive our frame of understanding from our social interactions and cultural life. In other words, we do not invent our ways of understanding the world. We learn them from the culture around us. We adapt these ways of understanding and knowing to serve our sense of individuality but they are, nevertheless, not purely ours alone. Ways of understanding are cultural, they are shared by many, they pre-exist individuals yet they are not fixed or given. They are historical and political.

One traditional 'problem' of Western epistemology that has been much written about is that we cannot know 'the world as it is': we can only know it through our sense perceptions. We have no way of knowing if our sense perceptions are deceiving us. You could be dreaming that you are reading this book. You have no way of being absolutely certain that you are not. There is a further problem with this truism. We cannot 'know' the electronic impulses that are our senses. We can only interpret them, that is, we can ascribe meaning to them by finding words that seem to express what we feel. For interpretive researchers, the language we choose to describe our experience is particularly important since it reveals something of the culture of which we are part. We draw on this culturally learned knowledge to make sense of the world we encounter.

In this book all 'research' is taken to entail interpretation. This includes the interpretation of primary data, of secondary data, of our own personal experience, and of the theories and models that we encounter in research literature. All interpretation is based on working assumptions that enable us to make sense of the social world. Interpretive traditions are sets of working assumptions about interpretation that have been made explicit in part and are used by researchers to develop bodies of distinctive research-based work. Research itself entails the interpretation of data or of other kinds of text. We interpret data sets to make sense of them in terms of our prior experience or our current stock of theoretical knowledge.

'Framing' research projects in theoretical terms

Interpretive research traditions do meld into each other: distinctions blur and many traditions share very similar positions on epistemology, method and scope. Some published researchers take a broad stance and frame their work as 'interpretive' (e.g. Hirschman, 1989; Szmigin and Carrigan, 2001) or 'qualitative' (Spiggle, 1994). Many other authors frame their work in terms that emphasize particular approaches or traditions, such as 'naturalistic' research (Belk *et al.*, 1988), phenomenological research (Thompson *et al.*, 1990) or semiotics (Holbrook and Grayson, 1986). Specifying the research tradition that influences a research project can be useful because of the different emphases of each tradition. In addition, a research project that explicitly states that it draws on a particular theoretical perspective immediately makes favourable signals to the person reading and assessing it. A defined theoretical perspective implies that the researcher has attempted to think through the implications and scope of their research question or issues. It also implies that the researcher is aware of the need to make assumptions explicit and to refer to previously published research. Finally, it suggests that the researcher will attempt to write a research report that is coherent: its aims, method and analysis will all 'hang together' and makes sense in terms of each other.

Theoretical perspectives may, as portrayed in Box 5.1, have a high degree of internal logical consistency. On the other hand, particular methods and types of question have sometimes become associated with particular perspectives by usage and habit. The usefulness of these associations is debated by researchers. For example, in university business schools it has become almost axiomatic that an empirical research study should involve a questionnaire survey, regardless of the scope of the study or the nature of the research aims. The survey questionnaire was devised by attitude researchers, but many studies are now conducted that use this data-gathering method without any reference to the assumptions and complexities of attitude research. This over-use of surveys has arisen from habit and familiarity.

There is an element of choice in research design: it was mentioned earlier in this book that multi-method approaches, combining useful features of more than one approach, can be fruitful. Many research studies are innovative in adapting data-gathering methods that are typically used in one research design for use in another. However, all such adaptation requires some understanding of why particular aims, methods and analyses seem to fit together while others do not. The theoretical coherence of the research study is important. A useful way of addressing this is to set the research study within a given theoretical perspective and to ensure that the scope, method, questions and implications cohere within this perspective.

Some theoretical perspectives become so widely used over time that they become taken for granted as the only way to do research in a particular field. This taken-for-granted aspect of theoretical perspectives can give them the character of a 'paradigm'.

Box 5.1 The role a theoretical perspective plays in 'pulling a research project together'

Theoretical perspective	Includes assumptions about ontology, epistemology, nature of social research
Research questions or issues	Type and scope of research aim(s) are consistent with the stated theoretical perspective
Research methods	Approach to data gathering and/or literature review is given by the theoretical perspective and consistent with the aims
Analysis and implications	The kind and scope of implications that can be inferred from findings are implied in the theoretical perspective, aims and methods

'Physical' and 'social' scientific 'paradigms'

A scientific 'paradigm' is a term popularized by Kuhn (1970). A paradigm is a set of explicit and implicit assumptions about how research should be conducted in the pursuit of scientific knowledge. Academic management and marketing researchers often argue that certain 'paradigms' or sets of assumptions are more correct or better in practice than others. For example, there has been a widespread assumption that questionnaire surveys subjected to statistical analyses closely approximate natural scientific methods. This is not agreed upon by all researchers. Many have argued that 'natural' science, that is, research that investigates the physical world of atoms and molecules, has its own set of interpretive methods that do not usually include survey questionnaires. It can be argued that research investigating the social world of human activity demands particular data-gathering and analysis methods that reflect the special character of social life. As one argument goes, life does not have to mean anything to an atom. In contrast, seeking meaning is a defining characteristic of human beings. Social research is concerned with people and their activities, including the activities of organizing, managing and consuming. As such it is concerned with meaning since the primary activity of humans in any given context is to make sense of their lived experience, to render it meaningful.

All books on research methods are highly selective about the methods and philosophies they deem appropriate for their readership. Although this book emphasizes particular approaches, it also takes the position that different scientific paradigms need not be seen as mutually exclusive. It assumes that interpretation is a necessary part of all scientific research. It also assumes that if the bases of interpretation are explored and made explicit in terms of everyday human understanding, then the scientific enterprise of advancing human knowledge of the natural and social worlds is served.

Kuhn's (1970) book drew attention to the way that certain data-gathering techniques and analytical methods become taken for granted over time as the only right way to do scientific research in a particular field. What is taken for granted can become so dominant that new researchers in the field are often not even aware that other ways exist. Alternative ways of understanding and doing research cease to be part of taught courses and texts. Consequently it takes a 'revolution' in knowledge to make people realize that what seemed a good way of conceiving of new knowledge for a long time was not, in fact, the only way.

There have been protracted debates about the relation research in marketing and management should have to research in the physical sciences. These 'philosophy of science' debates have passionate advocates on all sides. This book takes the position that different theoretical perspectives or research philosophies are not, necessarily, mutually incompatible. It takes the view that research is served by many differing approaches. Most importantly, it takes a pragmatic view on research: student researchers do not have to be adroit in philosophy of science in order to understand some of the philosophical issues that are debated and to employ these in a useful way in devising creative and coherent research designs.

Academic politics and research

Another reason why there is 'stickiness' in research ideas is that, for academics, ideas are political. The ideas we academics trade in can give us power over our careers. If one kind of research works for us, we are sometimes reluctant to acknowledge the value of other ways because we feel we have to defend our work. In fairness to academics, the arguments and debates over research are not merely self-serving and defensive. Academics can be passionate about ideas, especially when it comes to research, and are not likely to agree easily when they feel very strongly about a certain interpretation.

Letting go of a cherished belief can be difficult for anyone. In a sense, we all make sense of the world as informal scientists (to borrow a term from the personal construct theory of Kelly, 1955). We learn from our experience, form tentative hypotheses, then modify what we thought was true in the light of new experience. This part of learning is psychologically challenging whether you are a biological researcher, a consumer and marketing researcher, or a child learning about life. To let go of one belief in order to modify or change it in favour of another is a challenge to our need to feel that we understand and have control over the world we experience. So to say that social research in management and marketing is political is simply to acknowledge that it is done by people who have a psychological need for knowledge. The true social scientist meets this challenge by being 'open' to new ideas and tries to understand them in terms of his or her existing knowledge.

The lesson for the student researcher is to adopt a modest tone in research writing. If an assertion is made then it should be qualified carefully with reference to credible published works in reputable publications, or through careful argument and evidence-based reasoning. Academics want to see a quality of scholarship and good reasoning in student work, whatever the merits or shortcomings of their overall argument. The student researcher can, and should, have a view on the matters being discussed but his or her opinions should always be tentative, subject to modification in the light of new learning or evidence. This level of academic attainment, and the many intellectual and practical skills included in it, is what the research project is about. Pragmatically, taking the appropriate tone is a useful way of negotiating the political landscape of business school research.

Issues in interpretive research

Qualitative research and case studies

There can be little doubt that there is substantial blurring between the various qualitative data-gathering approaches and interpretive data analytical perspectives. The terms 'interpretive' and 'qualitative' are often used as synonyms. Strictly speaking, they are not. 'Qualitative' research refers simply to the kind of data being analysed. Qualitative data analysis often does apply analytical approaches that are taken from interpretive research traditions (Spiggle, 1994). However, the term 'qualitative' by itself does not tell you anything about the way the data set was interpreted, unless it is taken for granted that the interpretive process is the same for everyone. However, it can be a major mistake in research to assume that taken-for-granted values and assumptions are unquestionable and universal. It is therefore more precise to differentiate between the use of qualitative data sets and the process of interpretation applied to those data sets.

Similarly, the 'case study' has become a label for a method of research when, strictly speaking, it is merely a source of data. Saying that a research project is a case study leaves much unsaid, since it does not explain the theoretical assumptions that guided the choice of data sets and the analytical approach that generated findings.

The following chapters of this book do not include one dedicated to the case study. This omission deserves some explanation since the case study is perhaps the single most popular general approach claimed for research projects in business and management. The case study is well established and has a formidable history. The world-famous Harvard Business School made the case study the central pillar of their teaching. Originally, students would study the available information on a particular organizational management problem and would also visit the organization to see first-hand what its methods were and to speak to its managers. The students would then return to the classroom, offer their analysis of the business issues and problems facing that company, and debate this with the students and faculty. The aim of this was two-fold. By analysing the case and then debating their analysis with colleagues and professors, student researchers might develop skills of advocacy and critique (Contardo and Wensley, 1999). Through this demanding process they might happen on some general principles of management that could apply in a range of circumstances.

Case study research can take various forms. Many research studies that are labelled as using a case-study method rely on pre-existing information such as company and industry reports and other publications. Some employ an *ethnographic* style if the researcher can gain access to a company to observe processes from within. Others draw on data from depth interviews with company managers. Some case studies use a comparative approach by taking several cases and making comparisons between them of particular managerial issues or processes. Some case studies are conducted in a deductive style and test particular hypotheses. Others are conducted in an inductive research style to paint a detailed picture of the social life of the organization. All this variation in case study style means that the term is used to describe a variety of research approaches. There is no agreed 'case study method' as such. There is a wide variety of approaches to using cases to research management issues.

To claim that a research study uses a case study approach only tells readers that data was gathered about one or several organizations. It does not explain anything about the specific data-gathering techniques used (surveys, interviews, ethnographic observation) and neither does it explain how data sets were analysed. Finally, it does not explain the research design in terms of how research questions were formed and addressed. As mentioned above, some case studies have carefully formed *hypotheses* that are tested using case situations that are thought to be *representative* of wider groups of organizations. This would be called a deductive research design. The researcher has derived a specific question or questions from previous research and sets out to examine particular organizations to test that question.

Other case studies are inductive in that they do not set out with a specific research hypothesis but, rather, have broad areas of interest in an exploratory study. The inductive researcher does not know exactly what he or she is looking for: the data sets are sifted to see what they reveal about the phenomena that are under investigation. In a case study the findings may well be particular to one or two organizations. Such findings may well be suggestive of wider themes in many organizations, but a larger study would be required to establish this with more precision. Other case study designs attempt to set findings at a more general level by using cases that are representative of many others in important respects. In this way findings can be established which *may* be relevant to many organizations, but this would still be a tentative suggestion that required more research.

Interpretation and research 'method'

Another important theme for this section concerns the idea of research 'method'. Many student texts refer to methods and methodology (the study of methods). The difficulty with such discussion is often that 'method' is poorly defined. The word 'method' can imply that the research process is a little like putting data into one end of a machine and watching as findings drop out of the other end. 'Method' is used broadly to refer to a linked set of presuppositions about the nature of social research, a set of approved data-gathering approaches and a set of (often implicit) conventions concerning data interpretation, all grouped together.

This book seeks to pick apart these various stages of the research process. This is partly because the word 'method' can imply a somewhat mechanistic approach to social research that seems inappropriate to the creativity of interpretive research. Naïve use of methodological precepts can result in research that predetermines its findings. To illustrate this in another way, a hammer is a very useful tool for knocking nails into wood. However, there are problems for which a hammer is not the best tool, for example for turning a screw. It is a mistake in social research to take a hammer to every kind of problem by using one method regardless of its appropriateness to the research questions, aims and context. The one-method researcher might hit some data with their methodological hammer and then declare that the research design was appropriate because they definitely hit something. However, they would say, more hammering is required to generate more accurate findings.

In this book the broad idea of interpretation is used to position social (as opposed to physical) research as an activity that explores questions creatively through an interaction between methods, reflexive research reporting and critical analysis of systematically gathered data. Interpretive research uses methods but is not driven by preconceptions about what method is right. Rather, research is seen as a way of thinking and learning that is guided by sets of philosophical presuppositions linked with (usually qualitative) data-gathering techniques.

Applying strict methodological principles must, to some degree, presuppose the findings of research. Findings are invariably framed and constrained by the methodological assumptions researchers bring to the study. The spirit of research followed in this book is better expressed by phrases like research 'perspectives' or 'approaches' than method. In interpretive research the researcher's reflexive and philosophically informed interpretation of the data generates findings. The findings are not cranked out of a machine: they are not generated impersonally by a research 'method'.

Major themes of interpretive research

Interpretive research and 'rich' descriptions

It was noted above that while interpretive research traditions hold differing emphases on data gathering and analysis and use differing vocabularies, there are also many commonalities and overlaps between the various traditions. The interpretive stance is that social accomplishments of every kind are complex and enigmatic phenomena that cannot be represented by direct causal relations or boxes-and-arrows models without employing an extreme order of *reductionism*. Reductionism refers to the over-simplification of explanations. Such research tends to ignore contrasting perspectives in order to produce a simple, and simplified, process model. This can be useful where models and theories provide elegant and concise representations of particular phenomena or relationships. However, interpretive research is more often characterized by 'rich' descriptions of social phenomena that refer to all details and attempt to grapple with the complexity of social worlds. These rich descriptions tend to focus on the particular social context rather than the world in general.

Reflexivity

A feature of interpretive research that has been mentioned previously in the book is reflexivity. This concept has two main practical implications for the researcher. One is that the researcher is encouraged to try to be consciously aware of the values, assumptions and perceptions they bring to the research process. This reflexivity, or 'being aware of being aware', is brought into the research report through a self-conscious, and self-critical, writing style. In other research styles it is conventional for the researcher to write and behave as if he or she is detached and independent. The research report is written to minimize the identification of a thinking, feeling, interpreting individual as author. Interpretive research studies are often written in the 'third person' but nonetheless they should have a reflexive tone and self-conscious style. They can be written in the first person, that is, using the personal pronoun 'I' to represent the author. It can be more difficult to create an impression of rigorous scholarship in this style and student researchers are advised not to use it unless they are confident about their writing and analytical skills. Even then, it is strongly advised to obtain the view of the research supervisor.

Alvesson and Deetz (2000) suggest that, in interpretive research, 'people are not considered to be objects ... but are active sense makers like the researcher' (p. 33). The researcher's part in the interpretive process is, then, openly acknowledged. Researchers seek to use this involvement to deepen their understanding of the research process and they express it in their research reporting through a *reflexive* research reporting style that is open to self-criticism, honest about influences and biases and frank about limitations.

Meanings, facts and representation

Another important feature of interpretive research is a focus on meanings as opposed to a focus on facts. Interpretive researchers seek to understand how social life is actively produced by people's language, behaviour and social practices. There is a need to see particular social worlds from the point of view of participants. Just as ethnographic researchers have tried to understand soccer violence in the UK by joining a gang for a period of time and becoming part of the social process they are investigating, interpretive researchers do not seek to impose preconceived values or concepts on the people they are focusing on in their research. Researchers must seek to accept the world as it is produced by participants. Ethically, this does not mean that the researcher must agree with or encourage behaviour he or she thinks is wrong. It simply means that the integrity of the research process is best served if researchers seek to empathize with research participants. The emphasis on meaning results in a focus on meanings as they are constructed by research participants, rather than imposing the meanings and values of other groups on to the group that is being studied. In this way researchers can stand back from their research to try to understand why particular meanings become constructed and valued in a particular social setting.

For interpretive consumer researchers, buying products and services and understanding advertising and branding are all activities that people make meaningful by imposing values on them. Understanding meaning is considered to be the key to understanding motivation and behaviour. Interpretive management researchers are similarly concerned with management processes as aspects of human interaction in organizations. Managers are seen as thinking, feeling individuals, as are the people they manage. Work is an important site of meaning for human beings. Management is a class of organizational authority but it is also, colloquially, something all workers do: we 'manage' our lives, our relationships, our time and our activities. In managing our work we bring meaning to it and it is this meaning that interpretive researchers seek to tap into and use as a source of insight and understanding when they research organizational work and management.

Alvesson and Deetz (2000) remind readers that interpretive research reports are *representations* of a slice of social reality. That is, when the researcher writes about a management issue, he or she cannot claim that the research report is the reality of what has happened. It is, self-evidently, an interpretation written down in text. For Brownlie (2001) 'interpretive marketing research [is] a highly coded and situated form of representation ... that works to legitimize and privilege certain kinds of knowledge' (p. 48). For Brownlie (2001, p. 50) research does not merely 'reproduce a pre-existing world of marketing managers or consumers' but 'constructs the research domain' through 'scholarly artifice'. For example, it is not correct to assume that because ethnographic research seeks a rich and detailed description of a social phenomenon that this in some way produces a representation that is closer to reality. Ethnography is just another representational practice (Van Mannen, 1995).

'Representation' implies that whatever is written in research represents a viewpoint that is selective and reflects the educational, cultural and political influences on the researcher. It is appropriate, therefore, for the researcher to reflect on the interests that may underlie any particular representation. For Alvesson and Deetz (2000), representation is political in the sense that any representation of reality will concur with some interests and conflict with some others.

For example, much consumer research uses the concepts of consumer 'satisfaction' and 'choice'. However, there are circumstances in which consumption can be a source of dissatisfaction and a restriction of choice. A reflexive piece of interpretive consumer research would acknowledge the conflicting interests that may be invested in the use of particular representational strategies, such as framing consumer experience in terms of constructs like 'choice' and 'satisfaction'. As an example, some interpretive studies of management have painted a picture of organizational management as chaotic and stressful, and managers as unhappy, unfulfilled and stressed (e.g. in parts of Watson, 1994). Other studies celebrate managerial tasks and, by implication, managerial skills and produce a representation of the organizational manager as a folk hero (e.g. in Peters and Waterman, 1982). It does not question the integrity of such studies to discuss what interests may be served by such representations of organizational management.

Particular styles or modes of representation do tend to become accepted and conventional over time. For example, popular marketing management textbooks have developed distinctive rhetorical strategies that have become so familiar that it is difficult to articulate marketing issues through alternative representational strategies (Hackley, 2001, 2003). This presents a difficulty for researchers. A good researcher will not want to present a picture of the world that relies solely on conventional and perhaps stereotypical ways of representing the world. The challenge to interpretive social researchers is to see the worlds they research through the eyes of the people in them while also retaining a distance from that world, so that what is familiar to participants remains unfamiliar to the researcher.

What is considered to be normal and taken-for-granted thought, language and behaviour in particular social circumstances needs to be examined from an intellectual distance by the researcher. The researcher needs to ask just why is this way of seeing the world or behaving considered normal? Where did it come from? What does it accomplish in terms of group interaction or social positioning? Only by making the familiar strange can social researchers generate striking or original interpretations of social life. It has been suggested that the interpretive social researcher should be a 'professional stranger'.

Agency and situated freedom

Agency refers to the power of individuals to act and behave independently of social structures. Are your beliefs, likes, dislikes, manner and attitudes unique to you? Do they reflect your own personality? Are your decisions and accomplishments your own and no one else's? Or are they the result of the influences under which you grew up, your social class, the culture of which you are part, the kind of family you have? Are your actions, behaviours, your very thoughts the result of the social structures within which you exist?

Such questions as these have been the cause of much debate among social theorists and are usually referred to collectively as the agency-structure debate. The debate is important to researchers because it influences the kinds of findings that can be produced. If people behave because of the forces that are imposed on them through class, culture and other outside (structural) influences, then change can only come about through large-scale social change. If, on the other hand, people have the power, however curtailed and limited, to act, think and behave independently of the social structures around them, they are said to possess the power of agency.

Some interpretive research traditions (such as the phenomenological/existentialist) make this very assumption. They assume that people have some power, some limited or 'situated' freedom to define their own existence and to determine their own course of action. This is important because studies of how people create meaning within certain social situations would have little value if the people were merely playing out destinies that have been imposed on them by their social circumstances. The very idea of interpretation implies that there is some creativity and independence to the researcher's stance: he or she has the freedom to place creative interpretations on the research they conduct. This is important because it is assumed that the actions of consumers, marketing managers and other research participants are not simply determined by forces outside their control but are the result of their agentive action.

The assumption that people have the power of agency is not held by all interpretive research traditions. Some research approaches focus more on the effects that social institutions and structures have on the behaviour, thought and action of individuals and groups. Indeed, many traditions of consumer behaviour research are implicitly based on the assumption that behaviour is determined by factors outside the individual's control. Consumers are regarded as entities that 'behave' as if they are directed by the forces of organizational management. Factors in the consumer's social environment are regarded as variables in a buying equation. If management can put the right product together, the right information in the promotion, channel it to the right consumer, combine that with the appropriate marketing mix variables, then a purchase results. Such approaches to modelling consumer behaviour throw up many intriguing findings and theories. However, most interpretive traditions focus less on purchasing as a behavioural response to external and internal variables and more on purchasing as a response to a need for meaning that is directed by the reflections, experiences and emotions of the consumer.

Language and the social constructionist ontology

The concept of 'bias' is sometimes invoked to distinguish between the way events are reported by interviewees or survey respondents and the way they 'really' happened. In much interpretive research no such distinction is acknowledged. This is because the researcher is not in a position to speculate about a reality that lies beyond the accounts of research participants. All the researcher can do is to analyse the data he or she can obtain with as much care as possible so that the reasoning and evidence that give rise to their findings is derived systematically and presented clearly. For interpretive researchers using qualitative data approaches to language is not, necessarily, a window to underlying events and causes. Language itself is the reality that can be studied.

This general position implies a social constructionist ontology. The ontology of a research study refers to deep assumptions about the nature of the reality being studied. A social constructionist ontology regards social reality as something that people construct in interaction through their use of language and other social practices. This contrasts with the assumption (often attributed to natural scientists) that social reality is fixed, given and prior to language and social practice.

Not all interpretive research approaches assume a social constructionist ontology. For example, some traditions of *semiotics* assume that there are communication codes underlying the construction of meaning. These codes are seen as relatively stable, fixed and unchanging. However, not all semiotics researchers will agree that this is an important issue. The ontological position adopted by a researcher is an intellectual requirement, since high-quality intellectual work demands that implied assumptions are acknowledged in reasoning and are consistent with the implications claimed for the research. The ontology of social research is a working assumption, not a fully worked-through and defensible argument about the nature of reality. Social researchers state assumptions because these have implications for the kinds of findings and conclusions that can be generated from research. Social researchers cannot assume that assumptions are shared or taken for granted by all.

The social constructionist ontology is sometimes contrasted with the *realist* philosophical position. Social researchers invoke the philosophy of realism to support the contention that the social world of managers, organizations and consumers can be regarded as if it were like the physical world of plants, bodies and cells. This can be a rather oversimplified contrast: *realism* is a sophisticated philosophical stance that has many shades and subtleties. For example, *critical realists* hold that the world can and should be regarded as real in a material sense but only as a working assumption. Critical realists are agnostic on many philosophy of science questions. They take a pragmatic viewpoint.

The contradictions between realism and social constructionism do not need to be resolved by novice researchers before they can complete their first research project. They do, however, need some familiarity with philosophy of science issues so that they can be clear about the working assumptions they are bringing to their research. Social research studies in marketing, management and consumer research do not usually need to have a sophisticated grounding in philosophy of science, but they do need to have a sense of coherence. That is, the research question or issue, the data-gathering method (if there is one), the findings and implications have to hang together, to make sense in terms of each other. If new researchers have some working understanding of important philosophical concepts in social science, the challenge of coherence can be met.

The interpretive research stance: 'objectivity' and 'reflexivity'

An important principle of some experimental research traditions has been that the researcher stands apart from the research. The people who are in the research study are called research 'subjects', denoting the authority of the researcher (the scientist) to determine what they should be told, to control how they are used in the experiment and also to interpret their motives, actions and behaviour. The researcher, on this experimental model, stands outside what is being researched and attempts to generate 'objective' findings. 'Objective' here means findings that are independent of both the researcher and the research design.

The principle of objectivity has been the subject of much debate among researchers. Unfortunately it can be somewhat oversimplified. In social research no findings can be generated without human involvement so there is an unavoidable element of personal judgement involved. Physical science has been shown to be a very human affair with elements of subjectivity, judgement and culture-specificity (e.g. Woolgar, 1981, 1988, 1989; Knorr Cetina and Mulkay, 1983). Whether the design is experimental and the analysis statistical, or the design qualitative and the analysis interpretive, an attempt can be made to show how the findings might apply in other situations. In both styles of research findings can be well supported by data and reasoning. Similarly, in both kinds of research it can be shown that findings could be quite likely to occur in a similar way in differing situations. It all depends how findings are expressed, in other words, it depends on the scope and assumptions underlying the research.

The 'objectivity' of the researcher might be better expressed as 'integrity'. As researchers, we cannot understand our research except through our own frame of understanding, or culture, experience, judgement and learning. We can, however, try to make our findings and reasoning as clear, coherent and transparent as possible. In this way readers of research are in a position to judge whether the findings have broader relevance or, indeed, if they choose whether to carry out a similar study to see for themselves.

In many interpretive research traditions there is little emphasis on *replicability* of studies or on 'objectivity' of findings. Some studies expressly do not seek to generate findings that might be true in other situations or places. Many ethnographic studies, for example, seek to understand the ways in which a particular, specified, social milieu is produced. There is no attempt to reduce findings to direct cause–effect relationships or statistically supported correlations. Such studies do generate general findings in the sense that they contribute to the proposal that organizational management is a human enterprise that is produced by thinking, feeling actors who are idiosyncratic and emotional. As case studies they might also reveal features of successful, or unsuccessful, managerial styles that could be relevant to other kinds of organization. However, the major emphasis of ethnographic studies is on rich description, not testable cause–effect relations. Indeed, many interpretive researchers would argue that attempts to pin down social phenomena to direct cause–effect relations are doomed to failure because they misrepresent the complexity and human-ness of social life.

While interpretive research does emphasize high standards of theoretical coherence, transparency and rigour of data collection, it also acknow-ledges that the very presence of the researcher is a feature of the research that cannot be ruled out of the analysis. In other words, the interpretive researcher does not stand outside the research process but is implicated in it. There is, therefore, a need for the previously mentioned quality of reflexivity in research reporting. In conducting the research the researcher can try to be aware of his or her influence on events and be sensitive to that. He or she can demonstrate self-awareness in writing the research report by acknowledging the assumptions, predispositions and prejudices that he or she brings to the research as a whole.

Power and ideology: critical influences

A final concept that deserves mention here is power. Interpretive research does not necessarily seek to uncover the relations of power that frame social interaction. It is usually more concerned with revealing how social life is produced and sustained as a 'normal' thing through language and social practice in a given context. However, an awareness of how power is reproduced and played out in social situations is implicit in much interpre-tive research. If researchers ask the question 'why do these meanings seem to be important to this community of people?' then they must allow that one possible answer is that particular meanings serve particular interests, that is, they support the power of particular interests in some way. It is increasingly common for interpretive approaches to research analysis to be conducted within a 'critical' focus on power and interest.

Power has two broad meanings in social research. These are defined in the glossary for Chapter 8 but are worth mentioning initially here. *Structural power* refers to the ability of one person or group to coerce another person or group. This kind of power is commonly understood since it is usually very apparent, being vested in economic, class, law or other social institutions. It is extrinsic to social action, being imposed from outside a given social interaction. *Constitutive power*, on the other hand, is often less apparent since it refers to the ways in which we unwittingly reproduce *ideologically* imposed values through our everyday talk and action. It is intrinsic to a given social interaction because the language and social prac-tice of people in interaction does not merely reflect relations of power, it actively constitutes those relations of power.

For example, in many countries a way of speaking can categorize the speaker into a particular social class. This might be supported by the use of a particular vernacular and certain grammatical patterns, as in British 'working-class' or 'middle-class' speaking. Hence any interaction with a person of different social class is immediately framed within pre-existing ideological norms that set the terms of reference for the interaction. In Britain a regional accent was once a barrier to social and career advancement because it signified membership of a 'lower' class less worthy of responsibility and opportunity. While this is less true today, some would argue that it can still be the case in some circumstances. Within interaction and dialogue, people will draw (consciously or unconsciously) on ideological norms that pre-exist the interaction and they will reproduce these through language and social practice. Ideas of class membership reflect the economic and political dominance of particular groups at certain times in history. Constitutive power often takes the form of an ideology in the sense that it is apparent in implicit assumptions and values that come to be regarded as normal, given and beyond question.

In micro-analyses of social life, researchers can look at how language and social practice confers power on individuals. For example, a study of the construction of authority in a professional relationship such as management consulting might look at the ways in which rhetoric, gesture and language produce the effect of authority in particular relationships. A study of management on the shop floor might study the play of power and authority between management and 'workers' or staff. This could be seen in terms of factors affecting the credibility of the manager, such as personal style, use of language, negotiating skills and so on. Such a study would also look at the ways in which power and authority are resisted in management–staff relations. Published studies have focused, for example, on the disconnectedness of managerial power (Munro, 1997) and on the constitutive character of managerial power in a knowledge-based, professionalized industry such as advertising (Hackley, 2000).

Micro-studies can also employ another dimension of analysis. If particular gestures, bodily rhetoric (managers wear lounge suits, shopfloor workers wear jeans, etc.), sanctions and rewards characterize the relations between management and the workforce, then there may be historical reasons for this. In other words, there may be wider historical influences at work within the *micro-sociology* of particular relationships and groups.

Power is clearly important in many organizational contexts. The power of large organizations to change or maintain certain market conditions through the use of large advertising budgets is highly evident in fmcg (fast-moving consumer goods) markets. Some retail organizations have considerable power over suppliers to define price and quality specifications. On a micro-sociological level, formal management meetings are sites of the play of power from board level to shopfloor quality circles. Commercial organizations self-evidently have greater power over resources than individual consumers, but there is resistance to this power through consumer law, pressure groups and other means. Some commentators argue that the Internet has changed the power balance, shifting it towards consumers who can express their wants and dislikes directly. However, as some critical theorists point out, it is clearly in the interests of commercial organizations to claim that consumers have the power of choice. To what extent is this choice constrained or framed by commercial power? These questions and many others concerning power offer potentially fruitful lines of discussion for students doing research projects.

One very important aspect of the study of power concerns studies of gender and gender relations in organizational and consumption settings (e.g. Alvesson, 1998; Hirschman, 1993; Stern, 1993). Many student researchers have found that studies of the representation of gender relations in magazines and other media forms can provide fruitful material for speculation on the state of gender relations. Studies that, for example, content analyse advertisements and editorial of magazines from differing time periods tend to reveal striking differences in the ways that relations between genders are represented. In turn, the forms of representation reflect changing values and norms in the social world beyond magazines. What changing media representations of gender imply about the wider social world is a matter for the informed speculation of the researcher. Many other kinds of study focusing on power and gender have looked at career and promotion routes for women and men in different organizations and occupations.

A focus on power, then, implies that many aspects of social action and interaction, such as language, the rhetoric of gesture and dress, the rhetoric of gender relations, can be understood in terms of the power such behaviours confer on individuals. For researchers who draw on the Frankfurt school of critical theorists, power is a ubiquitous feature of social relations (e.g. Horkheimer and Adorno, 1944). For some researchers no interpretive study is complete without a focus on the ways in which wider structures of power, such as institutions of class, gender and economics, are reproduced at the level of everyday social interaction. Interpretive studies that are truly critical in this wide-ranging sense may be beyond the scope of most student researchers. In many cases, the aims of student research projects will be primarily managerial or interpretive/descriptive rather than truly critical. Nevertheless, the link between interpretive research traditions and critical studies that focus on power is too important to be ignored.

The selection of research perspectives for the following chapters

Interpretive research traditions that rely mainly on qualitative data have developed in many forms. There are numerous variations and adaptations of each tradition. They are interdependent: each tradition informs the others. There are also major areas of overlap. The various traditions have historical linkages and methodological commonalities. The aim of the following chapters will be to show student researchers how to conduct a research study by using any one of several major interpretive traditions, or by using combinations of concepts from differing traditions.

Many students and researchers may be intrigued by the research possibilities that lie in the perspectives that follow: they include phenomenology/existentialism, ethnography, critical discourse analysis, semiotics, postmodernism/poststructuralism, literary theory, gender studies and others. These and other perspectives are increasingly popular within marketing, management and consumer research. Other perspectives could have been chosen for this book. One important omission is the psychodynamic perspective which holds much potential for analysing topics such as intra- and inter-group relations within management and marketing, consumer motivation and behaviour, work motivation and organizational behaviour to name a few. However, it was decided that a suitable treatment of the psychodynamic perspective was beyond the scope of this book, and possibly too difficult for most first-time student researchers.

The perspectives outlined in this book were chosen because they are possibly the most accessible and directly applicable to the needs of marketing, management and consumer researchers. In addition they have a track record of use by researchers and publication in top-quality research journals. Students wishing to learn more about specific perspectives or traditions can follow the references to read up in more specialized writings.

The first chapter dedicated to a particular interpretive research tradition deals with phenomenology/existentialism. This would seem a useful place to begin, since many qualitative studies draw implicitly on aspects of phenomenology and existentialism. Indeed, for some researchers this is the major informing research perspective of qualitative research. This, and all the subsequent chapters, will develop a short exposition of the major principles and concepts of the perspective. It will then move into a section dealing with practical tips on how to frame a research project using the principles and concepts of this particular theoretical perspective. Each chapter will then illustrate the application of the perspective in research with examples of previously carried out research projects.

Glossary

Agency The power of the individual to control his or her own actions, thoughts and behaviour in spite of the influence social structures and institutions hold over us.

Critical realism Put simply, the position that the social world can be assumed to be real in a material sense for the sake of convenience. It is a pragmatic position that takes realism as a working assumption and a point of departure for research.

Ethnography A method of social research that entails a detailed and often long-term study of a particular social group. The aim is to understand the internal values of the group in terms of the lived experience of group members.

Ideology In a general sense, implicit values and norms that are carried within given modes of speaking, writing and thinking. Ideology is normally regarded as having a centre from which it emanates in support of particular (narrow) interests and groups. This centre is often obscured from view as ideological influences become widely accepted as the definitive way of regarding a subject or idea.

Micro-sociology The detailed study of how social life is produced within a specific group. It would normally entail a close examination of language, gesture and other social practices. Micro-sociological studies are often connected to larger-scale issues through consideration of the influence of ideological norms in the wider social and historical context.

Ontology A set of basic assumptions about the nature of social and/or material reality.

Paradigm A set of assumptions about the best way to pursue knowledge in a field regarding data-gathering methods, philosophy and analysis of data. The word 'paradigm' often refers to assumptions that have become taken for granted as the only correct way to do research in a particular field.

Phenomenological/existentialism Phenomenology was a branch of European philosophy associated with Brentano and Husserl that focused on the direct apprehension of experience. In modern psychology this tradition was developed into the experiential psychology perspective. In its modern form it has also been influenced by existentialists such as Camus and Sartre.

Realism In social research, realism is often invoked to mean that the social world can be assumed to be as solid and material as the physical world, at least for the purposes of research.

Reductionism Reducing complexity to simplicity by applying a particular form of explanation. The term is usually used in a pejorative sense to imply that the economy of a given form of explanation has been achieved at the expense of important detail.

Replicability The ability to replicate a research study, that is, to do it again within a different set of circumstances to see if the original findings re-occur.

Representation   Social researchers can only write about the worlds they investigate, they cannot reproduce those worlds, hence what they produce is a textual representation of the events they investigate.

Representative   Referring to sample choice in qualitative research: if a small group has similar characteristics to a larger group it is representative of that group. Findings from research with the smaller group may, therefore, reflect the views, behaviour or norms of the larger group.

Semiotics   Simply, the science of signs. In the tradition informed by C.S. Peirce, semiotics is the study of how signs come to have meaning in a given context. The task of the semiotician is to uncover the codes through which we interpret the meaning of signs.

Social constructionism   An ontological position that holds that the social world is constituted by and through language and social practice. In other words, people make up their social worlds in important senses. Social worlds are not fixed and logically prior to language and interactional practices. Language and interactional practices actively construct the social world.

Chapter 6

Phenomenology

Chapter outline

This chapter begins the discussion of specific interpretive research perspectives by drawing on two linked traditions: phenomenology and existentialism. It illustrates possible applications with research studies that could be adapted for use by student researchers. It also develops some of the major ideas, themes and techniques normally associated with each perspective.

Chapter objectives

After reading this chapter students will be able to

- explain the major themes and concepts of phenomenology as a research perspective
- apply these themes and concepts in a phenomenologically informed student research project
- understand certain phenomenological principles that have more general application in interpretive research studies

---

The phenomenological perspective

Social researchers of every persuasion have adapted philosophical systems and ideas for use in their own research. One particularly important philosophical theme that has been used in many research studies is phenomenology. Social researchers have linked the phenomenological emphasis on lived experience with the concern of existentialist writers for the experience of being and existing. Phenomenology has been placed in opposition to positivism in social research since the two research perspectives are usually characterized by assumptions that are mutually exclusive. Most notably, where phenomenological research assumes a socially constructed reality, positivism assumes that reality is external and objective. Easterby-Smith *et al.* (1991, p. 22) refer to this division and allude to ontological distinctions in Morgan and Smircich (1980). The contrasting ontological positions imply considerable differences in the conduct and analysis of research projects.

As with any philosophical traditions that have been adapted for social research, there are differing interpretations. Edmund Husserl's (1931, 1970) ideological phenomenology was adapted for social research by subsequent writers (Gurswitch (1974), such as Heidigger (1962), Sartre (1943, 1946) and Schutz (1932). Other strains of phenomenological research were developed, such as Habermas's (1970) interpretive sociology and the phenomenological social constructionism of Berger and Luckman (1966). These writers generally emphasized the embodied, agentive character of lived experience. Phenomenological social research takes the embodied, experiencing agent as a starting-point and explores the mutually constructed 'life-world' of participants, the world of lived experience from which all others derive. The phenomenology of Merleau-Ponty (1962a, 1962b) advocated a return to that experiential world that pre-exists science and knowledge.

Philosophical phenomenology was a development of Hegel's philosophy of knowledge: phenomenological knowledge was knowledge as it appeared in consciousness. The emphasis is placed on how people can access and describe their directly apprehended, lived experience. There is, therefore, an acknowledgement of the role of intuition, recognizing that much of our understanding is not articulated but, rather, is 'felt' or intuited. Phenomenologically informed researchers attempt to draw out this understanding by being open to the various personal ways people might describe this kind of experience (see Box 6.1).

For example, within organizations, managers are a category of person charged with particular responsibilities. 'Management' has, since the 1960s, been rather mythologized in that the skills, personal attributes and tasks of individual managers are held to be the reason for organizational success or failure. Phenomenological research can reveal how managers themselves experience this role. Do they recognize the heroic picture drawn in many popular management books? Do managers themselves feel that they have the skills, the knowledge and, in particular, the power to enact this role? Phenomenological research approaches would seek to access the subjective experience of managers to gain intimate insights into this experience. This results in a distinctive and penetrating research style.

Phenomenology also has many applications in consumer research. Consumer 'behaviour' is a long-standing tradition of marketing management research. The overtly managerial forms of research in marketing hold out the promise of predictability and control over consumers. If managers know how consumers react to a given advertisement, price offer or package this would take all the risk and uncertainty out of marketing. Phenomenology can conceive consumption not merely as behavioural response to external stimuli but as meaning-directed behaviour driven by

---

Box 6.1 Major features of phenomenological/existential research

Themes

A focus on the lived experience of actors

An emphasis on meaning, language, intentionality, agency and reflection

An empathetic stance from the interviewer as research participant

Assumptions

People are experiencing, reflective and agentive actors who collectively produce social events

The experience of existence, time and death are major aspects of what it means to be human

The integrity of the research data is paramount: there is no 'bias', only differing possible interpretations

The researcher is an active part of the construction of the research

Methods of data gathering

Qualitative, especially the audio-recorded, transcribed depth interview. Use of research field notes

Approach to data analysis

Focus on descriptions of experience, use of metaphor, the subjective construction of meaning, existential issues

Use of thematic analysis

Direct quotes used as exemplars of important themes to support findings

---

emotions, feelings and fantasies. In accessing the lived experience of consumers, phenomenological research can generate radically differing insights to traditional consumer behaviour research.

Phenomenological research themes

Intentionality

In phenomenological social research, the lived experience of people as they express it themselves is a most valuable source of research data.

Phenomenology focuses on intentional human experience. *Intentionality* concerns the sense in which experience is directed onto objects or phenomena, real or unreal. Literally, phenomenology refers to the study of appearances. Husserl was concerned with the way objects or phenomena appear to people. For researchers in management such 'objects or phenomena' could include marketed products, brands, managerial actions and interventions, marketing communications or any other aspect of organizational activity. Researchers drawing on this perspective are interested in accessing the emotions and subjective reflections of research participants in order to better understand the processes of management and/or marketing in which they are involved and which they jointly produce.

In phenomenological research the route to knowledge is to examine carefully what is felt, thought and perceived. People ascribe meaning to the objects that present themselves in consciousness. The task of the researcher is to explore events or processes by gathering first-hand descriptions of these feelings, thoughts and perceptions. Consequently the depth interview is an ideal data-gathering method for phenomenological research. Through this method, researchers can generate insight and understanding into marketing and management issues and processes from a human perspective by acknowledging that these processes and issues are done by thinking, feeling, reflecting people.

This last sentence calls to mind the section in the previous chapter that emphasized agency and meaning in interpretive research. In phenomenological research, people are active participants in social processes. They are not merely bodies that 'behave' according to external stimuli. Phenomenology emphasizes the human urge to derive meaning from experience. People are seen as actively interpreting their social worlds. Their interpretations and the meaning they ascribe to them are seen as the key to understanding social events and processes such as management and organizational or buyer behaviour. Most importantly, phenomenology sees people as independent thinkers with the power of agency. That is, people are thought to be able to initiate words, thoughts and actions. People's lives and thoughts are not simply determined by social structures and other forces.

Humanistic influences in phenomenological interpretive research

Hirschman (1986), among others, has written of the humanistic influence in phenomenological consumer research while Stern and Schroeder (1994) invoked humanism in their study of advertising imagery. Humanistic social research can be seen, historically, as a reaction to the dominance of experimental and statistical social research in the 1950s. The emphasis in positivist, experimental research was placed on people as organisms that learn from and behave in response to, external stimuli. The ability of people to be aware of how their action and behaviour is based in their own reflections and reasoning tended to be minimized. Many researchers wanted a more human level of understanding in social fields such as psychology, sociology and management studies. They felt that the model of the person in experimental research was flawed since it reduced the human being to an unreflexive organism without agency. This model also assumed that humans 'process' information much as computers do. By implication, humans were considered to have a strictly limited or zero capacity for reflecting on their circumstances and behaving creatively in response to reasoning and emotions. In contrast, humanism emphasizes the agentive capacity humans have to define our own existence and influence our own fate.

For humanistic psychologists such as Carl Rogers (1945) the phenomenological interview enabled people to reflect on their experience and, by doing so, change their perceptions and behaviour. The goal of humanistic psychology was, and is, self-realization. People are thought to have a capacity for reflection so that self-awareness can be increased and behaviour changed. Humanistic psychology has influenced the development of the field of counselling psychology today.

In social research in management and marketing, the same assumptions are made but the ends are different. While management researchers wish no harm on their research participants, the primary goal of the research is to generate insights and understanding about a particular issue or process, not to empower individuals with the ability to change their lives. The important thing for researchers (as opposed to therapists) is the assumption that people can stand outside their behaviour, so to speak, and reflect on it. This unique ability means that people are more than bundles of learned responses and reinforced behaviours. We are actively interpreting our experience in a search for meaning. This means that researchers must understand our experience as it appears to us in order to understand what motivates and drives behaviour.

Experience and existence in consumer research

The title of one study in the *Journal of Consumer Research* shows exactly what this theme emphasizes for consumer researchers: 'The experiential aspects of consumption: consumer feelings, fantasy and fun' (Holbrook and Hirschman, 1982). These researchers argue that consumption, or buying things, is not only done on the basis of a careful and explicit comparison of product or service features in the light of rational needs. They suggest that consumption can also be indulged in for fun and entails the fulfilment of fantasies. This insight may seem profoundly obvious to student researchers reading this book who have recently enjoyed a shopping trip, a meal in a restaurant or a night out dancing. The need for researchers to draw attention to the experiential reality of consumption arose because of the dominance in academic marketing research of theories which emphasized the economic rationality of consumers. This, in turn, arose because of the dominance of quasi-experimental and positivistic research methods which could not articulate experiential realities. The publication of articles such as the one referenced above represented a challenge to accepted research orthodoxy in consumer and marketing research.

The experiential perspective offered a radically new way of thinking about and therefore of researching buyer behaviour. Seen in this light, consumer research developed approaches that acknowledge the emotionality (Holbrook and Hirschman, 1982) and symbolism (Belk, 1988) of many buying decisions and consumer experiences. A later piece in the same journal develops a related methodological theme by emphasizing the value of research that draws on the links between 'experiential' consumer research and phenomenology. It is entitled 'Putting consumer experience back into consumer research: the philosophy and method of existential phenomenology' (Thompson et al., 1989). Much consumer research then and now has focused on the measurement of attitudes and consumer responses to survey questionnaires. In contrast, phenomenological researchers wish to tap into consumer experience as it appears to consumers, without the mediating influence of attitude scales or survey questions. They wish to understand the buying process as a phenomenon, as it appears to consumers. In this way phenomenological social research seeks to understand what consumption means for shoppers.

Phenomenology, then, was adapted in social research as part of the humanistic movement to find research perspectives that employed a richer model of the person and acknowledged the influence in social events of human emotion and agency. It acknowledged the human need to make experience meaningful and hence conceived of humans as seekers after meaning. One important part of what it means to be human is the experience of time and the certainty of death. This emphasis was incorporated into phenomenological research from existentialist writing.

The influence of existentialism

Existentialism is, broadly, the study of being. We are thrown into existence and have to face the reality, temporality and finiteness of our own existence. As agents of our own destiny, we make decisions about our lives. For existentialists, we are often unaware of our power to determine our own fate. Indeed, we are often scared by this power and escape from this knowledge by busying ourselves with trivial, everyday concerns and worries. This can represent a 'flight from freedom' whereby we deny our right to choose our destiny. Existentialist philosophy dwells on this extreme position on agency, suggesting that we live with choice and every moment we experience is governed by our willingness, or reluctance, to acknowledge this power of choice to ourselves.

The themes of being, existence and death may seem out of place in a research project about, say, the marketing of garden tools or the management of fast-food service operations. The existentialist influence is important for the analysis of qualitative phenomenological research data because of the interpretive position taken by the researcher. It is an extreme subjectivist position that focuses on our immediate experience of being and the ways in which we attempt to make sense of this experience. The ways we interpret our experiences as managers, consumers and workers can, then, be seen as ways in which we reconcile ourselves with the reality of mortality and the enigma of human existence.

Data gathering in phenomenological/existential research

Phenomenological researchers must generate verbal reports and/or written accounts of experience as their data. They must then organize and interpret this data. Clearly, the focus for research analysis here falls on language, since the route to inner thoughts and feelings lies in the accounts and descriptions that people give of their experiences. Language, written or audio-recorded, is the research data. Video and other texts (emails, letters) could also be used. This means that data gathering and analysis have a 'messy' quality, the data do not neatly 'fit' into categories and can be unwieldy to collect and collate. On the other hand, the value of this kind of data is that it can yield novel, striking and creative accounts that stimulate the researcher's interpretative imagination. This kind of data is also, often, intrinsically interesting in itself. When people feel relaxed and safe enough to talk about their experiences, the results can often be very engaging. When it is 'safe' to do so, we often reflect on our experience in ways which are new to us, we see things in new ways. The phenomenological interview has this quality in that it enables interviewees to access their experience in ways that had not been clear to them before.

The phenomenological interview

As mentioned earlier in the book, depth interviews can have varying degrees of formality. The researcher can use a predetermined script to list topics, or he or she can allow the interviewee greater scope for setting the agenda of the interview. However, it can be very useful for researchers to work to an interview guide which sets out the major themes of interest. This can be useful for remembering what topics to raise and for helping to jog the memory. It is a good idea to give the interviewee some advance knowledge of the topic or issues that will be the focus of discussion. On the other hand, it is important not to be too prescriptive. Part of the excitement of qualitative research is that the researcher does not know what he or she will find. People are interesting, creative entities and in phenomenological research studies the interviewee is always the expert. They have had the experiences to which you, the researcher, need to gain access.

A researcher cannot know for sure what will arise; interview agenda or guides should allow for this. This implies that phenomenological and existential research principles are not usually useful for testing theories. They are useful for exploratory research designs that set broad terms of reference and set out to discover things about a particular issue or process. Phenomenological researchers do know what they are interested in before they conduct an interview, but they do not know exactly what they will find out about it.

The degree to which the interviewee can set the interview agenda depends to some extent on the kind of topic or research question being addressed. It also depends on the scale of and stage in the research process. If a study entails a number of interviews then it is likely that the researcher's interests and understanding will grow as the research progresses. This will influence the interview agenda. In many cases research interviews become shorter as studies progress because the researcher has narrowed down the topics of interest. In many more cases the interviewee can raise unexpected and fruitful lines of thought and investigation.

Interviews that have no strict agenda have been used for many years in anthropology and sociology, and also in clinical and counselling psychology. Their history in marketing and management research is somewhat shorter. In humanistic psychology the open-ended interview was devised as a therapeutic intervention by Carl Rogers. In management research the aim of the interview is not client therapy, although in most cases the interviewee does find the experience fulfilling and enjoyable. It is rare for people to be invited to reflect frankly on their experience of their own work role and most find it refreshing. The interviewer's stance is non-judgemental and open to the interviewee's experience. The interviewer might intervene at times to help the dialogue along, or to probe particular responses to get at more specific themes. He or she might also need to gently redirect the interviewee back on to the topic of interest. However, in general, phenomenological research gathers better-quality data if the interviewee is made to feel comfortable so that they can be frank and insightful about their own feelings and thoughts concerning their working experience. In many cases they will not have had such an opportunity before: good interview researchers are capable of creating a rapport or empathy with interviewees which can help to generate striking and novel research data in the form of original and creative insights.

The phenomenological researcher stance

Conducting a phenomenological interview well is a subtle research skill. It is important that the researcher can empathize with the interviewee's perspective. The researcher must try to see the interviewee's world through their eyes. He or she must create a safe, open and confidential 'feel' for the interview. Many of the best qualitative interviews become like friendly chats: the interviewee becomes absorbed in their topic and forgets that the situation is, in fact, a relatively formal one. It helps if the interviewer has a specific interest in the topic, and a general interest in people and their thinking. It should be remembered that one-to-one interviews of this kind can be a powerful, moving and even threatening experience. Some sensitivity is demanded of the researcher so that they know when to probe for deeper answers, and when to leave alone. Of course, at all times the interviewee is free to terminate the interview, and they must be made aware of this at the beginning as a matter of proper research conduct.

Ideally, the researcher should be in a position to maintain eye contact and to attend to what the interviewee is saying. He or she might find it useful to make occasional notes, but this should be done with subtlety because it can make the interviewee feel uncomfortable. It is best to ask the interviewee for permission to audio-record the interview, then place a microphone in an unobtrusive position to pick up the dialogue. Later, the whole interview can be carefully replayed, listened to and transcribed. As a note of caution, it should be remembered that one interview can generate a vast amount of data. Fifteen thousand words is not unknown for one interview transcript. It is wise to keep interviews as short as reasonably possible; 30 to 60 minutes is adequate for most circumstances.

The interview tone

Good phenomenological interviews do develop their own momentum. It is important for the researcher to be sensitive to the tone of the interview. Some interviews seem to be socially difficult, the interviewee seems uncomfortable with giving responses. This is entirely natural, it can be difficult to create a rapport. Some interviewees are simply not comfortable with the directness and intimacy of the phenomenological interview. In such a situation the interviewer will have to work a little harder to generate good-quality data by (gently) asking more questions and generally leading the interaction. At the other extreme, some interviewees take some stopping once they realize that the situation is non-threatening and they have a captive audience to whom they can relate their entire life story. In such cases the interviewee might need to gently redirect the interviewee back onto relevant lines of discussion.

At the end of the interview the researcher/interviewer should thank the interviewee for their time and co-operation. They should be reassured that everything said in the interview will remain strictly confidential. Only the researcher and the readers of the research project will have access to the data. The interviewee's name will not be placed in the report unless they specifically agree to being named in the report. In most qualitative research interviewees are not named, either a pseudonym is used or interviewees are referred to by a number or letter (interviewee A said this, interviewee B said that). Many phenomenological researchers allow the interviewee to see the typed-up transcript of the interview to ascertain that it is a fair representation of the conversation. Some allow the interviewee to read the final research project report so that the interviewee can see how their comments were interpreted.

The pilot interview and developing interview skills

Conducting a phenomenological interview well is demanding on the part of the researcher. The topic area must be defined in such a way that the phenomenological interview can generate useful and relevant data. In many cases a pilot interview can be useful so that the interviewer can refine his or her interview agenda and get some practice at conducting the interview. The depth interview demands subtle and adept social skills. Listening intently and concentrating on keeping dialogue flowing can be extremely tiring, especially if several interviews are conducted in a short time. In a phenomenological interview, the interviewer's thoughts and opinions are not important: the focus of attention is entirely on the interviewee who has given their time and is prepared to be open about their experience. This in itself can be tiring but it is very important that the researcher/interviewer makes the interviewee the centre of attention for the duration of the interview. There is then the labour of transcribing the interview and/or making notes. Finally, some sense must be made of the interview; the researcher must write up the findings in a way that is structured and generates a useful discussion.

Analysing the transcript

When analysing data researchers should bear in mind the kind of research report they must produce. All qualitative research relies heavily on direct quotes to support arguments or to illustrate particular points in the research report. The direct quote is important research material for qualitative researchers of all kinds, so analysis of research data should bear this in mind. The direct quote might be indicative of a general theme that emerged in interviews. It might be a particularly pithy expression of an important issue or concern. It might illustrate something about the research issue that requires explaining to the reader of the research report.

A quote might be important in showing how particular metaphors or tropes of speech are used to describe or account for particular actions or events. Whatever their particular purpose in a research report, direct quotes make the research tangible for the reader. When analysing research data the importance of quotes should be borne in mind.

Description, empathy, metaphor, existential dimensions

The analysis of phenomenological/existential interviews emphasizes several major issues. In the research interview there is a description of the interviewee's experience in relation to a particular object, process or event. The researcher must be careful to interpret this description with integrity by adopting an 'insider perspective' informed by an empathy with the interviewee's point of view. The initial description should reflect the interviewee's view of the world. Of particular interest is the interviewee's use of metaphor. When we talk or write, use of metaphor is unavoidable. The metaphors we choose are powerful in informing the meaning we draw from our experience. As mentioned earlier, there is also a concern with existential issues: how does the interviewee deal with issues of time and existence?

Such themes might seem very abstract and difficult to extract from interview texts. Indeed, the analysis of interviews as a whole can be time consuming and difficult. The important thing is to find themes which can form the structure for the analysis/discussion. These themes may not be apparent straight away. They can come from extensive reflection on the data. The audio tape and/or notes and transcript might be read through several times before the structure, tone and themes of the text begin to emerge for the researcher. Particular phrases or words might not strike you as interesting or revealing at first but may do so after more reading and thought. The researcher should think about the interviewee's 'take' on events, how they arrive at that take, what it reveals about the meaning of their experience. What metaphors does the interviewee use to describe their experience? Do these metaphors re-occur? Are they of a particular kind?

After some reflection, particular themes might emerge that can form the basis for the research analysis. Such themes would act as the organizing structure for the findings and subsequent analysis/discussion in the research report. For example, an interview or series of interviews might be characterized by the use of particular kinds of metaphors. The researcher could use these metaphors as a basis for an analysis/discussion which speculates on why these metaphors and not others have been chosen, why they are powerfully expressive for the research participant, what they imply about the phenomenon being studied.

For example, one student researcher conducted a series of phenomenological interviews with entrepreneurs. The study was conducted to provide research data concerning the meaning of becoming and being an entrepreneur, so that insights could be found about the nature of entrepreneurial motivation and success. The analysis focused on the interviewees' biography, their origins and the ways in which life events had informed their entrepreneurial drive. One metaphor that seemed important was the interviewee's use of a 'no big deal' manner in discussing his transition from employee to self-employed entrepreneur. After reading the transcript many times, the researcher realized that the interviewee often played down the difficulty or unusual-ness of what he had accomplished. This seemed striking: having a salaried profession for 30 years and giving up that security for the risks of private business is a significant change, or at least so it seemed to the researcher. It appeared as though the dismissive 'no big deal' playing-card metaphor worked to deflect the realization of the risk that had been undertaken. Paradoxically, the metaphor revealed exactly what the interviewee was attempting to play down: the risk of and intense motivation required for, entrepreneurship.

The interview approach was idiographic in the sense that the interviewee's entrepreneurial behaviour was considered as part of an evolutionary process tied in with his origins and life experiences. A similar interviewing approach towards a different interviewee resulted in a published paper on the 'social construction of entrepreneurship' (Mumby-Croft and Hackley, 1997).

Doing phenomenological research

Phenomenological research designs, then, normally entail first-hand descriptions and accounts of events from people who directly participate in those events. For example, a study of the effectiveness of in-store merchandizing techniques in the clothes sector might generate data by interviewing and/or observing shoppers in stores. Interviews could also be conducted in other environments so that shoppers might reflect on their past experiences of in-store merchandizing. The phenomenological interview is usually a retrospective account of events or experiences. In retrospect, interviewees can often reconstruct experience and make sense of it in ways that were not available immediately after or during the experience.

Student researchers have conducted phenomenological interviews with other students to generate insights into the experience of undergoing higher education as a mature student. Phenomenological interviewing can be particularly powerful in chronicling personal change and transformation. It often allows people to reflect on deeply personal issues of motivation and meaning that they have not reflected on before, at least not with the mediating influence of another person. The counselling psychology movement is premised on the power of the interactional process that occurs when one individual is given the space and time to reflect frankly on their experience in the presence of another non-judgemental person. While the research interview is not designed to foster personal change and transformation it can be a powerful event for both parties, and researchers should remember this. The phenomenological interview is an intimate setting and should be handled sensitively by the researcher.

Shopping experiences as phenomenological research data

Other researchers have explored the experience of shopping as an aspect of consumer behaviour studies. Shopping, reduced to a price and value information processing phenomenon by many consumer behaviour models, is revealed as a rich and powerful experience by a phenomenological perspective. Brown and Reid (1997) had students in Northern Ireland, UK write down their stories of shopping experiences in short essays. Vivid experiences were recounted that revealed something of the complexity and value-laden character of shopping itself. Brown and Reid (1997) used a narrative analysis (discussed in Chapter 10) to focus on storytelling around shopping experiences. People recounted the many meanings of their shopping experience as they appeared to them from a deeply personal perspective. The stories were frequently vivid and compelling, and shopping experiences were woven into complex narratives that encompassed relationships, identity, social positioning and other profoundly personal issues. It was apparent that people go shopping to cheer themselves up or to distract themselves from the cares of everyday life. It was also evident that shopping is an integral part of contemporary culture and forms a landscape within which everyday life takes place.

Another phenomenological study focused on the consumption practices of expectant mothers and how these practices were mediated by considerations of time. Shopping was a part of this study but more important were the insights gained into the complexity of the lives of expectant mothers and the strategies they used to manage time and their consumption behaviour (Carrigan and Szmigin, 2002). For some people, shopping becomes pathological: like drug addicts, they simply cannot stop (Elliott, 1994; Elliott and Gournay, 1996). Interpretive research approaches that focus on subjective experience, like the phenomenological approach, are able to capture just what it is in shopping experiences that many people find so compelling.

Possible topics in phenomenology

In principle, any topic in social research could be the subject of a phenomenological study. Since phenomenology has not been a mainstream research perspective, there are many topics in marketing and management that could be subject to a reappraisal from a phenomenological perspective. Research project topics do need to connect fruitfully to an important or topical area of research and thought, even if the nature of that connection is a critical one that emphasizes gaps, oversights or methodological limitations in previous studies.

There is scope for student researchers to use the phenomenological interview to enhance a study based mainly on secondary information and data. In a 10–20,000-word project the scope for wide-ranging phenomenological interviews is, clearly, limited. However, it can be salutary for student researchers to use phenomenological principles to get the experiential perspective of organizational managers or consumers on various topics. Experienced managers can offer insights that encourage students to think hard about the application of the management principles they learn in taught courses. Similarly, interviews with consumers can generate useful material for reflection and discussion.

Phenomenologies of organizational management

One wide-ranging phenomenological study conducted by a research student offered a particularly useful example of the way that existing research traditions can be reappraised and further developed through an interpretive, in this case a phenomenological, research perspective. This study was undertaken as part of a PhD, but student researchers at other levels could adapt it for a smaller-scale approach. The study explored the current state of marketing planning practice from the experiential perspective of senior marketing managers. The researcher's motivation arose from an interest in marketing planning research (e.g. Greenley, 1988) and a feeling that questionnaire-based survey research did not offer the richness of insights into marketing planning practice that phenomenological interviews could. He interviewed marketing managers from several different kinds of organization. It took a long time to get the access the researcher wished to senior marketing managers. Interviews were extensive, taking around an hour each. The interviewer took care to establish a rapport with interviewees through early telephone contact and initial general discussion. More than twenty interviews were conducted over a time period of several years.

The rapport established by the researcher was evident from the candid and spontaneous interview responses. The interviews were audio-recorded and fully transcribed. The researcher focused on the use of metaphor in his analysis of transcripts. Interviewees drew on telling and novel metaphors to express their experiences and to offer accounts of their action and behaviour. These metaphors formed the organizing structure for the discussion of findings. The research found that most organizations did not engage in formal marketing planning processes, a finding that was consistent with previous research. However, unlike previous research, the study revealed a novel experiential viewpoint of managerial experience in marketing. It suggested that marketing management in general, and marketing planning in particular, were activities always mediated by local organizational conditions. This particularism, consistent with interpretive research principles, was a striking contrast to the generalized nature of popular marketing models and frameworks. Indeed, the study was in part a refutation of the legitimacy of generic 'one-size-fits-all' marketing management axioms.

The study was in part an implicit critique of previous marketing planning research because it addressed the topic from an alternative methodological perspective. In addition to offering a rich description of marketing planning managerial practices, the study also concluded with an alternative, narrative-style marketing planning model.

In common with many interpretive studies, it was difficult for the researcher to write up the research in a clearly structured manner. The nature of the study was expressed as a wide-ranging discussion. The interviews were also wide-ranging in the topics they touched upon. Qualitative research usually has this 'messy' quality, but the messiness is a source of richness in findings. The researcher in this case organized the write-up in a creative way, using the metaphors used by interviewees as chapter and section headings in the discussion of findings. However, the research questions and major findings did need to be stated clearly at the beginning of the write-up. It is easy for first-time interpretive researchers to forget that their work must satisfy some generic guidelines of social research. Whatever the particular interpretive tradition drawn upon, empirical researchers are, still, looking out into the world to see if they can generate findings that might feed into and develop previous research-based knowledge in that field. Therefore, a clear statement of research objectives, method and major findings is necessary.

The above study was positioned as a development of existing marketing management research. Phenomenological studies are particularly apt for developing a new 'take' on an old research topic.

Phenomenological approaches can be useful in framing research that addresses a novel or new topic area. This may occur if the student researcher's topic of interest has arisen from his or her work experience or from a special interest. Business practice is developing so quickly that possible topic areas arise far too quickly for the academic community to develop established perspectives on every possible topic. Phenomenological studies can examine a wide range of topics from the point of view of participants and hence they offer a theoretically well-informed route to vivid and relevant research studies in many topic areas.

Glossary

Existentialism The existentialist literary and philosophical movement focused on the human experience of being and existence. It became linked with the phenomenological perspective in social research because each perspective takes the experiencing, sense-making individual as a starting-point.

Humanism A movement in literature and art that has been echoed in social sciences. In social science it draws attention to the agentive, creative experiencing individual and places this model of the person at the centre of research and theorizing.

Intentionality In phenomenology, the idea that consciousness is directed onto objects.

Chapter 7

Ethnography

Chapter outline

Ethnography is one of the most important informing traditions of interpretive research, along with phenomenology/existentialism. Anthropologists developed the ethnographic method in their study of indigenous populations. In social research in management and marketing, ethnography has been widely used in adapted forms to generate qualitative insights and to understand these phenomena from the point of view of the participants. This chapter introduces important concepts and principles that student researchers can use in their own research projects.

Chapter objectives

After reading this chapter students will be able to

- understand that the research tradition of ethnography is associated with cultural anthropology
- appreciate that management and marketing researchers can adapt ethnographic approaches to suit the kinds of question they need to ask
- apply some important concepts and principles of ethnographic research in student research projects

---

Introduction to ethnography

Elliott and Jankel-Elliott (2002) describe how ethnography evolved from 'armchair' sociology based on surveys and second-hand information. A view emerged that first-hand research might be a better way of understanding alien cultures. Short field trips and interviews with members of a culture became one method; much more prolonged immersion in a social group became the accepted method for some anthropologists (e.g.

Malinowksi, 1922). At least a year of immersion was recommended so that the researcher could become truly one of the group he or she is studying. Chicago sociologists of the 1930s began to study subcultural groups in the USA as if they were studying the indigenous tribes of isolated islands. This became known as 'streetcorner sociology' as it studied the deviant subcultures of America (Downes and Rock, 1982, p. 36).

Ethnography is an approach to research that is often associated with cultural anthropology. For Banister *et al.* (1994) ethnography is characterized by

- the use of multiple data sources including conversations, interviews, observation and documents;
- a focus on everyday behaviour rather than experiments;
- using a relatively unstructured data-gathering approach in the early stages in order to clarify questions and allow themes to emerge from creative interpretation;
- seeking in-depth understanding of a small sample of circumstances.

Organizational management has been an area of interest for anthropological researchers since the 1920s (Wright, 1994). The ethnographer engages in close study of a particular social group in order to understand the cultural norms, values and behaviour of that group. This study has often been conducted over a long period of time so that researchers can gain a truly insider perspective. Management and marketing researchers have also adapted ethnographic approaches to use in shorter periods of research. Ethnographic principles have been used to study consumers and consumption in order to better understand the effects and implications of strategic marketing management actions (Arnould and Wallendorf, 1994). For example, Elliott and Jankel-Elliott (2002) have used ethnography in strategic consumer research for many global brands, while Clarke *et al.* (1998) studied the culture of the British 'pub'. Ritson and Elliott (1999) used ethnographic principles to research the social uses of advertising among UK adolescent advertising audiences. Many classic studies of organizational management have, as Wright (1994) shows, used principles derived from ethnography. Ethnographic research can construct representations of managerial experience and from that can offer useful insights into the process and practices of organizational management (e.g. Watson, 1994).

Ethnographers seek to understand social phenomena through the eyes of the group participants, while retaining a sense of scientific detachment so that they can understand the meanings and dynamics of a social group better than the participants themselves. With its emphasis on qualitative data gathering techniques and focus on experience and meaning, ethnography is sometimes regarded as a counter-position to traditional social scientific research approaches that focus on facts and causation. It is widely accepted that ethnographers seek rich, insightful descriptions of social phenomena as opposed to *nomothetic* generalizations that are founded on large samples and tests of statistical significance. However, ethnography and quantitative, causal research shares a concern with empirical data. It (ethnography) seeks to generate interpretive representations that derive from first-hand observation and study. It is, hence, an *applied* research tradition. In applied social research, ethnographic approaches have been used to understand soccer hooliganism, gang violence, drug addiction and other socially marginalized subcultures (Hammersley and Atkinson, 1983). In management and marketing research, the applied tradition of ethnography is often reflected in the problem-focused nature of much research. Ethnography is used as a tool to help in the design of management interventions and processes.

Opportunities for ethnographies of marketing, management and consumption

Ethnographers study behaviour and experience in natural settings. In practice this can mean taking part in that group as a quasi-participant so that the researcher can understand the jargon, the jokes, the local language and, hence, understand the shared meanings within the group. The researcher must understand the experience of being one of these people in this particular cultural setting in order to understand their motivations and behaviour. Clearly, for researchers, taking an unobtrusive part in a group over an extended period of time is not always easy. It may be possible to acquire a useful ethnographic understanding by being an observer in the group, perhaps 'shadowing' managers or simply joining in day-to-day routines. Many ethnographic researchers have reported that after initial suspicion people in a workplace or other social context come to accept the researcher's presence and even to use the researcher as an outlet for things they want to say but cannot, under normal social conditions.

There are various opportunities for ethnographic research. For example, student researchers are also consumers. Consumption affords a rich area for ethnography. Students can sometimes gain first-hand access to consumption settings through holiday or part-time jobs, or through their experience as consumers of entertainment, books, holidays and other products and services. One student used her part-time job to research the ways in which theatre audiences use local advertising of prestige products. She was able to gain interviews with audience members (with the permission of theatre management) because she worked in the theatre as a front-of-house assistant. Students quite often work part-time in retail environments and can use their contacts to arrange access to shoppers. Students can also use their own colleagues as research participants in studies of consumption of clothes, holidays, leisure activities, such as clubs and music, and other products and services.

Another student researcher explored the subculture of hip-hop music through his deejay activities. He was particularly interested in the clothes associated with hip-pop and how manufacturers gained access to the group. Yet another was interested in the extent to which holiday consumers are influenced by tour operator brands when they search the Internet for cheap holidays. She sat with consumers as they surfed the holiday deals on the Internet and spoke to them during the process to investigate their motivations and responses to the sites and information they saw. There have been a number of examples of 'netography', whereby researchers use Internet chat-rooms or emailed interviews and surveys to gain ethnographic insights into consumption or other issues.

Organizational management can be more difficult to research because of the need to arrange access. It is common for student researchers to send off letters requesting interviews or other forms of access only to find that their letter never receives a reply. A reply is far more likely if the student knows an individual in that organization and can direct the request to that person. Organizations are busy places and they receive many such requests. Many organizations are sensitive to granting access to someone they do not know. If access can be arranged it does not have to be unconditional or open-ended in terms of time. If an interview is granted with a manager at the organization's premises, then the student researcher can use the opportunity to observe the style and tone of interaction within that organization. Relatively short periods spent as a fly on the wall in an organization can also be useful as they familiarize the researcher with the shared meanings of staff so that, when the time comes to offer a creative interpretation of the research data, this interpretation can be informed by some understanding of the local cultural context.

Indexicality in ethnographic research

An important ethnographic principle is that of seeking to understand social phenomena in their social and cultural context from the point of view of group participants. This principle can also prove fruitful in interpretive studies that are not necessarily framed as 'ethnography'. The interpretation of, say, a depth interview is always conducted within a frame of presuppositions. The researcher can only understand what an interviewee is talking about to the extent that he or she understands their work and the organization they work in. The interpretation of qualitative data will necessarily entail suppositions on the part of the researcher that are drawn from his or her impressions of the context of research. The researcher must understand enough about the context of research in order to know just exactly what the interviewee is talking about.

This touches on the issue of *indexicality* of language and gesture. In a famous example, a wink (of an eye) can mean different things depending on the context (Geertz, 1973). A wink can be complicit, seductive, friendly, sexual, patronizing, funny, even threatening, depending on the context. Without an understanding of the context, a wink cannot easily be interpreted. Indexicality refers to the contextual meaning of things people say and do. Our language has a context: if an engineer uses the technical phrases and concepts of engineering in talking about his or her work, then an interviewer who does not have any knowledge of engineering will not fully understand what is being said. In the same way ethnographers feel that interviewers must have first-hand knowledge of the social context of which a research participant is part in order to understand what they are referring to in their interview. Ethnographic principles dictate that we cannot take this understanding for granted. We must go into 'the field' and get to know something of the shared meanings and symbolic social practices in a particular social realm in order to properly understand what people are talking about. Taking account of 'ethnographic context' means interpreting ethnographic research data in the light of a broader understanding of that social context first-hand in the field.

Particular comments and gestures may carry subtle shades of meaning that are not apparent to an outsider who has no knowledge of the group culture of the interviewee. Language, gesture and social practice have an 'indexical' property in that they refer to a particular social setting for their meaning. The principle of indexicality derives from the *ethnomethodological* sociology of Garfinkel (1967). The researcher carrying out an interpretive analysis of interview transcripts or other primary data cannot 'repair' the indexicality of comments and gestures without this knowledge. Repairing indexicality refers to the ability of the researcher to interpret language and gesture according to its meaning in context. Social understanding and the appearance of social competence are far more complex than they may often appear. The ethnographic researcher generates insights into social life by understanding the meaning that language, gestures and other social practices have for participants.

'Doing' ethnography

Arnould (1998) suggests that ethnography aims to 'clarify systematically the ways that culture (or sub-culture) simultaneously constructs and is constructed by the behaviours and experiences of members' (p. 86). He suggests that this entails four main principles:

1   ethnographic description;
2   experiential participation in cultural context;
3   a focus on particular rather than general insights;

4   multiple methods of data collection.

'Doing' ethnography, like doing any interpretive research, entails particular methods of data collection and analysis. But, more importantly, it entails using a set of broad principles that inform the researcher's whole engagement with the subject matter. Interpretive researchers draw on a theoretical perspective: they do not mechanistically apply a 'method' (see Box 7.1).

Box 7.1 Major features of ethnographic research

Themes
'Rich' ethnographic description of a social context

Focus on local shared meanings and the reproduction of cultural norms

Researcher immersion in the cultural context being studied
Importance of indexicality

Assumptions
Social and cultural life is created by people through symbolic interaction

To truly understand a social milieu a researcher must experience it

Qualitative research data is interpreted through a frame of presuppositions: ethnographic interpretation entails an understanding of the local cultural context

Methods of data gathering
Multiple methods including observation, interviews, informal conversations and exchanges, field notes and records

Approach to data analysis
Creative interpretation based on researcher knowledge of the social and cultural context in question

Focus on particular phenomena, not generalized truths

The researcher creates an imaginative representation of the social life in question in an attempt to convey something of the meanings, motivations and experiential understanding of participants

Focus on 'repairing' the indexicality of language and gesture

The ethnographic research study involves, first, gaining as much 'insider' knowledge as possible about the subject in question. For management researchers, this might involve reading all the available published information about a particular organization or brand before the primary research is begun. It may mean establishing links with a particular organization to try to engage members in discussion. A research study into a particular consumption practice or a specific consumption group would begin with a thorough investigation of secondary sources. The research would then progress to a first-hand engagement with the contexts of consumption. For most student researchers in management and marketing a prolonged period of field research is impractical. Even if access is granted, the time and resources are rarely available to students. But this need not rule out the application of ethnographic principles. Indeed, many management and marketing research studies apply the principles of ethnography to much shorter periods of field work.

The use of ethnographic principles in an advertising project

As mentioned earlier, ethnographic principles can be drawn on pragmatically to enhance the interpretive framework for qualitative studies undertaken by student researchers. For example, a student researcher with no first-hand experience of the advertising industry wanted to investigate how advertising effectiveness is assessed within advertising agencies. She studied the available literature to find that there are many approaches to measuring advertising effectiveness. Some researchers argue that it cannot be measured, that advertising's power to persuade or inform must be taken on trust to some extent. Others argue that the answer to the question 'how do you know if an advertisement has been effective' is always 'it depends on the objectives that were set for the campaign'. If a given advertising campaign has clear, distinct objectives its effectiveness can be measured relatively easily.

For example, a clear objective might be 'to raise awareness of brand X among a convenience sample of shoppers by 20 per cent over the campaign period'. The agency could conduct street interviews before and after the campaign to measure awareness of the brand. If a campaign does not have clear objectives then, clearly, measurement of its success is far harder. The student researcher felt that the published literature did not adequately reflect the practical problems of assessing advertising effectiveness and decided to get first-hand agency data on the issue. She wrote to several advertising agencies and one large international agency replied. Account team professionals agreed to talk to her and she went along to the agency in London.

The agency proved very helpful and the student researcher conducted six interviews over several days. Two were conducted over the phone prior to going to the agency. Notes were made on these. The other four were conducted in an office on the agency premises. These interviews were audio-taped. Field-notes were made of her impressions of the agency, her sense of the organizational culture and management style and her subjective impressions during the interviews. She also took note of informal conversations and encounters with agency personnel. After the interviews had taken place the researcher asked some supplementary questions by email. She also made use of agency documentation that she was given by helpful interviewees, such as creative briefs, agency publicity, case studies and other documentation. Her overall goal was not only to understand the issue she was researching but to appreciate something of what it meant to work in that industry and that agency. Her period of direct contact with the industry was short, but in that time she was able to gain a powerful first-hand impression of what it meant to work in that agency. She was able thus to earn a sense of what the 'problem' of advertising effectiveness meant for advertising professionals. Equipped with this understanding she hoped she could make a well-informed interpretation of her research data. In each interview the researcher asked the account team professional what he or she meant by advertising effectiveness and how it was addressed in that agency.

What she found was that advertising professionals are very aware of the need to be accountable to clients, and to shareholders. Everyone wants ads to be effective. The disagreement within agencies comes about when some people feel that measures of effectiveness themselves risk stifling the creativity of ads and, by doing this, actually make ads less distinctive. If ads are less distinctive, so the argument goes, they are less effective than they would otherwise have been regardless of what they scored on an awareness survey. Besides, some advertising professionals argue that while there are some sophisticated ways of applying measurement to advertising, the relevance of what is actually being measured to effectiveness is not always evident. For example, 'awareness' of a campaign is irrelevant unless the client's sales or other objectives are met.

The student researcher found that the priorities and values that professionals hold within advertising agencies are not always evident from published research studies. The issues in practice are invariably more complex and the shades of argument more subtle. This student used depth interviews for data gathering and only a short time in the field, but she also gained a rapport with staff, she saw first-hand the working style and tone within the organization, she spoke informally to agency staff between interviews and at lunch. In other words, she was able to repair the indexicality of interview data to some degree.

Clearly this student researcher's understanding might have been deeper if she had spent months in the agency. Nonetheless, she was able to offer some interesting and well-supported insights into a major advertising industry issue because she integrated her qualitative data-gathering method with ethnographic principles and took a holistic approach to the interpretation of data. She did not apply a mechanistic 'content-analysis' to the transcribed interview data. She actively interpreted it in the light of what she had learned from her brief first-hand encounter with the agency.

Formal and informal ethnographic data

Part of the goal of ethnographic research is to provide a rich description of a social process or phenomena by acquiring a thorough first-hand understanding of that social process or phenomena. This would normally imply multiple methods of data gathering since ethnographic researchers can acquire ideas about a cultural context from many sources. This could include depth interviews, analysis of other textual data such as emails or telephone interviews, historical documents, observation and field-notes of researcher reflections and ideas.

Typically, ethnographers combine formal data-gathering methods with informal methods. The formal methods will include the usual qualitative techniques of interview, observation and focus or discussion group. However, our understanding of social contexts is often acquired more intuitively through things we overhear, accidental observations we make, casual phone conversations or off-duty encounters with people who live and/or work in that particular social context. All such sources are potentially useful for the ethnographic researcher.

For example, it is far from unknown for an interviewee to say one thing in a formal interview then to offer a much more candid opinion in the pub afterwards. Indeed, informal social settings, such as staff restaurants, the bar or pub after work or other work-related social gatherings, can be particularly valuable for the ethnographic researcher. It would hardly be appropriate for a student researcher to take an audio-recording device along if he or she was invited to the bar or pub at lunchtime with work staff. However, the off-duty comments, jokes and ways of talking about work issues and personalities can offer important routes to understanding what happens in more formal work settings.

Researchers have found that the formal research interview held, say, in an office of the host company might yield very different insights to a subsequent interview that is conducted in a less formal setting off-site (Easterby-Smith and Malina, 1999). Such informal settings can 'round out' a researcher's understanding of a topic because the research participant may be more relaxed and less defensive. The author has conducted many interviews with marketing professionals and has had several experiences of people taking him aside to a quiet corner of the office to offer a franker viewpoint than could be offered in a more public setting. The ethnographic stance gives researchers the licence to use this kind of insight actively as research data.

High-quality informal data often emerges if the researcher has established a useful rapport with the research participants/interviewees. Indeed, in ethnography as in most qualitative research, the quality of this rapport often dictates the quality of insights generated (Agar, 1996). Easterby-Smith *et al.* (1991, p. 90) refer to the importance of establishing trust between researcher and participant. The research participant is more likely to be candid and spontaneous if he or she trusts the researcher to use their discretion and not to reveal the sources of any potentially embarrassing quotes or opinions. In many research contexts in which employees or managers are the research participants, they do worry that the researcher might name them as the source if they express a criticism of organizational policy or scepticism towards organizational aims and methods. It is important for the researcher to develop sensitivity for organizational politics and to establish an informal sense of rapport with the research participants.

However subtle and skilled the researcher's interviewing technique, there is no getting away from the fact that a research interview is a formalized encounter, especially if it is held in a formal setting such as an office. There may, therefore, be some ritual attached to the interaction. An interviewee may be suspicious that what they say may be read or heard by management. Even if they are not suspicious, interviewees are in a position of having to justify and account for their working practices. Few of us, faced with a research interview, would claim that we don't know what we're doing, we aren't very competent and we rely a lot on luck in our jobs. In any interaction we are faced with a social need to construct and maintain a persona that we feel is appropriate for that encounter.

Interviewing people about their professional role and working practice entails a social requirement that they present themselves as competent professionals. They must, therefore, make their responses to questions sound like plausible stories that attribute certain causes to certain effects. They must, in general, sound like a competent professional. For example, one study found that many marketing managers interviewed spoke of their use of theories and concepts that are found in popular marketing management textbooks. Yet when the researcher was shadowing these managers in their day-to-day work they did not seem to use any such models. Their interview answers were, it appeared, post hoc rationalizations. To some extent, they were saying things they felt that an academic researcher in marketing might expect to hear in a research interview.

Research interviews, then, are formal social encounters that involve expectations, codes and rituals and the performance of roles. However informal the interaction may seem, there is a difference between the informality of a relaxed research interview and the informality of ethnographic research data that comes from overheard comments, casual or unexpected observations, informal chats and conversations in non-work settings and so on.

Practical ethnography

Ethnography makes use of small samples of research participants. Often these samples are chosen simply because they are convenient. The important thing for ethnographers is to generate a 'thick description' of social behaviour which seeks to understand, and then describe, the complexity of social life (Geertz, 1973). Elliott and Jankel-Elliott (2002) refer to the distinction between 'inductive' ethnography and 'interpretive' ethnography (citing Alvesson and Skoldberg, 2000). The former research style tries to ground findings very securely in a detailed analysis of empirical data. The latter 'interpretive' style of ethnography attempts to render bold or striking creative interpretations of limited data sources. The best ethnography, arguably, falls part way into each camp with detailed and systematic data gathering providing the basis for creative insights that go beyond logical induction into the realm of imaginative representation.

As already discussed, data gathering for ethnography can take many forms. In practical ethnography in marketing and management research it is seldom possible for researchers to spend long periods of time living with the research participants. 'Quasi-ethnography', often used in commercial applications (Elliott and Jankel-Elliott, 2002) makes use of shorter, often opportunistic periods of data gathering. Elliott and Jankel-Elliott (2002) describe several studies. Rust (1993) describes a commercial study in which researchers loitered in supermarkets waiting for families with children to enter. They would then record some information about the family and follow them (discretely, one supposes) around the store. After the family left the researcher would make notes on what they had said and done to generate insights into shopping practices and family interaction.

The researcher-as-voyeur position may imply some ethical research issues that would need to be addressed on a study-by-study basis. Privacy is important to many people, and personal safety is important for researchers. If a student researcher is thinking of conducting a study like that of Rust (1993), then the explicit permission of the organization in which the research will be conducted must be obtained. If permission is granted then great care must be taken in gathering the data. It may be possible to simply 'hang-out' at places of interest. Many famous sociological studies into youth subcultures were conducted by Chicago-based sociologists in the 1960s. As part of their method researchers would make it their business to be where the group of interest would be so they could observe behaviour and listen to talk.

In consumer research applications researchers have adopted ethnographic principles by, for example, spending time in kindergartens and primary schools to understand how infant children become aware of brands. In one study the researcher convened 'focus' groups in which he showed pre-school children brand logos and elicited recognition. In another a female researcher discussed consumption practices with young girls with regard to their clothes, make-up and toys such as dolls. Commercial researchers seek to understand how children recognize and understand brands for commercial purposes. Academic researchers might have broader terms of reference. Whether the terms of reference for research are commercial and exploitative, or ethically informed and investigative, the ethnographic principle of simply hanging out with group members in the places where they hang out is a powerful one for the generation of insights into group meanings and actions.

Some more examples of practical student ethnography

For example, one undergraduate student researcher was interested in understanding the effects of alcohol advertising on young people of age 16–18. She found some published research studies that had addressed this topic, particularly Ritson and Elliott (1999). In this published study the researchers had undertaken an extensive ethnographic field-work period in UK sixth-form colleges. The lead researcher had actually gained employment as a teacher in exchange for privileged access to the students. He conducted interviews and also observed and listened to the students in their school context, and also in informal setting such as the common room. The study found that adolescents use advertising as a discursive resource in their conversation and jokes. Used in this way advertising was an important feature of adolescents' social positioning and identity-formation. The advertisements they liked or found funny signified group membership.

The student researcher conducted a smaller-scale study guided by her specific interest in the role of alcohol advertising on the social lives of UK adolescents. She convened focus groups of four to six people aged between 16 and 18 at three local sixth-form colleges in the West Midlands region of England. The focus groups were conducted in the school premises and were audio-recorded, then fully transcribed. Analysis of transcripts was thematic: the student researcher read and re-read the transcripts until major themes emerged that seemed to represent important issues and categories for the research participants. The researcher had a predetermined focus group discussion schedule and she explained this to the participants before the groups were convened. However, her goal was to establish a rapport so that the discussion would be as spontaneous as possible. The transcripts showed that she was largely successful. Researcher intervention was confined to asking supplementary questions and to providing stimulus material of several printed and video-recorded advertisements. With these stimuli, the groups embarked on energetic discussions about what particular advertisements meant to them. Many stories were offered about alcohol-related rites of passage.

The study supported previous studies in that it found advertising to be a powerful means of identity formation and group identification for people of this age. Alcohol advertising seemed particularly powerful in this respect. From an ethical perspective it also appeared that such advertising exposed young people to alcohol drinking practices considerably before they had attained an age (18 years) when it is legal to drink in the UK. The student researcher was able to utilize her own understanding of this phenomenon since she was only twenty years old herself and had previously attended one of the colleges in which focus groups were conducted. This insider-understanding gave her insight into the vocabulary and meanings of the focus groups discussions.

The focus group comments also provided insight into the subtle segmentation strategies of alcohol manufacturers. For the research participants, there were 'alcopop' drinks (fruit flavours with alcohol) that they felt were appropriate to drink as an under-age drinker but they would not drink now they were 18 years old. There were also strict codes about what it was appropriate for boys to like to drink and for girls. Several boys referred to drinks that they liked but would not order in a bar because their friends might comment adversely on their choice of drink (it might be a 'girl's drink'). These product meanings were assimilated from advertising and applied whether or not the person speaking actually did drink a particular drink. The collective effect of alcohol advertising seemed to place considerable emphasis on drinking as a rite of passage into adulthood. Few focus group participants admitted to not drinking alcohol in the presence of such peer pressure.

This study took the form of a small number of focus groups lasting only 30 minutes each. This data was supplemented with field notes, thoughts, reflections and subjective impressions of the researcher. In spite of the small scale of the study, it did generate striking findings that largely supported previous published research findings about the role and importance of alcohol advertising on and for young people in the UK.

Field notes and ethnography

In another alcohol-related study Clarke *et al.* (1998) explored the cultural meanings of the British 'pub' by using a combination of depth interviews and questionnaires administered in pubs. They also drew on semiotic influences to interpret the audio-recorded data. *In-situ* studies such as this allow researchers to utilize rich sources of field data. 'Field notes' are the impressionistic and relatively un-formalized reflections and ideas of the researcher. In a service industry context it is clear that researchers can make great use of such first-hand observation to enrich their understanding. For Spradley (1980) field notes can include comments on such things as the physical space in which interactions take place, descriptions of the people involved, the things they are doing and the objects that are present, and the timing and sequence of events and the feelings expressed or indicated. Researchers can draw on field notes as they seek interpretations of formal data such as interview transcripts. They can interpret data in the light of their understanding of the social context that is reflected in the field notes.

Internet and IT ethnography

As mentioned earlier, it is possible to conduct Internet-based ethnography ('netography') in some cases. Web-based chat-rooms can be useful sources of candid information. One student researcher explored perceptions of a particular brand of motor car using chat-rooms. She would post a question and record the responses. She could not, of course, interpret the responses in the light of considerable indexical understanding. She did not know anything about the respondents. In some cases net researchers have begun a dialogue and then, later, revealed their purpose and asked respondents for some information to help with the interpretation of data.

Internet behaviour is still largely uncharted territory for social researchers. The ways in which people interact with the technology, the motivations for Internet consumption and the kinds of fulfilment that come from this peculiarly solipsistic activity are little known. Student researchers are ideally placed to map this kind of behaviour with regard to particular contexts, applications and settings.

More broadly, the ways in which technology changes and influences human behaviour and social interaction can be a fertile source of ethnographically informed research. People now use laptop computers in highly personalized ways as personal diaries, records of events and relationships, organizers, work-machines and sources of entertainment. The laptop is clearly an important sociological event, just as the Sony Walkman and McDonald's burger were in their time (and indeed still are).

The computerization of work has changed working practices radically with the development of call-centres and related service provision. The ways in which IT influences work and social practices by, for example, blurring the separation of 'home' and 'work', might be a useful ethnographic study for a student researcher. Indeed, the student experience of higher education itself has been transformed by information technology. IT permeates pedagogy, it is relied upon as an information resource, literature reviews are largely conducted on IT through databases of journal articles and web-published papers. Most of the topics in this book have dedicated web sites for enthusiasts. How has all this changed the meaning of being a student? This and many other topics could form fruitful areas for the ethnographically informed study of student researchers.

Glossary

Applied 'Applied' is a term attached to research focused on a practical problem or issue as opposed to research that seeks to enhance theoretical understanding.

Indexicality The idea that the meaning of particular words or actions depends on their social context.

Nomothetic A nomothetic research design seeks statistically significant generalizations that hold true for all conditions independently of time and culture.

Chapter 8

Critical research and critical discourse analysis

Chapter outline

This chapter offers a general outline of the idea of 'critical' research, building on the introduction to critical thinking earlier in the book. It suggests concepts and ideas for developing critical perspectives in marketing and management research and illustrates these with a number of published studies and theoretical works. The chapter then goes on to introduce one important tradition of critical research: critical discourse analysis.

Chapter objectives

After reading this chapter students will be able to

- explain important concepts of critical research
- understand some distinctions between the colloquial usage of the word 'critical' and the more specific usage associated with particular theorists
- apply principles of critical discourse analysis in research projects
- understand some of the limitations and intellectual aims of critical research

---

The idea of 'critical' research

The idea of 'critical' intellectual work has been introduced earlier in the book. In this chapter we examine the notion of the critical in a wider application concerning research philosophy, methods and aims. In many management texts the word 'critical' is used as a synonym for 'important', as in 'marketing is a critical business function'. In educational contexts 'critical' intellectual work refers to a deep engagement with the subject matter, an uncompromising examination of the assumptions of any given point of view or theory, and an independent stance that acknowledges that versions of the truth in social science may serve particular interests more than others. In this sense all research writing should have a critical dimension since it should rigorously evaluate the intellectual and moral grounds for claims. Intellectual work that is critical in this sense engages with the explicit and implicit assumptions of any given research perspective to explore what these assumptions might entail or imply.

In social research 'critical' can have a much more specific meaning. For many researchers 'critical' research implies a particular theoretical stance that is informed by Marxist theorists such as Horkheimer and Adorno (1944) and the 'Frankfurt school' of writers and developed by writers such as Althusser (1971). Critical historical sociology (e.g. Foucault, 1977) has also been an important influence. In marketing, management and consumer research, critical research traditions have been invoked with two broad aims. One has been to contribute to an intellectually viable management education agenda that moves away from 'how to' consulting prescriptions and develops the critical awareness of managers. A second main aim has been to promote a fundamental reappraisal of the aims, methods and ideologies of both management education and organizational practice.

From a managerial perspective, critical theorists point out that much management theory is *ideological* in character and this tends to place limits on the intellectual scope of representations of theory in the field. One argument is that one cannot faithfully evaluate the use or truth of a theory or model unless one asks whose interests are served by this particular form of representation. From a broader ethical standpoint, critical theorists seek to critically reappraise the ways in which practice and representation impose narrow values and reproduce narrow interests. Critical research questions the moral conduct of organizational marketing and management and attempts to put forward alternative agenda from the point of view of less powerful parties, i.e. consumers, citizens and employees.

These aims have been developed in a wide range of published academic writing and research. Alvesson and Deetz (2000) have already been mentioned as writers who have developed critical approaches in a variety of subfields of management research. Alvesson and Willmott (1992) have written an accessible introduction to critical management studies that takes perspectives from several management subfields including marketing, accounting, organizational psychology and information systems. In consumer research the critical theory point of view has been put forward by, for example, Murray and Ozanne (1991) (see also Murray *et al.*, 1994; also references to feminist and gender consumer research studies in Chapter 10).

Marketing, it is generally accepted, has a less well-developed critical tradition than some other management fields. Arguably this may be because the marketing management point of view is widely accepted and propagated as an ideology heavily informed by consulting and other financial interests. In other words, the marketing 'philosophy' and attendant concepts are often put forward as unquestionable organizational and managerial virtues, even though the reasons why the marketing philosophy is so beneficial are more often taken for granted than precisely explained. Marketing does, nevertheless, have a growing body of critical research and writing (e.g. Brownlie *et al.*, 1999; Hackley, 2001) and a new US academic journal that specifically takes a critical stance towards marketing and consumer research, called *Consumption, Markets and Culture* (Routledge).

The critical research 'stance'

Language and power in critical research

Critical research can be characterized by a number of priorities and precepts. In this introduction one particularly important precept deserves special mention. This is the position that language is assumed to be *constitutive* in the sense that it constructs, or constitutes, its objects. That is, language does not merely refer to entities and concepts like 'marketing' or 'management': it actively constructs them. This 'linguistic turn' in (critical and interpretive) research is reflected in a concern with language, texts, discourse and narrative in research approaches. Because of this concern with language and representation, interpretive approaches to social research in management fields fit particularly well with critical analyses.

Critical research in marketing and management does not focus solely on the managerial problems of how to do marketing/management more effectively. Rather, it focuses on the ways in which language is used to construct marketing/management as legitimate and accepted things. Organizations, in whose name much academic business research is conducted, are powerful entities. An important part of their power lies in the ability to define what is normal and valuable. It is this power that is placed under scrutiny in critical research. This does not necessarily mean that critical research is anti-capitalist or anti-organizations. Indeed, critical research has been turned to managerial purposes, since it can offer insights into marketing and management activity that are not available to other research perspectives. Critical research acknowledges a political reality, that is, the interests of large commercial organizations may not always coincide with those of citizens, consumers or employees.

Critical research practices

Critical research does not conform to a particular method or accepted set of procedures. It is, rather, an intellectually (and politically) informed perspective. The critical researcher does not settle for easy, conventional or superficial explanations but 'unpacks' concepts and develops a reflexive dialogue with the reader. This is accomplished by using the research data (whether primary or secondary) as material to develop lines of discussion, argument and investigation that do not simply accept the apparent order of things but question it in order to reveal obscured relations of power and control. There is no critical research 'method' as such. Rather, critical research entails a stance or a series of related axioms and concepts around which argument and discussion are organized. Box 8.1 is, therefore, necessarily simplified but attempts to capture some of the major concepts and practices of critical research.

Qualitative data are usually the most appropriate for critical empirical research studies. However, the critical stance applies more importantly to the interpretive strategies and representational practices that the researcher brings to their objects of study. The critical perspective informs research design but can also be applied in the literature reviewing and analysis/discussion aspects of any research study. Critical research adopts or adapts many of the concepts in Box 8.1 in varying combinations and with differing emphases.

Social critique, discourse and power

Researchers familiar with the work of the Frankfurt school of political/economic theorists understand critical research as a more radical approach than one that demonstrates (only) intellectual values. For those researching in the Frankfurt school tradition it is capitalism itself in its many forms that is the object of critique. Capitalist *discourses* are considered to be repressive in the sense that they exclude and rule out ways of talking, thinking and being that may be more fulfilling of human potential. Discourses of marketing (that is, ways of talking and writing about marketing) are said to reproduce structures of control and domination, especially the domination of corporations and allied political institutions over the social and psychological life of citizens. Critical social research then has a role in revealing, through critique, how these structures of domination are reproduced in everyday working and consumer life. By so doing critical research creates discursive space for resistance, thereby making possible a form of *emancipation*. Critical perspectives encourage a questioning stance towards ways of thinking and talking that are taken for granted. It promotes reflexive awareness of how language and discourse construct particular relations and ways of being and working.

Much managerial research is decidedly non-critical in this important sense. It seeks to reproduce a social order and make it seem a natural, unquestionable thing. The authority of managers, the social benefits of organizational marketing and the desirability of ever greater levels of consumption are taken for granted. Managerial research perspectives tend to

Box 8.1 Major features of critical research

Themes
Power; discourse and language; ideology; emancipation; class; history

Assumptions
Social constructionist ontology

Language actively constitutes its objects, it does not merely refer to them

Social relations are infused with power: social structures and institutions exercise deep influence over the ways in which people talk, think and feel

Agency is strictly constrained by social structures and institutions

Indeed, a sense of agency may be illusory if people have simply internalized values and norms that reflect assymetrical relations of power

This sense of agency may unwittingly serve other interests, for example in management initiatives to 'empower' workers

'Normality' and 'common sense' are taken to be things that are produced in social life under the influence of social structures and institutions that have a historical basis

Critical perspectives are thought to have moral force as agents of practical change and individual liberation as well as being intellectually powerful in their own right

Methods of data gathering
Qualitative, naturalistic, phenomenological, observational

Approach to data analysis
Interpretive approaches (such as critical discourse analysis) are used to draw categories, metaphors and other themes from data. These are used to develop lines of discussion that seek to generate insights into the ways in which interests and values are reproduced in 'normal' and 'everyday' interactional practices

exclude or play down consideration of other interests such as environmental concerns, gender relations, the ability of citizens to resist the power of corporations, and issues of free competition. Critical research seeks to overturn the apparently 'natural' or 'given' order of things to explore how these have become taken for granted. The aim is to achieve a greater integrity in research by openly revealing the interests bound up with particular ways of knowing and describing. The assumption is that all representations of knowledge are political in the sense that they serve some interests more closely than others.

Ideology and critical research

Ideology is a central concept in critical social research and cultural studies. Althusser (1971) broadened the Marxist notion of ideology as a system of *structural power* (see comments below) by drawing attention to its *constitutive power* to form *subjectivities*. He suggested that social institutions such as education, religion, law and the media perpetuate values, practices and interests that serve the state in ways which become so taken for granted that they form our very subjective system of values and presuppositions, and hence inform our thought and behaviour in subtle and penetrating ways. Edgar and Sedgwick (1999) suggest that the word 'ideology' derived from French educational philosophy that associated ideas with some underlying cause in biological, social or material conditions. Napoleon ridiculed the *idéologues* and ideology became a pejorative term. For Marx, ideology referred to the ideas of the economic ruling class that invariably became the accepted way of seeing the world.

In later social theory ideology becomes a more subtle notion that manifests in the micro-practices of everyday life and is continually reconstructed and renegotiated through social practice and interaction. Ideology does not refer to a delusion or untruth, as it did for Marx. In contemporary social research ideology cannot be counterposed to an absolute truth of which it is a distortion. Ideological beliefs are simply part of the socially constructed world of ideas that reflect differing perspectives. Hirschman (1993) adopts Eagleton's (1991) definition of ideology in her investigation of the influence of masculine ideology in consumer research. Ideology refers to the ways in which a 'world-view or value-and-belief system of a particular class or group of people' (Hirschman, 1993, p. 538) is reproduced through certain kinds of representational strategy.

The notion of ideology is sometimes used in marketing, management and consumer research to refer broadly to sets of ideas and implied relations that have become taken for granted. Since ideas are always political in the sense that they emerge from particular sets of historical circumstances, they serve interests that are not immediately apparent. The use of the term ideology in social research does not necessarily have pejorative implications even though it is often used in a highly critical context. Alvesson and Deetz (2000) note that academics in management studies are often viewed as ideologists (p. 84) in that 'they serve dominant groups through socialization in business schools, support managers with ideas and vocabularies for cultural–ideological control at the workplace level, and provide an aura of science to support the introduction and use of managerial domination techniques'. While Alvesson and Deetz (2000) do not intend this as a compliment, many management academics suggest that they are entirely satisfied with the role of ideologist. Prominent researchers in marketing who claim no critical agenda readily concede that marketing is ideological in character (e.g. Deshpandhe, 1999; Gronhaug, 2000).

Ideology critique and management ideas

In critical management research ideology critique focuses on 'worker's self-understanding of experience' (Alvesson and Deetz, 2000, p. 83, citing Willmott, 1990; Gramsci, 1971 and Burawoy, 1979). Workers, a category into which most of us fall one way or another whether we are a CEO or a managerial trainee, articulate the experience of being a worker in ways which reflect the ideological norms we have assimilated. In business schools and through our reading of popular texts we may have absorbed ideas as if they are taken for granted. These ideas inform our preconceptions and values which, in turn, underlie our values and behaviour as workers. An important thing to note regarding the comment on 'self-understanding' is that it is the subjectivity of workers that is formed by ideology. That is, as workers we deeply internalize particular values because we accept the assumption that they are consistent with our own interests. In this sense ideology critique attempts to dig deep into our 'self-understanding' as workers to see where our internalized values came from and to recover the implications these have for our subjective sense of identity and personal realization.

As an example, it has been suggested that marketing management students are used to assimilating sets of ideas that are presented in many introductory texts as unquestionable and ethically neutral. Marketing students and managers often feel that the marketing curriculum produced through popular texts consists of ethically neutral problem-solving techniques and practical concepts. These techniques and concepts are presented as if they are in the interests of all: they create wealth for society, promote opportunity and growth for individuals and corporations, and they confer expertise and privilege on the managers who learn and espouse them.

However, these ideas can be seen in an entirely different light. For some critical commentators they are loaded with unfounded presuppositions, lacking in intellectual coherence and bereft of empirical support. Furthermore, they support narrow views of the world and reproduce relations of power that serve certain consulting and corporate interests at the expense of other groups. Marketing management concepts are derived from particular historical conditions. They emerged during a huge rise in wealth in Western Europe and North America after the Second World War. They were popularized by a growing group of management 'gurus' with origins in business consulting. Many of these gurus then took their ideas into the academic world as business schools became established in universities. Through publishing enterprise, these ideas become widely accepted as authoritative and taken for granted. In fact, marketing management assumed the characteristics of an ideology that is perpetuated through the use of particular rhetorical strategies (Hackley, 2003; and see also Meamber and Venkatesh, 1995; Firat, 1985; Firat and Venkatesh, 1995a; Furusten, 1999).

Whether or not marketing management ideas are managerially useful, socially beneficial or intellectually sustainable is not the main issue here. The suggestion that they are ideological in character has implications for how they are judged as intellectual products. It also has implications for how we understand the ways in which people draw on marketing and management discourses to account for and justify events and practices in the contexts of work, management and consumption. Of course, how they are judged as intellectual products may well, in turn, have implications for how people view their managerial usefulness and social value.

Organizational management and power

Critical research normally assumes a social constructionist ontology. That is, it assumes that social life is constructed in interaction through language and social practice. Interaction and social practice is, in turn, framed by social structures and institutions. Our power to act freely and in our own interest in local interactions is constrained by social realities of economics, social class, gender, ethnicity, education and other social structures and institutions. The social constructionist ontology implies that there is an important distinction between two kinds of power. On the one hand there is *structural power*: structural power derives from a particular arrangement of social institutions and allows certain individuals to coerce others into co-operation. Constitutive power, on the other hand, is a more subtle concept, since it alludes to the ways in which power is manifest in and through language in interaction.

To offer an example, a manager might have structural power over an employee because he or she can impose sanctions for non-compliance on that employee, such as pay deductions, the denial of promotion opportunities or disciplinary action. However, it might be .the case that the employee is better educated than the manager and is a member of the social class of more senior managers even though he or she does not hold that rank in the organization. In such circumstances it may be difficult for the manager to negotiate his or her authority against the background of class superiority that frames interaction with the subordinate.

The authority of a manager in the workplace, then, is partly a matter of structural power. This refers to a manager's ability to coerce workers into co-operation. His or her power derives from the social institution of management, from the ability vested in them by the corporation to exact penalties for non-compliance, and their control of resources such as pay levels, promotion opportunities and other worker benefits. However, in spite of their apparent authority, many managers do not always feel powerful. It is well documented that middle and senior managers can feel under intense pressure. Some managers might be more successful than others at exacting compliance from subordinates. Some managers in fact feel powerless in spite of their apparent authority because they feel that they lack the necessary support (from the organization, or from their subordinates) to accomplish the tasks they are set. They also often feel that there are severe limitations to their coercive power because, for example, they cannot impose adequate sanctions against the incompetence or non-performance of subordinates.

Many managers feel under stress because they feel that they are subject to differing kinds of demands from their own senior managers and from their subordinates. When managerial discourse is examined it can be seen that, while managerial power is derived from the office of management, power is also negotiated in interaction. Constitutive power refers to the ways we unwittingly reproduce relations of power through our everyday language and discourse. Some workers are able to exploit this to resist managerial power. Some managers are unable to exert power in spite of their advantages because they reproduce their own sense of powerlessness through their everyday language and discourse. Managerial power, then, is not only something imposed through unquestionable authority vested in the manager by the organization and supported by structures of other social institutions such as social class, level of education and the power invested in them by labour law. It is also something that is renegotiated and reconstructed in each interaction between a manager and other levels of staff within the organization, both subordinates and senior managers. In this sense managerial power is constituted through language in interaction in addition to being the result of structural power.

Constructing managerial authority

Managerial authority is sometimes regarded as a given, a taken for granted aspect of organizational life. Books such as *In Search of Excellence* (Peters and Waterman, 1982) have shown management in a powerful light as the class of worker that can make or break an organization through their skills of analysis, leadership and problem-solving. Other, academic studies have shown management in a different light, as people trying to cope with enormous organizational pressures in difficult circumstances (Watson, 1994); still other studies have shown how the idea of managerial power is itself highly questionable (Munro, 1997). Some studies have shown that managerial power within some organizations can be seen as a discursive effect produced not by explicit sanctions and rewards but by expropriating certain forms of language and imposing certain values on employees (Hackley, 2000). Given this indeterminacy, managerial power can be seen as something that must be constructed and maintained through the language and interactional practices of managers.

Constitutive power, then, refers to the ways in which power is manifest in particular ways of talking and acting that have historical and cultural origins. A particular manager might, say, wear a dark lounge suit to work and exhort the workforce to be more 'customer-facing'. The lounge suit carries with it overtones of authority because of its class-based history. In many countries the suit (still) signifies membership of a non-manual class of workers that has access to education and wealth. A manager might feel that he or she would be taken less seriously if he or she wore casual clothing to work. Language is another important rhetorical aspect in constructing managerial authority. Invoking management buzz-phrases such as 'customer-facing' or 'customer-focused' has become a particularly powerful resource for managers to extract compliance from workers in organizations. The jargon of managers is important in producing managerial authority since it can imply that managers have technical knowledge and, therefore, hold power over subordinates. Much management jargon also implies that individual action is part of a collective enterprise that cannot be questioned. If a call-centre worker is disciplined for not being sufficiently 'customer-sensitive', it can be very difficult for him or her to defend such charges because the notion of being 'customer-sensitive' is so widely accepted as an unquestioned virtue in itself. Managers have the power to define exactly what terms like this mean in terms of behaviours in the organizational context.

Critical research and interpretive analysis

As mentioned above, critical studies often use qualitative data-gathering techniques. Alvesson and Deetz (2000) draw attention to the common ground between interpretive and critical research and suggest that critical perspectives can often usefully be conjoined with interpretive approaches, such as ethnography and discourse analysis. They cite critical ethnography (Thomas, 1993) as a useful approach and offer examples of work that have combined ethnographic principles with varied data-gathering approaches such as direct observation and interviewing to powerful effect as with Kunda (1992). Critical research, like interpretive research, tends to focus on the particular rather than the general. It is situational in that its main concern is to conduct micro-sociological studies of power in a given organizational or other context. In the discussion and analysis of such studies it may sometimes be possible to go beyond the particular social context to trace the historical and cultural origins of a particular form of social relations or interactional practices, such as where local asymmetries of power result from a history of class relations.

While nomothetic, statistically supported causative generalizations are not possible from such research it can offer general, qualitative insights into what may happen in other similar situations. If a particular study reveals elements of how power is constructed and maintained in one organization, then it may offer qualitative insights into that same process in other organizational and social contexts. Such insights cannot be verified formally but may be powerfully suggestive nonetheless. One broad aim of interpretive research is to reveal how social life is constructed in many differing contexts. If the centrality of power and the constitutive effect of language is revealed plausibly in many different studies, then it can inform a far more general understanding of how social life is actively constructed and maintained. For the critical researcher, this understanding might then inform individual reflexivity and, perhaps, act as a catalyst for social change. A greater understanding of the ways in which language, social practice and social institutions interact in the production of social life might lead to a reappraisal of fairness and equity in social relations.

Doing critical research: critical discourse analysis

Student researchers can apply a critical orientation to their work in various ways. A critical approach can be used to define the terms of reference for a project and to frame the entire process. Critical influences can also be drawn on in part, in the data analysis and discussion/analysis sections. The literature review too can, and should, have a critical dimension. While critical research does not conform to a method as such, there are techniques that can be used to make critical research projects systematic in their data gathering and analysis. This chapter will now introduce one such approach that is well established among marketing and consumer research as it is in other social science fields, such as social psychology, organization studies and cultural studies: critical discourse analysis.

Critical discourse analysis is part of a wider movement to establish a new agenda for the understanding of social phenomena. It employs a distinctively critical perspective since it seeks to reveal how social life is constructed within a context of power and contest. It can be seen as part of the poststructuralist movement in its focus on language and discourse as a site of contest and negotiation. Unlike postmodernism, poststructuralism can provide powerful techniques for empirical research through deconstruction, critical ethnography and critical discourse analysis (Elliott and Ritson, 1997).

Doing critical discourse analysis

Approaches to discourse analysis reflect wide variation in researchers' views. The view developed here will draw particularly on a tradition of discourse analysis developed within social psychological research (Potter and Wetherell, 1987; critical perspective in Burman and Parker, 1993 and see van Dijk, 1984, 1985) and applied in various ways in marketing (Elliott, 1996), advertising (Cook, 1992) and consumer research (Ritson and Elliott, 1999). This tradition is informed to varying degrees by other research traditions including *ethnomethodology*, semiotics and *conversation analysis*.

Discourse analysis has also been a significant development in organizational sociology (Fairclough, 1989, 1995). The techniques of discourse analysis may differ, but the notion of 'discourse' and the associated focus on the role of language and social practice in constructing social reality has become widely employed in critical marketing and management studies (e.g. Morgan, 1992). This section will discuss the notion of discourse before outlining an approach to the analysis of discourse for research projects.

Language and discourse

Critical discourse analysis focuses on the ways in which we construct our sense of social reality through language in interaction. Language is a major feature of discourse, but the term 'discourse' can refer to other interactional and representational practices in addition to language. 'Discourse' is referred to as a 'a system of statements that construct an object' (Parker, 1992, p. 5). 'Discourse' is also described as anything that can be described, and hence can be represented as text; it therefore refers to both speech and writing (Stubbs, 1983). It is regarded by some authors as a broader concept still, referring to all genres in which someone 'organizes language to an audience' (Benveniste, 1971, p. 208). In its non-technical sense discourse refers simply to conversation. The use of the term in interpretive and critical social research implies that it is considered to be a central concept in understanding social, and also psychological, organization. Discourses are ways of organizing, describing and talking about certain events or things. They can be drawn upon by individuals to make sense of the world and to account for actions or events. We might also draw on certain discourses or 'ways of talking about' things to produce a sense of normality. We might adapt discourses to form our own strategies of social positioning and identity formation in local contexts. Studies of discourse focus on language as a major feature of constitutive social interaction.

Foucauldian influences have been important in framing the use of the concept of discourse in management and organization studies. For

Foucault (1977) discourses embrace all the presuppositions, historically derived rules and institutions and social practices that make certain forms of representation possible (Mills, 1997). In this poststructuralist sense discourses are the preconditions for everyday knowledge. The task of the critical researcher is to critically interrogate and unravel social phenomena so that the preconditions for their production become apparent. In other words, the task is to see how particular ways of seeing the world become accepted and 'normal'. Outside management research a focus on discourse has been used in ideology critique to explore, for example, how a particular scholarly discipline ('oriental studies') consolidated certain ways of understanding and thinking about colonialism (Said, 1978). Foucault (1977) famously explored the ways in which certain social groups acquired and sustained their own power over others by defining the terms of normality. 'Discursive closure' (Deetz, 1992) occurs where a given and accepted way of expressing things excludes or closes off alternatives. In this way particular discourses can be powerful in perpetuating particular ways of seeing the world. The idea of discourse, then, in ideology critique, becomes closely linked to ideology (Gramsci, 1971) in that discourses act as vehicles for the reproduction of and perpetuation of, ideological norms.

Discourse is an important feature of the organization of individual psychology because of the link between structural power in society and individual subjectivity. Through our language and interactional practices, we may feel that we are asserting our individual sense of agency and realizing our own 'personality' when in fact we are drawing on historically derived discourses that reproduce the power of other groups and sustain our own relative powerlessness (Edwards and Potter, 1992). Discourse analysis seeks to recover this sense of the history of certain forms of discourse as well as revealing the detailed process of how social life is produced in local contexts (see Box 8.2).

Seeking structure, function and variation in social texts

A social text such as a transcript of a depth interview or a set of written documents can be analysed for these three characteristics: structure, function and variation. With regard to *structure*, the text is likely to display features that seem to recur. A person talking may use particular strategies of accounting for events and actions, particular metaphors, tropes of speech, grammatical techniques or tone of voice that become evident on reading and re-reading the text. The same may be true of any kind of text: there are likely to be structural regularities of some kind, whether these are stylistic, thematic or grammatical. Very often such structural characteristics are not evident on first listening or reading but become so after the text has been reflected upon and re-read over a period of time.

Box 8.2 Major features of critical discourse analysis

Themes
Focus on language and discourse as constitutive features of social interaction

Focus on ideology and the reproduction of relations of power through everyday talk and social practice

Performativity of language and social practice

Assumptions
Social constructionist ontology; but the possibility of agency is heavily circumscribed by social structures and institutions

Discourses as broad categories of speech, writing and representation carry ideological influences and preserve particular forms of understanding

We perform acts of social positioning and identity formation through our language and other interactional practices

Methods of data gathering
Qualitative, any methods that can generate descriptive text: depth interviews, ethnography, focus/discussion groups, analysis of published texts, e.g. press reports

Approach to data analysis
Seeking structure, function and variation in social texts: evidence of structure regarding recurring themes, tropes of speech, metaphors, evidence of variation in accounts; analysis of the rhetorical function of these positions and accounts in terms of the maintenance of particular meanings that have implications for social positioning and identity formation

Emphasis on revealing 'interpretive repertoires' or discourses that account for and justify particular ideas, actions or procedures

Function and accounting practices

Once a text has been analysed for structural regularities the researcher needs to reflect upon what rhetorical purpose they may serve, that is, what is their *function*. This idea of function in discourse reflects a tradition of linguistic philosophy that took as axiomatic the idea that words do not merely refer to concepts or things, they *do* things as well (Austin, 1962).

Language has a *performative* role in this sense. As ethnomethodological researchers seek to show, speakers seek to accomplish certain social effects by their speech. If I am lecturing a class, I want to engage their interest by referring to theories and practices in my field. However, I also have to accomplish a professional role, that of lecturer. To this end I have to try to sound plausible as an academic researcher and lecturer. Performative speech-acts can also take tactical forms, such as when you ask someone a question not as a genuine query but as a social gambit at a party.

In discourse analysis, as in rhetorical analysis (discussed in Chapter 10), what is said is important not only in itself but with regard to what it leaves unsaid (Antaki, 1994). That is, one kind of expression tends to omit or gloss over other, alternative expressions. For example, in a piece of the author's research (Hackley, 2000), one advertising agency's account team professionals tended to account for actions and decisions in terms of a corporate way of doing things. It was 'the way we do things here'. This way of accounting for particular actions and decisions was, among other structural regularities, called upon frequently by junior account team staff during depth interviews.

The 'interpretive repertoire'

The 'corporate way' accounting device seemed to constitute an *interpretive repertoire*. This expression is used by Potter and Wetherell (1987) to mean a particular device or technique of accounting for and justifying particular actions or ideas. The way these authors use the term 'interpretive repertoire' is similar to the way the term 'discourse' is often used in poststructuralist writing. However, they usually use the term to refer to one specific linguistic device, while the term 'discourse' is more often used to refer to a collection of such devices that, together, support and reflect a particular view of the world and justify certain positions or actions. In the author's research, it appeared that justifying actions in creative advertising development in terms of the corporate style or techniques of agency served certain functions for the speakers. It positioned them as being team players who acknowledged and respected the agency's traditional way of doing things. By so doing they performatively signified that they were not maverick individualists; rather, they wanted to be seen to defer to the agency's processes and were good, corporate citizens and competent professionals.

Variation in accounts

This analysis led to another issue. Function in social texts can often be revealed through the *variation* in accounts that people offer. In the agency, the way that creative advertising campaigns developed did not appear to conform to a regular process. As one person admitted, every brief was different and things varied a great deal. Furthermore, the corporate way of doing things was very difficult to specify. It appeared to be almost infinitely flexible because there were so many variations in the development of different campaigns. Finally, more senior members of account teams tended not to refer to this (perhaps mythical) agency way of doing things with anything like the same piety as junior members. Instead, they accounted for processes and decisions in terms of particular circumstances and individual knowledge and skills. The more senior staff did not, perhaps, feel such pressure to appear to conform to company policy. They were more confident of their status and position. However, while acknowledging this, their accounts of how advertising was developed in an ad hoc and particularistic way further undermined the idea of a specified set of procedures or actions.

In this example, then, structural regularities in social texts were found in terms of 'interpretive repertoires' or ways of accounting for and justifying particular actions and decisions. The research then used variations in these accounts to speculate on the function such accounts might serve in terms of social positioning and the maintenance of a professional identity. The performative dimension of language was important in this respect. The things that interviewees say could be seen as devices designed to accomplish certain social tasks, such as the social task of appearing a competent professional in a given organization. This does not imply that the interviewees were not competent professionals. It simply acknowledges the self-evident truth that, in our various social roles, we must accomplish certain effects in order to be perceived as plausible and credible, and socially competent.

Concluding suggestions for critical student researchers

The analysis of discourse, then, takes as its starting-point the assumption that humans construct social life through language and social practice within a framework of ideology deriving from social structures and institutions. We are autonomous individuals but we act within social structures which sharply constrain our freedom and power to act in our own interests. The analysis of language and other practices of social interaction is central to critical research because language is said to be constitutive of social life, that is, language does not only refer to social reality: it actively constructs it.

Language is also important in critical studies because of the ways in which we use it. In critical discourse analysis it is assumed that language does not merely refer to concepts or things. Language also *does* things, it has a character of performativity. The things we say have a performative dimension in that we try to accomplish social acts through language. This accomplishment is targeted both at others and at ourselves in the sense that we seek to maintain a particular world-view. As ethnomethodologists have suggested, we try to accommodate the preconceptions of others, and our own wishes about our status and aims, into the positions we take and the things we say. This accommodation depends on our understanding of the social context of the interaction. We constantly interpret words as signs to understand what is meant (to construct meaning) in specific social contexts. The analysis of social texts can reveal this process of construction through structure, function and variation in accounts.

For many student researchers, this highly theoretical form of critical research may seem daunting. Student researchers should, certainly, only consider a critical research project after careful discussion with their academic supervisor. However, critical discourse analysis has many advantages for student researchers. For example, the focus on power can generate novel and striking perspectives that are, to many researchers, far more interesting than managerially inclined projects. For many critical researchers academic managerial research is fatally flawed because, while it purports to generate commercial solutions, it never can because such solutions are invariably grounded in highly specific cultural contexts. Academic research that seeks to reveal general rules of business success may be a futile pursuit. Paradoxically, the kind of research that is classed as 'critical' because of its focus on power and its non-managerial vocabulary and aims, may be more effective than managerial research in revealing how organizations accomplish commercial success. It can be argued that commercial success is invariably the result of the appropriation and exploitation of power.

This need not be thought of in pejorative terms: it can be seen as a necessary truth of capitalist activity. In competitive markets organizations cannot rely on monopolistic market conditions to protect their profits but they can and do try to create quasi-monopolies through branding. In an important sense Nike, Coca Cola or Kodak have a monopoly over their respective brands. If they can persuade consumers to seek out their brand and ignore competitors, then they have in effect created a kind of monopolistic market situation. Marketing organizations try to create a competitive advantage by differentiating their brand(s) from those of competitors. They use their purchasing power to source cheaper, better-quality components and ingredients, their economic and technological power to make production more cost efficient, and their huge advertising budgets to promote their products' attributes and to make their brands memorable to the consuming public. Corporate power is implicit in all kinds of commercial success. Whether this power is exercised for good or for ill is a matter for individuals to decide. Critical research in general seeks to open up such issues so that they can be properly considered.

Glossary

Constitutive   Language is said to constitute its objects rather than merely refer to them. Language actively constructs the meaning of terms and concepts. In the context of power, constitutive power refers to power that is reproduced in and through particular discourses. Language and discourse are said to actively constitute relations of power and not simply to reflect them. Constitutive power is intrinsic to social interaction.

Conversation analysis   Associated with ethnomethodology, conversation analysis takes a minute and detailed interest in the way that everyday interactions are ordered, produced and controlled. It has been widely used in positivistic research to document particular interactions. Topics of study have included the role of pauses in conversations and the negotiation of turn-taking and conversational topics in telephone conversations.

Discourse   In common usage, a dialogue between speakers. In interpretive social research 'discourse' means 'that which can be described'; it is a broad term that refers to sets of conventions for talking or thinking about a given object or idea.

Emancipation   The critical research stance is that discourses can be repressive. In its moderate form 'emancipation' refers to the critical research aim of promoting reflexive awareness about the ways in which ideologies are formed and reproduced.

Ethnomethodology   Refers to an approach to the sociology of everyday life promoted by Harold Garfinkel (1967). It focuses on how participants jointly produce a sense of everyday normality in social life and places great importance on the agency and social competence of individuals. Less emphasis is placed on the influence of social structures and institutions over local interactions and practices.

Function   In discourse analysis, refers to the function of speech-acts with regard to the social positioning they are intended to achieve.

Interpretive repertoire   A linguistic device which accounts for and/or justifies a particular view of the world or specific acts.

Managerialist   Managerialist research reflects and supports the apparent aims, given assumptions and taken-for-granted priorities and values of organizational managers. It is usually positioned as an attempt to address or solve a managerial 'problem'.

Performative This refers to the distinction between language use as a referring device to indicate objects and concepts and as a social positioning device through which we signal particular motives or claim status. In other words, we *perform* social accomplishments through language and other social practices.

Structural power The power to coerce and gain compliance through the implicit or actual threat of tangible or intangible sanctions. Structural power is extrinsic to social interaction since it reflects power relations that pre-exist a particular interaction.

Structure In the discourse analysis of social texts researchers seek structural regularities with regard to tropes of speech, metaphors or ways of accounting for actions, ideas or decisions.

Subjectivities Subjectivity refers to unreflexive personal consciousness. This subjectivity may appear to be private and unique but can be shown to be socially derived in important respects. We may absorb certain historical, linguistic and cultural practices and ideas so that they intimately form our values and assumptions. We may take these values and assumptions as taken for granted and forget that, in fact, they were learned.

Variability In social texts the accounts given to justify actions or ideas may vary in different circumstances. This variation may be revealing with regard to the rhetorical function that it served in that version of events.

Chapter 9

Semiotics in marketing and consumer research

Chapter outline

This chapter outlines some of the main principles and concepts of semiotics in the context of research in marketing and consumer studies. There are differing approaches within semiotic, or semiological, studies of visual or linguistic phenomena. This chapter draws on the concepts and terminology of semiotics used in North American traditions of consumer and marketing research to illustrate important subjects of study and to suggest practical applications for student researchers.

Chapter objectives

After reading this chapter students will be able to

- understand some important principles of semiotic analysis as applied in marketing and consumer research
- appreciate the contribution of semiotics to understanding marketing and consumption phenomena
- apply semiotic analysis to varied kinds of data in student research projects

---

Semiotics/semiology: origins and scope

Semiotics is, broadly, the study of signs and their meaning in communication. A sign in this sense is something that can stand for something else. 'Semiotics' or 'semiology' is etymologically derived from the Greek *sema*. It can be traced back to the ancient Greek medical techniques of Hippocrates and Galen who inferred medical conditions from the symptoms reported or presented by patients. The word semiology is usually associated with the study of linguistic signs. The tradition of semiology deriving from European linguistics is associated with Ferdinand de Saussure (1974).

The North American tradition (known as semiotics) reflects work by philosopher C.S. Peirce (1953–66, 1986). Scholars have borrowed indiscriminately from each tradition so the distinction between the two is blurred in many research studies.

This chapter emphasizes the concepts and terminology of the North American tradition. In 'semiotics' the focus of study is on any signs whatever in regard to their capacity for communicating and generating meaning. 'Semiosis' is the process of extracting messages and significance from signs, and thereby generating meaning. In human semiosis the central problem is to understand how signs come to have meaning. Some traditions of semiotic analysis attempt to reveal the codes through which humans draw meaning from signs in particular cultural contexts. However, such codes need not be stable or enduring: they may not pre-exist the relation of sign and *interpretant*. The meaning of signs is arbitrary. In principle, anything could stand for anything else. It is the cultural context that frames the interpretation of signs and imbues particular signs with localized meanings.

Danesi (1993) explains how the colour red can have many different meanings, depending on the cultural context for semiosis. A red traffic light, a blushing cheek, a red armband can all communicate different messages. Red faces in Western cartoons often signify anger, while in China red is a lucky colour. An open window, footprints in the snow, a bloodied knife are classic signifiers in detective stories (Hackley, 1999, p. 137). The Marlboro man, a classic marketing sign, stands for 'American culture, independence and self-reliance, but may also stand for rebellion, chauvinism, fatalism, ill-health or the genocide of Native American Indians, depending on the communication context and the particular interpreter' (Mick, 1997, p. 251). National flags are such powerful signs that some are revered in one country and regarded with contempt in another. The variation in cultural contexts means that people can bring quite differing interpretive strategies to the same signs.

Semiotic studies have been developed in a wide range of human fields. For Mick (1997) semiotics is 'one of the richest sources of principles, concepts and tools for studying communication and meaning' (p. 260). There have been studies of the semiotics of cinema (Metz, 1974), communication (Fiske, 1982; Fry and Fry, 1986), theatre and drama (Elam, 1988) and language (Barthes, 1968; Eco, 1976, 1984). For some semioticians, semiotic study can form a superordinate human science of communication (Sebeok, 1991), ranging from the communication of single cells to the communicative codes of entire cultures. Semiotic studies of non-marketing fields have considerable relevance to research in marketing. *Semiosis* in marketing and consumption occurs mainly through language (both spoken and printed) and other visual and aural signs. Marketing can be seen as a system of signs that communicate values through brands, packaging, prices, advertisements and a plethora of other signs.

Semiotics and marketing

While marketing as a whole has been a fertile site for semiotic analysis (e.g. see Umiker-Sebeok, 1987; Umiker-Sebeok *et al.*, 1988; Larsen *et al.*, 1991; *International Journal of Research in Marketing*, special issue 1988, vol. 4, nos 3 and 4) two particular marketing fields have proved especially interesting for semioticians. These are advertising and consumer research. Researchers such as Williamson (1978) and Bertrand (1988) have explored the semiotics of advertising in depth. Sherry and Camargo (1987) developed a semiotic analysis of the use of English language words in Japanese advertising. Consumer research has also proved important in stimulating semiotic analysis (Holbrook and Hirschman, 1993; Holbrook and Grayson, 1986; Mick, 1986, 1997; Mick and Buhl, 1992).

The symbolic character of human communication is seen as a 'central and differentiating aspect of the species' (Mick, 1986, p. 196) and nowhere is this more evident than in the worlds of marketed consumption. The world of consumption is replete with signs, as Mick (1997) notes: 'Examples of signs in the consumer world are everywhere a person wished to look, listen, smell, feel or taste: brand names and logos, lyrics, melodies and tempos in music; deodorants and perfumes; wool sweaters and silk pillows; pizza and whiskey...' (p. 251).

Marketing can be seen as a vast site of signification since marketing signs permeate economically advanced countries through ubiquitous mediated communications. One can, in fact, find little social space that is not populated by marketing signs in some form. Even in the English countryside it is common to see discarded branded confection wrappers and soda tins. In urban areas marketing signs are a pervasive presence bombarding the consumer at every turn (Hackley and Kitchen, 1999). Marketing messages are composed of 'strings of signs' (Sebeok, 1991, p. 146). The meaning, and meaningfulness, of these juxtaposed signs depends on the social and cultural contexts in which they are constructed and interpreted.

From a managerial perspective, the better an organization understands the communication practices of its targeted consumers the more likely it will be to construct strings of signs into messages that are plausible, interesting and persuasive to consumers. Brand names and logos, advertising, public relations coverage, product design and packaging are some of the most obvious areas of semiotic importance for producing organizations. Marketing management itself can be seen as the management of consumer semiosis in a sense. Marketing specialists have the task, through communications strategies, of trying to manage and control the semiotic interpretation consumers place on company signs (and those of competitive rivals). All of marketing management in its consumer context can be seen in this way as the management of interpretation. Seen as such the central role of communication in consumer marketing is revealed.

Theoretical value of semiotics in marketing and consumer research

Semiotics offers a way of theorizing marketing communications and signification issues that is radically different from the prevailing linear information processing approach. Marketing theorists borrowed theoretical frameworks from post-war cognitive psychology theorists such as Herb Simon. These frameworks used a man–machine analogy to try to understand human thinking and perception. The analogy was based on a computer and people were considered to 'process' sensory data much in the way that computers process binary data. In popular marketing management and marketing communications texts, the information processing model and its many variations remains the most commonly used way of articulating communications issues (Buttle, 1995). This model resulted in the hierarchy-of-effects theories (Lavidge and Steiner, 1961) of 'how advertising works' that, still, dominate marketing theory (Vakratsas and Ambler, 1999).

There is not space to critique hierarchy-of-effects models of advertising here, but the view taken in this book is that while they offer economy of explanation they only account for some kinds of advertising effects. It is important to note that, although hierarchy-of-effects advertising theories and linear information processing models of human cognition, communication and consumption are not the same thing, they do share important assumptions. Holbrook and Hirschman (1982) suggest that the information processing model has failed to address important issues in consumer behaviour. One such important issue is the extent to which it emphasizes rational information processing and neglects the symbolic character of much human understanding.

Semiotics offers an alternative approach. Information processing models of communication applied in marketing contexts privilege the economic rationality of consumers and the notion of 'information' in advertising, packaging and so on. Semiotics offers an entirely different way of looking at and talking about, the way consumers make sense of marketing communications. It therefore implies a different model of 'how advertising works' based not only on a rational appraisal of product or brand information but also on the semiotic interpretation of marketing symbols. As Williamson (1978) points out, advertising cannot be understood by asking how it 'works': one has to ask how advertising comes to have meaning. Semiotics offers a route to this kind of understanding. The semiotic perspective therefore provides an intellectually distinctive way of re-appraising communications issues in marketing and consumption as a whole.

Marketing is of interest not only to students of management and managers themselves but also to those interested in cultural studies. Cultural studies seek insights into how culture and collective understanding is formed and sustained. Marketing signs are fascinating to many non-managerial researchers because of what they suggest about general cultural values and communication experiences. Elsewhere in this book published work is mentioned that focuses on the cultural importance of marketing innovations like the McDonald's hamburger (Ritzer, 2000) and the Sony Walkman (Du Gay *et al.*, 1997).

When semiotics researchers study marketing and consumption they are studying an area of huge significance in contemporary economic life. We forge our sense of identity and social positioning within a matrix of marketing signs. The semiotic arena of marketing reflects and constitutes the wider cultural setting for semiosis. Anthropological researchers such as Leach (1976), Belk *et al.* (1988) and Wernick (1991) emphasize the revealing nature of consumption and promotional and marketing culture. They show that marketing appropriates values and signs from non-marketing culture and attaches them to marketed entities to serve corporate aims. This seems to have happened to such an extent that is it now difficult to suggest that there is a non-marketing culture in developed economies because of the extent and reach of marketing commodification. Your ownership of branded goods can signify much about you, such as your social status, the groups to which you claim membership and your aspirations and fantasies about your self (Belk, 1988).

Not only products but education, experiences and even relationships are rendered into commodities in contemporary economic life (for example, dating agencies, paid-for distance education, paid-for ballooning, racing driving or theme-park thrill ride experiences). Research studies that investigate the ways in which we make and sustain meaning within this symbolic realm are of great social scientific interest. In particular, when we view advertising and try to derive meaning from it we draw on our vocabulary of culturally constituted semiotic codes to interpret the signs from which advertising is composed. Our interpretation of marketing signs such as brand logos and advertising images is a matter of enculturation: we are, effectively, taught the meaning of these signs. We cannot understand or 'read' marketing signs without a considerable amount of cultural knowledge (Scott, 1994a). Advertising agencies acquire this knowledge in order to place marketing signs within a recognizable cultural setting so that we 'get' the idea that is conveyed (Hackley, 2002). Marketing signs seek to exploit culturally extant semiotic codes in order to cue particular meanings. For example, in a culture that places high prestige on sporting success, Nike ensures that its 'swoosh' logo is seen in multiple settings of sporting achievement so that the culturally resonant setting for the logo ensures a 'transfer of meaning' (McCracken, 1986).

Semiotics, then, is an intrinsically cross-disciplinary field in that its scope of investigation falls across all human sciences. While certain areas of activity, such as marketing and consumption, are especially fertile for semiotic analysis because of their use of many forms of imagery, semiotics is itself a form of study that potentially connects different fields of study. As we have seen in this brief introduction, semiotics connects the study of management, marketing and consumption with anthropology and cultural studies.

Themes and concepts of semiotics

Semiotics is concerned with the ways in which signs constitute meaningful messages. However, like any intellectual tradition, it is far from unified. This chapter necessarily plays down disputes and controversies within different traditions of semiotics and semiology in order to offer student researchers an introductory route to doing semiotic analysis in a research project. It offers one of various possible 'takes' on practical semiotics. Student researchers should not, in any case, consider the existence of controversy and disagreement to be a reason for not exploring any given research tradition. For academics, disagreement and controversy is their professional life-blood. Their 'business' is ideas and their expression. Each has an individual 'take' on any given research approach. Indeed, accepting that research activity is not black and white but grey is an important part of the student's education. If student researchers can engage with research texts in a spirit of well-informed critical enquiry, then both their educational ends and the need of every research community for critical contributions are equally served.

The semiotic perspective, then, has much to contribute to an interpretive research agenda because it draws attention to the arbitrariness of meaning. What this implies is that anything can, in principle, stand for anything else. In another world the word-sign 'dog' could refer to a shoal of fish: a red traffic light could mean 'extinguish cigarette'. The fact that these interpretations seem absurd to a person familiar with Western culture reflects the extent to which semiosis is culturally acquired. Meaning, then, is seen as a cultural construction. Signs are 'read' and their meaning interpreted in terms of cultural codes which we have to learn in order to make sense of the signs around us.

In contrast, positivist modes of research often assume that meaning is fixed and objectively verifiable. For example, information processing research in marketing communications normally assumes that meaning is fixed, stable and synonymous with the construct 'information' in any given communication. The distinction between meaning as something interpreted and context-dependent and meaning as something fixed and given is important because of the implications it has for research design and interpretation of findings. If anything could, in principle, stand for anything else, then the interpretation of, say, a silhouette of a man on a toilet door becomes a far more complex and significant act than it may at first seem. Why do we assume that this silhouette means that 'men' can gain access to bathroom facilities through a door marked with this sign? We do so because the use of this sign, and the provision of separate public bathrooms for the use of each gender, are cultural products that we can understand because of our immersion in relevant forms of cultural understanding. Signs could be arbitrary, but they are not because understanding is culturally mediated. The meaning that we draw from and read into signs is a product of our cultural understanding. Information processing research cannot acknowledge the culturally situated character of meaning construction. Its critics have suggested that it tends to universalize aspects of cognitive activity that are, in fact, constituted through culturally specific forms of understanding.

For student researchers, semiotics is an opportunity to take a fresh look at marketing or consumption phenomena in terms of the meaning these phenomena have for particular parties. Meaning-making can be shown to be a product of local, contextualized communicative codes. Whether such codes have the character of an enduring underlying material reality, or whether they emerge through the process of semiosis, is an argument that semioticians have not resolved. Some semiotic studies conceive of semiotic codes as relatively enduring things that reflect an underlying *structure* of reality, not unlike a material reality. On the other hand, semiotics is often conducted without this ontological assumption. Communicative codes, it is assumed, are not necessarily fixed or logically prior to semiosis.

Sign, symbol and icon

There may be many ways in which signs signify (sixty-six for Peirce, according to Mick, 1997, p. 253; also see discussion in Leach, 1976, p. 10). Three particular forms of semiosis are often used as the basis for analysis. These three forms of semiotic relation are not mutually exclusive: they do overlap but nonetheless can be useful organizing categories for researchers. When a sign acts as an *icon* it is like the thing it represents. Iconicity may reside in a relation between, say, a map and the terrain it represents. It might reside in a relation between a picture of Marlon Brando in *Rebel Without a Cause* and the idea of youthful rebellion. The second form of relation occurs when a sign acts as an *index*. An indexical sign points to or indicates something else. For example, a wavy line on a road sign might 'point to' bends in the road a few hundred yards ahead. A picture of a silhouette of a man on a door might 'point to' or indicate that a men's bathroom is right here behind this door. The third form of relation is *symbolic* which, in semiotics, means that something stands for (is symbolic of) something else, such as when a red cross stands for an international medical service, or a red sports car in an advertisement stands for vigour, youth and the 'good life'.

As we have seen, semiotic meanings may vary according to the perspective of the interpretant. For example, the red sports car above may represent the 'good life' in a rather materialistic sense. To another person it might represent capitalist decadence, to still another it might represent a rather infantile male fantasy of the 'good life'. Meanings may also vary over time as cultural values change. The author sometimes shows a videotape of television beer advertisements transmitted in the UK between 1960 and 1995 to students of advertising. The video is a compilation of advertisements for Courage beers made by advertising agency BMP DDB Needham of London, UK. It is striking to see how social mores and values have changed, so that the representation of women and men in 1960s' advertisements would be unthinkable today.

Women in the older ads are represented in the advertisements as men's jailers. The men, in contrast, are represented as rather childlike but endearingly so, always seeking ways to escape from the domestic prison of the home to the male conviviality of the 'pub'. They are often pursued by a 'nagging' wife. The ads are, of course, intended to be funny and were probably thought so in the 1960s. By the 1990s the position is reversed, with women represented as independent and confident, symbolically realizing their freedom from men by consuming alcoholic drinks in what was previously an exclusively male domain: the British pub. The men are the same men as in the earlier advertisements, objects of fun interested only in trivial things. In the UK the ways in which gender and the relations between genders can be represented in broadcast media has changed radically in 40 years and this is neatly reflected in this compilation of beer ads. The cultural meanings of gender have, in a sense, changed over time.

In this example it might be argued that representations of men and women have not fundamentally changed at all. The 'punchline' of the joke has changed: in old beer advertisements, the joke is that men come out on top. In the later ads, the women have the last laugh. However, as some gender-based studies (cited in Chapter 10) suggest, gender representations in beer ads are open to varying interpretations. If women are now portrayed as men once were, as seekers after pleasure through alcohol, as hedonistic, individualistic and self-indulgent, what does this imply about the wider social status of women? Does it reflect women's greater economic power, independence from men and social status? Or is it just another way of portraying women as less powerful than men? Semiotic analysis of advertisements and other marketing signs can offer interesting, sometimes provocative analyses that reflect the cultural variability of semiosis. Signs that are usually interpreted in one way in one era acquire quite different interpretations in another era in any given cultural context.

Semiosis, then, 'takes place on a boundary of cultural, historical and sociological analysis' (Hackley, 1999, p. 141). This cultural dimension has been neglected in some studies that over-emphasized the individual, private aspect of interpretation. As Wernick (1991) has pointed out, many studies of advertising 'eclipsed attention both to the historicity of promotional texts and to their contextual dimension' (p. 25). In other words, our interpretation of signs is culturally mediated. We must learn the cultural codes that predetermine particular modes of interpretation. These cultural codes may be highly specific, so this is not the same as saying that there can be only one culturally correct interpretation of a sign, since signs and interpretants are necessarily embedded in a given (and highly specific) cultural context.

Intertextuality and semiosis

Wernick's (1991) comment above about the 'historicity' of promotional texts is linked to the concept of *intertextuality*. Intertextuality is an important concept in semiotics (for a useful discussion see Chandler, 2002). It refers broadly to the sense in which the meaning of one text is interdependent with the meaning of others. Just as the meaning of a phoneme depends on the other phonemes with which it is combined to make a word-sound, a sign has meaning in terms of other signs. Intertextuality is particularly apparent in media texts such as advertisements, newspapers and movies in which meaning is signified through semiotic reference to other examples of advertisements, etc., or to other genres such as classical music, literature or current news events and popular press stories.

Intertextuality is invoked in poststructuralist and postmodern writing to refer to the indeterminacy of authorship of any text. That is, since any sign is reassigned within a pre-existing sign structure, the source of meaning becomes difficult to establish. This is particularly apparent in writing. Barthes (1977) has suggested that 'it is language which speaks, not the author' (p. 143). In this book the author ('I') is/am reproducing ideas that are not mine when I cite others or refer to ideas that have been established some time ago in various fields of study. Yet that is also true of the authors whose works 'I' cite. The authors of academic books seek to construct and direct meaning by drawing on other texts to which they have been exposed and to which they refer for authority. The infinite regress which can be implied might appear to contradict common sense, yet the notion of intertextuality does illustrate how taken-for-granted presuppositions (about, for example, authorship and meaning) can dissolve under closer scrutiny to reveal something of the complexity of social phenomena.

Polysemy and triadic relations in semiosis

The meaning of signs such as those composed of and in texts is, furthermore, constructed by readers who themselves are under the influence of other texts to which they have been exposed. Hence texts have a *'poly-semic'* character in that they can generate a wide range of possible meanings depending on the context of interpretation. The context of interpretation is important because of the differing cultural codes that may be drawn on for interpretive cues in differing cultural contexts. Seen in this light, meaning is something that authors attempt to control or influence, but texts are subject to unpredictable interpretations. Consequently, imposing authorial meaning on the interpretation of a text is a delicate balance and a complex achievement. Advertising agencies that understand this know that they must take great care to isolate the right groups of consumers and to understand them as an 'interpretive community'. Agencies must also create ads that attempt to impose particular meanings in powerfully suggestive but subtle ways by drawing on the semiotic codes that are used within a given interpretive community.

The process of interpretation can be seen as a dyadic or triadic relation. For Peirce, semiosis has a *triadic* character since it depends on a relation between the sign, the object and the interpretant (i.e. the interpretation). This contrasts with Saussure's ideas about semiosis as a *dyadic* relation between the sign and the signified. As Mick (1986) suggests, the interpretant refers to the interpretation placed on the sign and not to the entity (such as a person) doing the interpreting. The interpretant (interpretation) will vary depending on the cultural context. It will also be influenced by the extent to which its meaning in a particular context is dependent on previous interpretations of the same object.

For example, the Skoda motor car brand was portrayed in UK advertising as a cheap alternative to mainstream brands. However, negative reports about the car's reliability and engineering quality resulted in media stories and jokes in the UK that poked fun at the brand. The Skoda brand and its associated signs (the word-sign Skoda and the brand badge on the cars) were interpreted in terms of a communicative code that denigrated the brand. However, a reorganization of the brand, re-engineering of the car and a re-launch with new advertising has changed this code in the UK. The Skoda brand signs are now interpreted much more positively because of favourable quality reports in motor trade magazines and generally positive media coverage. The advertising campaign intertextually (and humorously) referred to Skoda's old negative image so that people bought into the new interpretation of Skoda. The relation between the object (Skoda motor cars), its various signs (the word-sign 'Skoda', the brand badge, the advertising) and the interpretant (the interpretive reaction the sign elicited) changed as a result of a change in cultural understanding. For people to understand the new meaning of Skoda from the new advertising, they had to understand the references the ads made to the old meaning of Skoda.

'Doing' semiotics

As evidenced by the published work cited above, semiotics can be a useful approach in empirical research studies that seek insights into the constructed, arbitrary and culturally mediated character of human understanding. It is particularly so when the research data include pictures or other kinds of visual image, such as advertising. However, many other contexts of consumption could be useful areas for semiotic research, such as, for example, food consumption, product design in differing industries (motor cars, entertainment), the design and the consumption of retail environments, retail architecture, the use of Internet web sites, and marketing issues in the fashion and magazine industries. Semiotics can prove fruitful as part of multi-disciplinary studies into gender and visual media representations or into aspects of environmental (and organizational) psychology when the physical spaces of consumption are the subject of interest (see Box 9.1).

Practical semiotics entails the deconstruction of meaning in given contexts. In semiotics as with all interpretive research the obvious, everyday and taken for granted must be made strange and unfamiliar. The object of the researcher is to understand the complexity and arbitrariness of taken-for-granted modes of meaning-making. To do this researchers have to try to understand the world-view of particular groups while also standing outside those groups. This is precisely because much of our everyday understanding is unreflexive. We are not aware of the assumptions and cultural knowledge that are built into our common-sense, subjective understanding. The task of the social researcher is to go beyond the taken for-granted to speculate on its implications.

As a starting-point for semiotic analysis of advertising, the check-list in Box 9.2 is offered, adapted from Hackley (1999), p. 145.

This check-list is designed to help student researchers to deepen their semiotic analysis of visual material such as advertising. Many first-time researchers find that beginning the process of deconstruction of an advertisement is difficult. Until one acquires the habit of deconstruction, meanings can appear to have a 'given' and 'common-sense' character. Box 9.2 focuses on specific aspects of an advertisement. If the student researcher can begin to understand the complexity of apparently simple advertisements as 'strings of signs', then he or she has taken a step towards deconstructing the way in which an advertisement seeks to tap into particular cultural codes of communication in order to frame and privilege particular interpretations over others. The way in which advertising evinces particular meanings is often spontaneous and unreflexive: we take for granted the meanings (or lack of meaning) in an ad. Without careful reflection it is easy to overlook the mechanics of semiosis.

For example, the actors chosen in an ad might appear, to some viewers,

Box 9.1 Major features of semiotic analysis

Themes
Semiotics is the study of signs and their meaning

Focus on semiosis as meaning-making in a given cultural context

Humans are interpreting creatures: the universe is suffused with signs. Semiotics is an inter- and cross-disciplinary field

Important concepts include the sign, icon, index and symbol

Assumptions
Human understanding is often abstract and symbolic as opposed to literal and rational. Indeed, the symbolic interpretation of signs is a defining characteristic of human understanding

The relation of sign and signifier is arbitrary: in principle, anything can stand for anything else. It is the cultural context of communication that frames semiotic interpretation

Methods of data gathering
Semiotic studies have often used judgement samples of advertisements or other visual data

The ways in which consumers interpret particular signs could be investigated through focus groups or other qualitative data-gathering techniques

Approach to data analysis
Focus on revealing the semiotic codes that cue particular interpretive strategies in a given context

Any kind of sign can in principle be subject to semiotic analysis such as marketing brand logos, packaging, advertising, the spaces of consumption such as shopping malls, other media texts such as movies, radio jingles, etc.

Semiotic interpretation can be subjective and/or inter-subjective

to be well educated and 'middle class', attractive and healthy. By using casting, costume, make-up and scene settings to suggest this, the ad is seeking to symbolically associate the brand with such people in the minds of consumers. The clothes actors wear in the ad, their speech (vocabulary, accent and tone) and their manner might well signify particular class-based values or norms. For example, in a series of UK advertisements for a brand

Box 9.2 An approach to semiotic deconstruction

Questions to ask:	What does X signify to me?
	Why does X signify this to me?
	What might X signify for others?
	Why might X signify this for others?

Possible sources of X:

Objects (visual semiosis)	For example, clothes, hairstyles, make-up styles, the ways objects are used by people, use in press ads of printed copy, typeface, use of logo/pictorial symbolic image, the spatial inter-relationships of objects
Gesture (bodily semiosis)	For example, body types, facial types, expressive gestures, facial expressions, posture, gaze, juxtaposition of bodies, juxtaposition of bodies with products
Speech (verbal semiosis)	For example, use of idiomatic expressions, regional or national accent or dialect, use of metaphor/metonymy, tone and volume of speech, pace of delivery, use of voiceover, use of humour, emphasis on particular words/phonemes

of instant coffee, the interaction between the main (female and male) actors implied a possible romance. The characters were attractive and the setting was affluent. The physical environment, and the physical appearance and interaction of the characters, provided a lifestyle setting in which the coffee appeared to be a natural part. It might well be thought that instant coffee is exactly what one would not drink if one is affluent and cultivated. The ads, therefore, sought to create a suggestion that ran counter to many attitudes. It sought to make instant coffee drinking aspirational and a natural event in affluent environments.

The romantic storyline of the ads caught the public imagination in the UK and the ads were hugely successful, both in terms of coffee sales and also in terms of the generation of a great deal of free editorial coverage in the press. The juxtaposition of actors who represented values that are widely prized in Western culture (such as physical attractiveness, affluence, professional success and romance) with a brand of coffee produced a cross-over effect as these meanings were transferred from the setting to the brand. Student researchers can find many such examples of advertisements and other marketing signs that, placed suggestively in lifestyle settings, seek to transfer particular values from culture to brand. Semiotic deconstruction of marketing and other texts can reveal how this process takes place.

Semiotics and rhetoric

Semiotics is linked with the study of rhetoric (discussed in Chapter 10) in that, in commercial contexts, semiotics is often used to persuade. For example, the classical music of Beethoven, Bach, Wagner and many other composers is often used in the musical scores of Hollywood movies. This is because of its power to draw out emotion in the listener. A cleverly constructed musical score can be so persuasive that it can make up for shortcomings in acting or characterization by persuading the viewer to sympathize with a character or with the depiction of a scene. A semiotic study could investigate how music can come to have meaning, that is, how listeners interpret particular musical passages in terms of human emotions. Used in the context of a movie, music seeks to persuade the viewer to believe a given scene and hence has a rhetorical purpose. If it is to be successful in this purpose, the director of the movie would need to understand and anticipate the viewer's semiotic interpretation of the music juxtaposed with the visual scene, actors, dialogue and so on. In advertisements music, or 'jingles', are conventionally thought to be devices to trigger recall. However, the role of advertising jingles can be seen to be far more important and complex than this (Scott, 1990) since music is itself a powerful signifier.

The rhetorical purpose of an advertisement is to persuade consumers to like the brand or to persuade them to accept some more specific claim about the brand. Semiotic analysis attempts to reveal the cultural communication codes that the advertising agency creative staff intuitively tap into to try to persuade consumers to form the desired interpretations. This can be illustrated with a well-known story about a brand of cigarettes called 'Strand'. This brand was advertised in British cinemas in the 1960s. The visuals portrayed a man on London Bridge late at night, lighting a Strand cigarette in the smoky London haze. The strapline went, 'You're never alone with a Strand.' The advertisements were unsuccessful because (the story goes) people interpreted the ads to mean that people with no friends smoke Strand cigarettes. Even if this tale is somewhat apocryphal, it does illustrate the potential instability of meaning in advertising. Creative professionals hope that they understand the cultural codes through which consumers will form meanings on exposure to their advertising. However, if they do not, then the consumers might place an interpretation on the ad that is quite unexpected and not at all what the client would wish.

Student semiotic studies

One of the author's students conducted a comparative study of Japanese and UK advertising for particular brands of motor car (briefly mentioned earlier in the book). She collected a variety of press ads and found that the advertising was significantly different for two brands in the respective countries. As a Japanese person studying in the UK, she was able to carry out a semiotic deconstruction of the meaning of both the UK and the Japanese ads because of her knowledge of each language and culture. There have been a number of studies that have done similar analyses (e.g. Tanaka, 1994; Sherry and Camargo, 1987). The student researcher sought to understand how meaning was produced in the ads and thereby infer the marketing rationale behind them in terms of the desired segmentation and positioning strategies.

Such an analysis is necessarily subjective but there are ways in which it can be made more scientifically persuasive. For example, other people (from each country) can be involved to see if interpretations converge. However, it should be remembered that semiotics as an interpretive approach cannot discover the definitive meaning of any sign. The researcher must conduct a thorough analysis in order to write a persuasive account that is transparent and also acknowledges that alternative readings may be equally legitimate.

The author has found to his cost that interpretations of advertisements are never final or beyond contest. When an international MBA or MSc class is asked to interpret particular ads the response can be lively and diverse, with interpretations offered that had never occurred to the teacher but which, on reflection, seem perfectly plausible. What this seems to illustrate is the way in which advertisers need to try to understand the interpretive codes within the local communities to which they are directing their advertising. Meaning can be extremely culturally specific.

Another student research project drew on semiotics to conduct an investigation of advertising ethics. The study sought to understand how a selection of consumers interpreted ads that were considered ethically dubious or controversial. Focus groups were convened in which ads were used as stimulus material and the various interpretations offered were analysed using a semiotic perspective. The approach was useful because it did not proceed on assumptions about what was of interest to consumers. Instead, it offered a flexible approach that allowed consumers to articulate their own interpretations of the ads. The student researcher was interested in how young people (university students) interpreted ads in terms of their ethical standing. The study allowed the researcher to get away from preconceived notions of what in advertising is ethically acceptable or not. The findings were interesting in that the ads that provoked ethically critical comments were not those that might have been predicted. The interpretation of ads was subtle; for example, the use of nudity in itself was not considered offensive but the use to which nudity was put was sometimes considered unethical in particular marketing contexts.

As mentioned earlier, while advertising and other marketing signs have proved extremely popular sources of research material for semioticians, student researchers need not confine semiotic study to these fields. Studies of retail environment design, product design, packaging, work place design, corporate image, industrial architecture and corporate reputation, to name a few, could also be enhanced or supplemented by the application of semiotic theory and practice.

Glossary

Dyadic Relation with two dimensions, as when one interviewer interviews one interviewee (a dyadic interview).

Icon A sign that is similar in some way to its referent, in the way that a photograph bears a resemblance to the image it portrays, or an onomatopoeic word resembles a sound, such as in 'plop' or 'roar'.

Index A form of semiosis in which a sign points to or indicates something else, such as where the word 'TAXI' lights up on the top of a yellow car.

Interpretant The entity (usually human) that interprets the sign. The word 'interpretant' is also used to refer to the interpretation.

Semiology The study of linguistic signs and their relation to concepts.

Semiosis The process of semiotic interpretation.

Semiotics The study of signs and their interpretation.

Sign For C.S. Peirce, a sign is anything that can stand for something else.

Structuralist The term is often used in social research to imply a realist ontology. That is, explanations for social phenomena can reveal universal structures of meaning that underlie social processes.

Symbol A form of semiosis in which something acts as a symbol of something else, such as when a clenched fist symbolizes aggression.

Triadic A relation with three dimensions, e.g. in Peirce's model of semiosis with sign, object and interpretant.

Chapter 10

Other approaches

Literary theory and narrative analysis, feminism and gender studies, postmodernism and poststructuralism

Chapter outline

This chapter looks at several important and useful research perspectives that are often used in combination. While these perspectives develop distinctively different kinds of 'take' on social research, they also have a number of important overlapping areas which makes them particularly useful for multi-perspective studies. The chapter introduces important concepts and explains some ways in which these might be applied in data analysis by student researchers.

Chapter objectives

After reading this chapter students will be able to

- appreciate some important commonalities between interpretive social science research and literary studies
- understand some major principles and concepts of selected literary theories and gender and feminist studies
- see how concepts and ideas from postmodernist writing have become influential in interpretive social research

---

Literary theory and the study of rhetoric in marketing and management

Literary theory has offered many concepts and insights that have been used by researchers developing qualitative, interpretive approaches in management and marketing studies. In the UK and the USA this has been reflected in many articles in the leading research journals (e.g. Stern, 1989, 1990; Easton and Aráujo, 1997; Brown, 1999; Holbrook, 1990). Rhetorical analysis has played a major role in the 'linguistic turn' in interpretive marketing and consumer research alluded to by Brown (1995, p. 147),

Elliott (1996), Holbrook and O'Shaughnessy (1988) and discussed in Beckman and Elliott (2001). This 'turn' has emphasized the constructive character of language and the value of research perspectives deriving from the humanities for generating insights into marketing and consumption.

The word 'rhetoric' is often used in a pejorative sense to mean insubstantial or empty. Tonks (2002), writing of marketing rhetoric in consumer contexts, dates this pejorative usage of the term back to Plato who criticized the Sophists' teaching of rhetoric for being 'mere cooking' associated with 'trickery, deceit, immorality and superficiality' (Kennedy, 1963, p. 15, in Tonks, 2002, p. 807). Aristotle took a rather more benign view and the study of rhetoric became a key part of the school curriculum right through to medieval times. Rhetoric, in fact, became regarded as the overarching intellectual discipline, unifying the sciences because of its integrative 'epistemic' (Tonks, 2002, p. 810) character. It was studied as part of the school and university curriculum throughout the medieval era and, in the UK, up to the 1800s.

The interest in rhetoric has returned in many studies that consider it not only as a part of literary analysis but more fundamentally as an organizing principle for thought and argument. There is no necessary implication that to use rhetoric is deceitful or cunning. It is, simply, the means by which humans argue and persuade. Language and, hence, thought itself, are rhetorically organized to produce certain (rhetorical) effects. In the context of the social scientific emphasis on the constitutive character of language in constructing and maintaining social life, rhetoric has once again assumed major importance in social study.

Rhetorical 'privileging' and 'silencing'

The literary study of rhetoric, then, focuses on the persuasive character of particular forms of written language. It is important to note that rhetoric is not simply about what is written, or indeed, what is said. It is also about what is excluded. Expressing a view or idea in a persuasive or plausible way distracts attention from other possible ways of expressing that idea. Alternative forms of expression with quite different implications might seem equally plausible. Forms of expression tend to privilege certain ways of seeing the world and accounting for events while, by default, silencing alternatives. Social psychological researchers Edwards and Potter (1992) note that a major feature of rhetorical analysis is 'the demonstration of how, in order to understand the nature and function of any version of events, we need to consider whatever real or potential alternative versions it may be designed to counter' (p. 28, citing Billig, 1988, 1989).

In accounting for events, mental states or actions we are, in effect, arguing a point of view to others, and also to ourselves. As we construct particular accounts we make sense of them: we fill in the account with implied motivations and explanations. Other accounts or explanations then become rhetorically less forceful or persuasive: they become 'alternative' rather than accepted 'common sense'. In this way the rhetorical use of language is highly significant in not only describing but also in constitutively forming our psychological states.

Particular writing or speaking strategies invite the question: what potential threat or criticism was this way of putting things designed to counter? If I come home and my son opens the door and says 'it wasn't me, Dad' I immediately wonder what he's done wrong. What potential accusation or criticism is his denial intended to counter? If a marketing text proclaims that 'This book is focused on practical marketing management', a focus on rhetoric might prompt questions like 'why write that? In what way is marketing management not practical? What does the text accomplish by saying this?' Rhetorical strategies seek to exclude possible alternative accounts or claims (such as the claim that marketing management textbooks fail to adequately explain marketing practice). Marketing is a textual genre in the sense that marketing ideas, research and thought are produced, sustained, perpetuated and defended through writing. These words and phrases then become the instruments of managers and others in organizational settings. Marketing is, then, a prime site for rhetorical analysis.

The role of rhetoric in the art of persuasion

It is not uncommon for a politician to be praised for ability in the art of rhetoric. Rhetorical skill can persuade doubters to support a particular policy or course of action. It can even make a politician popular in a general way by persuading people that he or she is likeable. Clearly, ability in rhetoric is important for chief executive officers and other managers. Unlike politicians, managers may not be able to employ speechwriters. They must, nevertheless, generate support and co-operation through the use of language. University lecturing, too, has a rhetorical dimension. Academics use language to construct intellectual authority in their research books and articles. Academics who have ability in rhetorical arts can persuade others of the plausibility of their point of view. They can persuade students they know about their subject. This need not imply that an academic who lectures unconvincingly does not know his or her subject. Without skill in rhetoric academics may find it more difficult to persuade others of their knowledge and understanding.

Within the field of organizational management words and language have always been important tools for generating co-operation, support and compliance. The management field is often criticized for being too concerned with the latest 'buzz' phrase or trendy management technique. Business Process Re-engineering, Quality Management, Relationship

Marketing and many other techniques have brought fame and wealth to the management 'gurus' who popularized them. Most of these techniques fall out of favour after a time and people start to point out that the claims made for them were a little overblown. One aspect of the analysis of rhetoric focuses on just how such techniques or buzz-phrases seem, for a while, to be so compelling and persuasive.

Rhetorical analysis is inherently a critical method since it seeks to reveal the mechanisms by which consensus and agreement are produced. The study of rhetoric is therefore bound up with the issue of power. The power of particular rhetorical devices and strategies to persuade can be seen to have a historical basis in particular social structures and institutions. 'It's only rhetoric' is sometimes a comment levelled at political or commercial claims and discourse that suggests that rhetoric is trivial and reflects a mendacious, half-truth approach to accounts and claims. In social research, rhetoric is far more than this. The study of rhetoric is the study of how meaning and persuasion are mobilized through language and social practice.

Rhetorical analysis in marketing and management

The top marketing and management research journals have published rhetorical studies that analysed uses of rhetoric within those fields. For example, Brown (1999) drew on literary analysis to compare the rhetorical styles of two leading marketing writers and consultants, Professors Theodore Levitt and Morris Holbrook. Such an analysis is not always well received by business academics who feel that a focus on rhetoric demeans their work. They write as if they are offering solutions that can be applied in the practical worlds of business. Many do not wish attention to be drawn to the rhetorical skills that enable them to write plausibly in this way. The study of rhetoric is based on the truism that all knowledge is mediated: we cannot convey experience except through language and writing. Many business consultants have won influence and credibility through the ability to write and speak as if they are offering homespun wisdom deriving from direct experience of organizational management. This ability itself is a mark of high-order rhetorical skill, as Brown (1999) points out.

In another trenchant analysis of management rhetoric Case (1999) critically analysed the rhetoric of the Business Process Re-engineering trend made popular by management consultants Hammer and Champy (1993). His article prises apart the claims made for the re-engineering fad and focuses on the rhetorical devices that were employed to make those claims seem plausible and persuasive. Case's (1999) argument is not that business process re-engineering was just empty puffery. Neither does his argument impugn the sincerity of the management consultants and gurus who proselytize this or other management fads. Rather, Case's (1999) analysis draws attention to a truism that is often forgotten, namely that management ideas and consulting solutions are made up of words. The analysis of the rhetoric of management texts is, therefore, appropriate and necessary to help us to better understand their influence and popularity in contemporary culture.

Another important study (Furusten, 1999) has critically examined the popular management books of several management writers, including the influential Peters and Waterman (1982). This author's aim was to understand how such books come to be so popular and influential when they do not appear to have a scientific or intellectually well-founded basis for their claims. Their popularity can be seen as part of a broader cultural trend in which the words and ideas of management 'gurus' are treated with the kind of attention and interest that was, in other cultures, reserved for prominent philosophers or religious figures. Like Case, Furusten (1999) focuses on the rhetorical strategies of management writers and gurus to deepen understanding of this modern phenomenon. Each found that management ideas that do become particularly popular do so because of their powerful rhetorical appeal rather than purely because they have been proven to be especially effective or well founded.

It was mentioned above that marketing is a particularly rich site for rhetorical analysis because of the vast number of texts which preserve and popularize marketing ideas and formulae. Hackley (2003) critically analysed the ideological rhetoric of popular marketing management text books. Hackley (2003) picks through a selection of popular US and UK marketing management texts in order to try to set out the major rhetorical strategies through which these texts seek to be persuasive and plausible. In this article rhetoric is linked to ideology since it is through rhetorical strategies that ideological norms are reproduced as normal and unquestionable things. The focus on rhetoric implies a deeply critical orientation towards the subject matter of such works. It implies that they achieve their aims through persuasive rhetoric as well as, and sometimes instead of, intellectually rigorous argument and carefully organized evidence. Rhetorical analysis acknowledges that, in order for a particular set of ideas to become accepted and popular, it is more important that they are rhetorically persuasive than intellectually rigorous.

Marketing rhetoric and management practice

As mentioned above, for some psychological theorists, rhetoric is more than simply a literary craft of persuasion. It is an important organizing principle of human psychology (Billig, 1987, 1991). In a sweeping sense we can be seen to depend on particular kinds of accounts of events and experiences to make sense of the world. We have explanations for our behaviours that seem, to us, to justify them. We understand our beliefs and actions in terms of accounts we construct of our lived experience.

For many marketing students becoming a marketing manager in an organization will entail using marketing rhetoric to acquire influence and to persuade. Marketing and brand managers use marketing texts to influence organizational staff to be more 'consumer orientated', to respond to 'customer needs', to look out into the market to track changes and trends and to change organizational behaviours to fit these changes. Managerial tasks are often focused on persuading and influencing. Rhetoric is a far from trivial topic of study: in important respects our sense of organizational and personal reality are rhetorical constructions. Within organizations the uses of rhetoric can usefully be studied by researchers interested in how people construct organizational reality and social relations in their particular contexts.

Student projects and rhetorical analysis

The articles cited above are advanced research studies published in some of the world's foremost academic management research journals but, in spite of their difficulty, they do have uses for student researchers. Some of the techniques and approaches can be borrowed for smaller-scale student research projects to examine rhetoric in organizational settings and contexts. In this way the study of rhetoric can be used by student researchers to try to pick apart the reasons why certain approaches are seen as compelling and persuasive and others are not. Throughout history some voices, views and opinions have become accepted as normal and right, and others have been regarded as marginal and illegitimate. At the time of writing, the rhetoric of marketing and management is powerful and influential. In previous eras, business and commerce has been regarded as intellectually trivial and not worthy of the attention of higher study or analysis. The study of rhetoric seeks to understand why this should be so.

For example, one marketing student recently conducted a research project for her MSc in Marketing based on a textual analysis of the rhetoric used by politicians and news media to work up political consensus. There was little similar work in this field on which to base her literature review. However, she was able to find useful references by looking at the literature of political marketing and also communication studies. These fields gave her a literature-based grounding for her analysis. She felt that a social scientific investigation of the ways in which politicians and other commentators seek to work up consensus through news media was relevant to the growing research interest in political marketing. One of the nice things about research in marketing is that research studies can often be connected to current affairs and media trends and events. This can give research in marketing and management a highly topical flavour.

Student research projects can engage with management and organizational rhetoric in many ways. The theoretical perspectives discussed in this book are not mutually exclusive: there are significant areas of overlap. A discourse analytic methodological approach drawing on Chapter 9 is a kind of rhetorical analysis since it analyses the ways in which texts organize thought, attempt to persuade and order reality. A phenomenological research design might also incorporate some consideration of the rhetorical structures and strategies used by research participants to achieve certain effects. Student researchers could usefully explore the popular management rhetoric of particular gurus or particular management text genres such as the studies cited above. They could, alternatively, focus on naturally occurring discourse in organizational or consumption settings to perform rhetorical analyses in those contexts. For example, how do consumers in particular settings justify, explain and account for their consumer behaviour? Rhetorical analysis could usefully generate insights into this and related questions.

Narrative analysis

Narrative analysis is another literary influence that has been drawn on in interpretive marketing, management and consumer research. A 'narrative' is a linguistic account of an event or events that is organized into a sequence or structure so it can be understood and connected. Some literary studies of narrative have focused on the structures of narrative and how these come to be imbued with meaning. Other approaches have emphasized the interpretation of narrative by focusing on the reading strategies that people employ in order to draw meanings from narrative accounts.

Academic research into management fields can be seen in terms of 'narrative projects' since it consists of literary texts that construct narratives, or stories, about, for example, marketing (Shankar *et al.*, 2001). In most popular marketing management books the text is organized persuasively to give marketing a sense of narrative. There is a familiar story of the evolution of marketing as a discipline that is referred to in many of these texts (Kerin, 1996; Keith, 1960). Marketing management theory is given origins (normally placed in the late 1950s in the USA), there is a time of struggle (the 'production' and 'sales' eras of business orientation) and it achieves great popular success in the modern era. Marketing has its pantheon of management guru-heroes and there are the trials and tribulations of misunderstanding and mistakes along the way (Hackley, 2001). The historical accuracy of these claims is not important: the textual organization marketing management texts give the discipline a striking and persuasive narrative character.

In postmodern and poststructuralist writing 'grand narratives' are, simply, big stories that frame our interpretation of other, smaller, stories.

For example, much marketing writing, such as that in popular marketing management textbooks, has been described as 'modernist' or 'progressivist' in that it assumes that marketing is part of the relentless upward progress of humanity (Brown, 1995). There is no space in modernist narratives for critical re-appraisal of basic values and assumptions. The assumption that marketing, as described in the text, is moving towards a utopia of perpetual organizational success and customer satisfaction is given in the narrative form (Brown *et al.*, 1996). In order to enhance this effect the rhetorical organization of popular marketing textbooks leaves little space for penetrating criticism. Lyotard (1984, xxiv) writes that 'I define postmodern as incredulity towards metanarratives.' For Lyotard the narrative form is a highly significant cultural artefact that frames the way we think. He seems to position postmodernism as an antidote in that it seeks to recover these narrative forms and, by questioning their unstated assumptions and exposing their rhetorical techniques, undermine their effect.

Narrative studies in marketing management

Literary tracts of all kinds have a narrative character, they tell a story and have a beginning, a middle and an end. For example, we are used to scientific research being presented as if it stands outside narrative because it is a discourse separated from storytelling by its objectivity and rigor. Yet (even) scientific research tracts can also be seen to have narrative characteristics (Latour and Woolgar, 1979). Scientific Research and Development, for example, can be seen as an enterprise that invents narratives to interpret compounds and substances in terms of new 'uses' for need satisfaction. The effects of the drug that became marketed as Viagra, for example, were known for a long time as an unacceptable side-effect before somebody connected the drug to the narrative of male sexual performance enhancement and made it into a huge marketing success (Letiche, 2002).

We are inculcated with narrative forms from the stories we read and hear from an early age. We expect the accounts we read and hear as adults to conform to these narrative characteristics. Our preconceptions about which narrative forms are appropriate in given contexts frame our interpretations. Traditional scientific reporting has a very distinctive written tone and style. Many scientific research studies have conformed to a particular narrative structure that emphasizes the research question as an investigation that springs from and extends existing knowledge. The written tone is impersonal and emphasizes the objectivity and universality of the knowledge that is sought. There is then a discovery of new knowledge that derives from the scientific application of a research method. There are then implications for more research in order to further refine and add to the knowledge. Narrative conventions applied to the production of scientific research texts are framed by the wider scientific discourse that sets our assumptions and guides our interpretation of such texts. Consumer research studies, that, for example, advocate a role for poetry and lyricism in consumer research (Sherry and Schouten, 2002; Holbrook, 1990), directly engage with and challenge the extant narrative conventions in social scientific research.

Much interpretive research in management and marketing has, in contrast, drawn attention to narrative conventions in order to generate critical analyses and interpretive insights. Brown and Reid (1997) employed a form of narrative analysis to draw out the ways in which shoppers wove their tales of shopping into broader narratives of life and living. Their research revealed that shopping was rich in meaning for many people and formed a vivid part of their lived experience. Shankar and Goulding (2001) have also adapted a narrative approach to the study of consumption. They cite authors such as Stern *et al.* (1998) and Grayson (1997) as evidence that narrative analysis is drawing wider attention among marketing and consumer researchers.

Shankar and Goulding (2001, p. 1) adapt a table of narrative characteristics from Gergen and Gergen (1988). These authors suggest that narratives have some important characteristics. Narratives have a point in the sense that they develop a moral or theme that is valued. The 'point' of popular marketing management texts is that they produce social progress through wealth creation and organizational efficiency, and personal progress through the enhancement of marketing 'skills'. Narratives have selected events that are ordered and causally linked to lead up to and support the main point of the story. In the case of marketing management texts these events are often the ones referred to above concerning the historical evolution of the discipline through three 'eras'. Finally, narratives have signs that they are narratives such as a middle, beginning and an end.

Narrative analysis might be applied in various ways. Most obviously it can refer to the interpretive analysis of depth interviews or written experiential accounts. Such accounts can be interpreted as stories in terms of the ways in which they seem to conform to narratives in order to make sense of events and to produce desired effects. For example, in a job interview one might describe one's 'career' in terms of conscious decisions and logical sequences of jobs and education undertaken. A franker appraisal might reveal that one's career decisions were opportunistic, idiosyncratic, accidental or dictated by circumstance. However, in a job interview we would often try to tell our working life as a story in order to conform to the narrative convention of a job interview and thereby to present ourselves in the best possible light.

Researching other forms of rhetoric in marketing

The rhetoric of prose writing and speech has not been the only kind of rhetoric analysed in management and marketing research. The previous chapter mentioned that music and visual images also have a rhetorical purpose in advertising. Scott (1990) has researched the rhetoric of music in advertising and has also focused on the need for a theory of visual rhetoric to better understand the persuasive use of visual images in advertising (Scott, 1994a). Cook (1992) has published a comprehensive research monograph analysing the persuasive character and social role of advertising from a discourse perspective particularly informed by applied linguistics. Tanaka (1994) drew on semiotics and linguistics to develop a pragmatic approach to analysing UK and Japanese advertising. Cross-disciplinary studies such as these can provide examples for student researchers of how literary theories and analytical concepts might be adapted and applied in smaller-scale research studies.

Another of Scott's (1994b) research studies deals with the adaptation of a well-known approach to literary analysis, reader-response theory, to the analysis of advertising responses. For this researcher, consumers can be said to 'read' advertising in important respects. This is in direct contrast to the major tradition of advertising consumer research that assumes that consumers 'process' advertising as data much like a highly advanced computer. The reading analogy (also employed in Cook, 1992) leads into the generation of new insights about how consumers understand and respond to advertising.

Stern and Schroeder (1994) point out that research into advertisements has often focused on the 'information' (price, quality, positioning) that is available to be 'processed' by consumers. Such research has neglected the view that consumers draw meaning from advertisements as a whole rather than in distinct parts. We do not look at advertising text, sound and imagery as distinct sources of information. All three wash over us as we are exposed to advertising. Little attention has been paid by information-processing researchers to the ways in which other components of advertising, especially the visual imagery, acts as a source of meaning that can influence the meaning of the other components of an ad. Their paper draws on literature and concepts from literary and art criticism to develop an approach to the analysis of visual imagery in advertising. This approach, again challenging the narrative conventions in much marketing research, is developed in other work such as in Brown and Patterson (2000).

Gender studies and feminist research

Research into gender studies and feminism has a well-established record of research publications in consumer research, often combined with literary theory perspectives (e.g. Stern, 1993; Hirschman, 1993). The extent to which marketing images mediate the construction of masculinity has also been a topic of research (Patterson and Elliott, 2002). Feminism as a broad research perspective is well established in consumer studies and management research, while its use is growing within research in marketing, reflected, for example, in a recent major collection of feminist research in marketing (Catterall *et al.*, 2001).

A major concern of such research is the way that social identity formation and relations of gender are informed by marketed images and values. Marketing is a pervasive influence in developed economies. Do the values and norms implicit in marketing activity reproduce particular relations of power and domination? For example, do magazine images reproduce male dominance as a norm? Some student researchers have found that, by analysing the visual imagery and/or editorial content in popular magazines over a period of time, they have been able to develop critical analyses of gender representations in such magazines. This might entail a focus on the portrayal of gender relations or a focus solely on the construction of masculinity or femininity in media representations. Of course, one implies the other but research studies can take one particular focus to sharpen their analysis.

Gender-based studies are sometimes conducted in a purely interpretive spirit by researchers who do not have a specified critical agenda but merely wish to understand the process of media representation in the context of gender construction. However, such studies have a critical dimension which it is difficult to escape. Analysis of gender representations has to engage at some level with the issue of power when the researcher asks why certain forms of representation are popular or prevalent and others are not. For example, Alvesson (1988) studied the ways in which gender relations were produced through the discourse of an advertising agency. Workplaces are important sites in the play of gender relations. Issues of equal opportunities and the 'glass ceiling' phenomenon of male-dominated promotion procedures can be investigated through such gender-based research perspectives.

Researchers could employ a phenomenological approach in seeking to understand the experience of being a man or woman in the workplace. This might generate experiential interview texts which could then be analysed as narratives that tell a story of the production and maintenance of gender and gender relations at work. Some professions, especially caring professions such as primary school teaching, are predominantly female occupations. Others, such as stock broking or civil engineering, are predominantly male. Does this state of affairs reflect skill imbalance between the sexes? Does it reflect ideologies of power that have long traditions and reflect wider inequalities? Is such imbalance of opportunity perpetuated by the ideological norms on management and marketing activity and teaching? Gender-based studies can elucidate these and many related issues in marketing and management.

The postmodernist critique of marketing

It suits the didactic purpose of this book to defer discussion of post-modernism and poststructuralism until the latter stages. This should not imply that their influence on interpretive research perspectives has been negligible. On the contrary, it could be argued that postmodernist themes (Harvey, 1989) (often linked, or conflated with, poststructuralism) have been singularly influential in developing the interpretive stance in marketing and consumer research. Firat and Venkatesh (1995a, 1995b), Firat *et al.* (1995), Featherstone (1991) and Brown (1994, 1995) have each set out themes of postmodernism in consumer research and in marketing respectively.

Postmodernism in marketing and consumer research has become a label for a set of precepts and positions which, collectively, challenge modernist notions of progress, unity and coherence. Postmodern influences have been important in art, architecture and literature (for a 'genealogy' of post-modernism see Firat and Venkatesh, 1995a, p. 241). Epistemologically, postmodernism indicates a reaction against modernist notions of epistemological unity, objective truth and linear historical progress. Prominent in postmodernist themes is a sense of the fragmentation of meaning into multiple contested meanings (or 'polysemy') and a break in the reliance on 'grand narratives' or organizing themes that, in previous historical eras, were thought to have ordered social structure and, hence, private thought (Lyotard, 1984). Postmodernist writing often emphasizes a 'de-centre-ing' of knowledge so that what might once have been unified, absolute, progressive and consensual is now fragmented, relative, temporally indeterminate and contested. Postmodern writing stands for experimental narrative forms, challenging prose styles and (purportedly) new ideas. It tends to be irreverent and sceptical, questioning norms and challenging convention.

Much postmodern writing remarks on the curious character of marketing institutions such as 'shopping centres, department stores, advertising campaigns, package designs, new product development and the entire consumption experience' (Brown, 1995, p. 8). Indeed, marketing has been identified as the quintessential site of postmodernism (Firat and Venkatesh, 1995). Postmodernist reflections on marketing point to the simulated character of vaunted consumption experiences as in the 'hyperreality' of Disneyland. It indicates the pastiche of differing styles and genres in advertising text and visuals, brand names and product design. For example, 'Retro' design in furniture, popular music and motor cars combines modern styles with classic designs to produce a new effect that rehabilitates the old. The culturally trivial nature of popular marketing phenomena and the privileging of style over substance is also addressed by post-modernist writing that refers, for example, to 'reality' TV shows and 'designer' clothes labels. In American television the modernist values and aspirations of the *Little House on the Prairie* have been replaced with the irony, parody and self-referentiality of the *Simpsons*. In UK product marketing the natural values of real dairy butter have been replaced with the ironically self-deprecating yet highly successful '*I Can't Believe It's Not Butter*' butter substitute.

In postmodernist writing the text is a major focus of attention and the media is a major source of texts. Postmodernist writing is often highly critical of conventional practice and beliefs and uses irony to undermine 'grand narratives' of belief and practice. Marketing, a 'narrative project' as noted above, has become part of the media complex with its big-selling textbooks, web-based resources and video-star management consulting gurus. Not only have marketing phenomena provided a showground for the literary talents of postmodern commentators: marketing writing has itself attracted the critical attention of postmodernists. As noted above, popular marketing writing's relentless progressivism (the drive to universalize marketing orientation) and essentialism (the 'core' concepts of marketing) make it particularly vulnerable to postmodernist critique.

Some of the most pungent criticism comes from Brown (1995): 'I don't think marketing has all, or even many, of the answers: I don't think the marketing concept can be applied to everything under the sun ... and I suspect that ... marketing theory seems resolutely stuck in a modernist time-warp' (p. 181). The certainties of marketing management texts never seem to change while postmodernism 'reminds us of the reflexive or circular nature of social knowledge, where the very existence of a concept influences and alters the phenomena to which it pertains' (Brown, 1995, p. 178). In mainstream marketing writing the text refers to a 'real' world of marketing practice that lies beyond the text. Postmodernist writers indicate that marketing as object is constructed through and by the text. Marketing reality is, therefore, not merely referred to by marketing texts. It is highly influenced by them because of the presuppositions texts impose on the understanding of marketing students, managers and wider spheres of influence. Indeed, marketing and management texts have a constitutive role in producing the texts of organizational and management practice.

Postmodernism and student research projects

While the postmodern tendency in marketing writing is avowedly critical of the verities of mainstream marketing management, it also points to the novel insights and intellectual vigour that can derive from postmodernist perspectives. Nevertheless, from the student researcher's perspective, a postmodern empirical research project is probably a risky undertaking, at least in most university business schools. Empirical postmodern marketing research might be quite implausible, or at least highly problematic (Brown, 1995, p. 172) so the student researcher interested in postmodernism is largely confined to a conceptual project that engages in a postmodern critique of a branch of theory or practice.

Postmodernist themes lend themselves aptly to critique of marketing culture and practices, especially writing and other text-based practices. The student researcher considering writing a conceptual research project will find that postmodern marketing writing offers a fertile source of ideas. Some of the most penetrating, vigorous and witty scholarship in the marketing field has been produced under the postmodern brand.

Students considering wading into the swirling waters of postmodernism for their student project would be well advised to discuss this carefully with their supervisor. They should be advised that mention of postmodernism can provoke heated (and heatedly negative) responses from some business school academics. For many academics postmodernism is a byword for obscurantism, literary self-indulgence, aimlessness and inaction. Postmodernism loftily critiques everything without having a position itself on anything.

Even those student researchers who gain approval for such a project should not congratulate themselves too quickly. They have a difficult task ahead of them. It could also be a rewarding one to the diligent and open-minded student researcher who is prepared to read a large number of difficult books and articles. The researcher could begin by reading some of the texts cited here (especially Brown, 1995). Student researchers can go from there to make their own observations on marketing culture, texts and practices. They can do this from their vantage point as consumers of products and services and aspirants to the status of marketers, and also as consumers of marketing itself.

Managerial marketing is an example of commodified knowledge that is produced (by management consultants), distributed (by academics, publishers and trainers) and consumed (by all the above plus citizens and students). A critique of one's own experience of consuming marketing education would make a distinctively postmodern research project (and one of the author's supervisees, mentioned earlier, did exactly that). To the extent that postmodernism attempts to find new ways of articulating and expressing our experience of our culture and its knowledge, such projects are ambitious and important.

Interpretive studies of marketing, management and consumer research: some concluding remarks

This book is written as a practical guide for the pragmatic student researcher and as a point of departure for the more ambitious. It has sought to introduce research perspectives and ideas that may not be familiar to many under- and postgraduate students in marketing, management and consumer research. It has offered many published studies to illustrate particular approaches and to provide useful sources of reference for student researchers wishing to pursue interpretive studies. A selective approach has been taken because of space limitations: there are many other interpretive approaches not developed in this book.

For example, Du Gay *et al.* (1997) have taken a cultural studies perspective to understand the cultural phenomenon of a marketing innovation, the Sony Walkman. Holbrook (1995) used subjective personal introspection as a methodological basis for essays on consumption. This approach, clearly potentially valuable for student research projects, has not been specifically developed in the book. It was mentioned earlier that psychodynamic approaches to social research have been excluded in spite of their value in interpretive research. Neither have ethnomethodology and conversation analysis (Garfinkel, 1967; Heritage, 1984) been given detailed treatment. There is far more work on the sociology of marketing and management practices that provides valuable insights for researchers (such as Ritzer, 2000) that has not been referred to here for reasons of space and organization.

However, while acknowledging the many omissions, the book offers an extensive introductory source of concepts, methods, practical suggestions and reference sources for those student researchers interested in developing interpretive themes in their work. In seeking a broad perspective to address the needs of a wide range of business-related students, the book has emphasized inter- and cross-disciplinary research. It has also acknowledged that interpretive approaches in some fields have proved more popular than in others. For example, consumer research has proved a fertile site for revisionist research perspectives that re-appraise old topics from an interpretive standpoint (Belk, 1991; Belk *et al.* 1989). In other management subfields, such as operations research and marketing management, there are fewer available published studies to which to refer for exemplars of interpretive approaches. Still others, such as organization studies, offer many examples of interpretive work that, arguably, are more appropriate for PhD level students than for inclusion in this book. The book has tried to balance the treatment of accessible research topics and themes in favour of the needs of the novice interpretive researcher while also offering a guide to useful sources for these who wish to specialize in particular fields and gain more advanced knowledge.

The commonalities among interpretive research traditions

Many researchers looking into interpretive methods for the first time are daunted by the sheer complexity of the task. If one takes a pragmatic approach emphasizing commonalities and overlaps between the various interpretive traditions, one risks a negative reaction from researchers who work exclusively in one of the many interpretive traditions. However, it should be apparent to readers of this book that interpretive approaches have significant common features. There is an emphasis on qualitative research data, a focus on using that data to support particular interpretations, and an emphasis on grounding research perspectives in stated philosophical terms of reference.

There are many philosophical similarities between interpretive traditions. Semiotics, for example, can be seen as a 'phenomenological doctrine of consciousness' (Zeman, 1977, quoted in Mick, 1986, p. 199). In the sense that semiosis reflects apprehended reality, this may well be a notable area of commonality with phenomenological research. However, for C.S. Peirce, semiosis reflects the reality not of experience but of the world of signs. Furthermore, the particular interpretation placed on any given sign depends on a socially agreed code for many semioticians. Phenomenology, in contrast, seldom emphasizes social agreement but, rather, focuses on private, unmediated experience.

Ethnography has much in common with some strands of critical discourse analysis, especially in the form of critical ethnography (Forester, 1992). However, traditionally, ethnography would seek to recreate the conditions of localized social life without necessarily offering a political critique of those conditions. The common features of data analysis would normally include a broad focus that took account of informal data and subjective impressions acquired through field work.

These comments are not intended to imply that interpretive research can be regarded as a unified category, and neither do they imply that qualitative research and interpretive research should be regarded as being synonymous. On the contrary, one of the aims of this book has been to show that the philosophical choices of research perspective are of crucial importance since they frame the questions that can be asked and presuppose the kinds of answers that can be offered. Furthermore, the choice of interpretive methods within the book was intended to show that academic research is an intensely personal endeavour in which subjective choices reflect the localized preconditions for academic research.

The book has sought to encourage student researchers to reflect on their own and other's presuppositions about social research in marketing, management and consumer studies in order to make the conduct of research projects a creative and intellectually rewarding experience. The book is written from a conviction that the student research project can and should be such an experience and that it can also constitute a positive aspect of the student's academic and personal intellectual development. As Rorty (1982) has remarked, choices between theories cannot be made solely on the basis of what theory is most efficient or correct. The choice should reflect questions such as 'What would it be like to believe that? What would happen if we did? What would I be committing myself to?' (p. 163). This book hopes to encourage students to investigate their own assumptions and to see where they lead in terms of research perspectives, methods and findings. In this regard the book is conceived as a point of reference for the creative intellectual endeavours of student researchers, and it is hoped, a point of departure for many such studies.

Glossary

Narrative   The organization of writing or language to portray accounts of events in a way which seems sequential and connected.

Polysemy   A feature of postmodern culture: a message or entity is said to be polysemic if it displays not one but many possible meanings.

Appendix
What is a 'good' academic journal?

Many student researchers embark on their literature searching unsure which journals have a high academic reputation. This list offers a starting-point for those unsure where to focus their literature searching. However, it is worth mentioning that many academic articles use specialized technical vocabulary and sophisticated statistical techniques. Student researchers seeking useful examples of interpretive research have to be prepared to be highly selective and to find papers that they can adapt, in whole or in part, for use in their own research design or literature review.

Most papers that appear in good journals have been through a lengthy process of review and rewriting before publication. Academic journals are 'refereed', that is, academics submit research papers that are judged by colleagues. The papers are commented upon, criticized and often rejected for publication. If the submitting academic is lucky and the paper is a good one, it might be returned for amendments prior to possible publication. The ranking of a journal is a subjective affair and depends on criteria such as how frequently work appearing in that journal is cited in other journal articles, how widely the journal is read internationally, and by the academic standing of journal contributors.

The following list is neither exhaustive nor definitive.

Management

Academy of Management Review
Administrative Science Quarterly
Journal of Management Studies
Academy of Management Journal
Strategic Management Journal
Journal of Management
Human Resource Management
Organization Studies
Management Learning
British Journal of Management

Journal of Business Ethics
Harvard Business Review
British Journal of Industrial Relations
Journal of Occupational and Organizational Psychology
Asia Pacific Business Review
Journal of International Business Studies

Marketing and Consumer Research

Journal of Marketing
Journal of Marketing Research
European Journal of Marketing
International Journal of Research in Marketing
Journal of Advertising
Journal of Advertising Research
International Journal of Advertising
Journal of Consumer Research
Qualitative Market Research: An International Journal
Consumption, Markets and Culture
Journal of Marketing Management
Journal of Retailing
Psychology and Marketing
Journal of World Business
Journal of Services Marketing
Journal of Personal Selling and Sales Management
Journal of Marketing Communications

References

Agar, M. (1996) *The Professional Stranger*, London, Academic Press.

Althusser, L. (1971) *Lenin and Philosophy and Other Essays*, London, New Left Books.

Alvesson, M. (1998) 'Gender relations and identity at work: a case study of masculinities and femininities in an advertising agency', *Human Relations*, vol. 51, no. 8, pp. 969–1005.

Alvesson, M. and Deetz, S. (2000) *Doing Critical Management Research*, London, Sage.

Alvesson, M. and Skoldberg, K. (2000) *Reflexive Methodology*, London, Sage.

Alvesson, M. and Willmott, H. (eds) (1992) *Critical Management Studies*, London, Sage.

Antaki, C. (1994) *Explaining and Arguing: The social organisation of accounts*, London, Sage.

Arnould, E. (1998) 'Daring consumer-oriented ethnography', in Barbara B. Stern (ed.) *Representing Consumers: Voices, views and visions*, London, Routledge, pp. 85–126.

Arnould, E. and Wallendorf, M. (1994) 'Market-orientated ethnography: interpretation building and marketing strategy formulation', *Journal of Marketing Research*, XXXI (November), pp. 484–504.

Austin, J. (1962) *How to Do Things With Words*, London, Oxford University Press.

Ayer, A.J. (1936) *Language, Truth and Logic*, London, Penguin Books.

Banister, P., Burman, E., Parker, I., Taylor, M. and Tindall, C. (1994) *Qualitative Methods in Psychology: A research guide*, London, Sage.

Barthes, R. (trans. 1968) *Elements of Semiology*, trans. A. Lavers, New York, Hill and Wang.

—— (1977) *Image–Music–Text*, London, Fontana.

Beckman, S. and Elliott, R. (eds) (2001) *Interpretive Consumer Research: Paradigms, methodologies and applications*, Copenhagen, Copenhagen Business School Press, Handelshøjskolens Forlag.

Belk, R. (1988) 'Possessions and the extended self', *Journal of Consumer Research*, vol. 15, no. 2, pp. 139–68.

—— (ed.) (1991) *Highways and Byways: Naturalistic Research from the Consumer Behaviour Odyssey*, Provo, UT, Association for Consumer Research.

Belk, R., Wallendorf, M. and Sherry, J. (1989) 'The sacred and profane in consumer behaviour: theodicy on the odyssey', *Journal of Consumer Research*, vol. 16, June, pp. 1–38.

Belk, R., Sherry, J.F. and Wallendorf, M. (1988) 'A naturalistic inquiry into buyer and seller behaviour at a swap meet', *Journal of Consumer Research*, vol. 14, March, pp. 449–70.

Benhabib, S. (1992) *Situating the Self: Gender, Community, and Postmodernism in Contemporary Ethics*, New York, Routledge.

Benveniste, E. (1971) *Problems in General Linguistics*, Miami, Florida, University of Florida Press.

Berger, P.L. and Luckman, T. (1966) *The Social Construction of Reality*, London, Penguin.

Bertrand, D. (1988) 'The creation of complicity: a semiotic analysis of an advertising campaign for Black and White Whiskey', *International Journal of Research in Marketing*, vol. 4, no. 4, pp. 273–89.

Billig, M. (1987) *Arguing and Thinking: A rhetorical approach to social psychology*, Cambridge, Cambridge University Press.

—— (1988) 'Rhetorical and historical aspects of attitudes: the case of the British monarchy', *Philosophical Psychology*, vol. 1, pp. 84–104.

—— (1989) 'Psychology, rhetoric and cognition', *History of the Human Sciences*, vol. 2, pp. 289–307.

—— (1991) *Ideology and Opinions*, London, Sage.

Brown, S. (1988) 'What's love got to do with it? Sex, shopping and subjective personal introspection', Chapter 8 in S. Brown, A.M. Doherty and B. Clarke (eds) *Romancing the Market*, London, Routledge, pp. 137–71.

—— (1994) 'Marketing as Multiplex: screening postmodernism', *European Journal of Marketing*, vol. 28, no. 8/9, pp. 27–51.

—— (1995) *Postmodern Marketing*, London, International Thompson Business Press.

—— (1999) 'Marketing and literature: the anxiety of academic influence', *Journal of Marketing*, vol. 63, pp. 1–15.

Brown, S., Maclaran, P. and Stevens, L. (1996) 'Marcadia postponed: marketing, utopia and the millennium', *Journal of Marketing Management*, vol. 12, pp. 671–83.

Brown, S. and Patterson, A. (eds) (2000) *Imagining Marketing: Art, Aesthetics and the Avante-Garde*, London, Routledge.

Brown, S. and Reid, R. (1997) 'Shoppers on the verge of a nervous breakdown: chronicle, composition and confabulation in consumer research', Chapter 4 in S. Brown and D. Turley (eds) *Consumer Research: Postcards from the Edge*, London, Routledge, pp. 79–149.

Brown, S., Doherty, A.M. and Clarke, B. (eds) (1988) *Romancing the Market*, London, Routledge.

Brownlie, D. (2001) 'Interpretation as composition: Debating modes of representation in marketing research', in R.H. Elliott and S. Beckmann (eds) *Interpretive Consumer Research: paradigms, methodologies and applications*, Copenhagen, Copenhagen Business School Press, pp. 47–86.

Brownlie, D. and Saren, M. (1992) 'The four Ps of the marketing concept: prescriptive, polemical, permanent and problematical', *The European Journal of Marketing*, vol. 26, no. 4, pp. 34–47.

Brownlie, D., Saren, M., Wensley, R. and Whittington, R. (eds) (1999) *Rethinking Marketing: towards critical marketing accountings*, London, Sage.

Burawoy, M. (1979) *Manufacturing Consent*, Chicago, IL, Chicago University Press.

Burman, E. and Parker, I. (eds) (1993) *Discourse Analytic Research*, London, Routledge.

Buttle, F. (1995) 'Marketing Communications theory: What do the texts teach our students?' *International Journal of Advertising*, vol. 14, pp. 29–313.

Carrigan, M. (2003) 'Guide to Dissertations', unpublished student guide, University of Birmingham Department of Commerce.

Carrigan, M. and Szmigin, I. (2002) 'Time, uncertainty and the expectancy experience: an interpretive exploration of consumption and impending motherhood', unpublished paper, University of Birmingham, UK.

Carson, D., Gilmore, A., Perry, C. and Gronhaug, K. (2001) *Qualitative Marketing Research*, London, Sage.

Case, P. (1999) 'Remember re-engineering? The rhetorical appeal of a managerial salvation device', *Journal of Management Studies*, vol. 36, no. 4, pp. 419–42.

Catterall, M., Maclaran, P. and Stephens, L. (2001) *Marketing and Feminism: current issues and research*, London, Routledge.

Chandler, D. (2002) *Semiotics for Beginners*, <http://www.aber.ac.uk/media/Documents/S4B/window.html>.

Clarke, I., Kell, I., Schmidt, R. and Vignall, C. (1998) 'Thinking the thought they do: Symbolism and meaning in the consumer experience of the British Pub', *Qualitative Market Research: An International Journal*, vol. 13, pp. 132–44.

Contardo, I. and Wensley, R. (1999) 'The Harvard Business School Story: avoiding knowledge by being relevant', paper presented at the conference *Re-organizing Knowledge, Transforming Institutions, Knowing, Knowledge and the University in the XXI Century*, Amherst, September.

Cook, G. (1992) *The Discourse of Advertising*, London, Routledge.

Danesi, M. (1993) *Messages and Meanings: An Introduction to Semiotics*, Toronto, Canadian Scholar's Press Inc.

Deetz, S. (1992) *Democracy in an Age of Corporate Colonization: Developments in Communication and the Politics of Everyday Life*, Albany, NY, State University of New York Press.

Deshpandhe, R. (1999) 'Forseeing marketing', *Journal of Marketing*, vol. 63, pp. 164–7.

van Dijk, T.A. (1984) *Prejudice in Discourse: An Analysis of Ethnic Prejudices in Cognition and Conversation*, Amsterdam, John Benjamins.

—— (1985) (ed.) *Handbook of Discourse Analysis*, vols 1–4, London, Academic Press.

Downes, D. and Rock, P. (1982) *Understanding Deviance*, Oxford, Clarendon Press.

Du Gay, P., Hall, S., Janes, L., Mackay, H. and Negus, K. (1997) *Doing Cultural Studies: the story of the Sony Walkman*, London, Sage.

Eagleton, T. (1991) *Ideology*, London, Verso.

Easterby-Smith, M. and Malina, D. (1999) 'Cross-cultural collaborative research: toward reflexivity', *Academy of Management Journal*, vol. 42, no. 1, pp. 76–86.

Easterby-Smith, M., Thorpe, R. and Lowe, A. (1991) *Management Research: An Introduction* (2nd edition 2002), London, Sage.

Easton, G. and Aráujo, L. (1997) 'Management research and literary criticism', *British Journal of Management*, vol. 8, pp. 99–106.

Eco, U. (1976) *A Theory of Semiotics*, Bloomington, Indiana University Press.

—— (1984) *Semiotics and Philosophy of Language*, London, Macmillan.

Edgar, A. and Sedgwick, P. (1999) *Key Concepts in Cultural Theory*, London, Routledge.

Edwards, D. and Potter, J. (1992) *Discursive Psychology*, London, Sage.

Elam, K. (1988) *The Semiotics of Theatre and Drama*, London, Routledge.

Elliott, R. (1994) 'Addictive consumption: function and fragmentation in post-modernity', *Journal of Consumer Policy*, vol. 17, no. 2, pp. 157–79.

—— (1996) 'Discourse analysis: exploring action, function and conflict on social texts', *Marketing Intelligence and Planning*, vol. 14, no. 6, pp. 65–9.

Elliott, R. and Gournay, K. (1996) 'Revenge, existential choice and addictive consumption', *Psychology and Marketing*, vol. 3, no. 8, pp. 753–68.

Elliott, R. and Jankel-Elliott, N. (2002) 'Using ethnography in strategic consumer research', *Qualitative Market Research: An international journal*.

Elliott, R. and Ritson, M. (1997) 'Post-structuralism and the dialectics of advertising: discourse, ideology, resistance', Chapter 6 in S. Brown and D. Turley (eds) *Consumer Research: Postcards from the edge*, pp. 190–248.

Fairclough, N. (1989) *Language and Power*, London, Longman.

—— (1995) *Critical Discourse Analysis: The critical study of language*, London, Sage.

Faulconer, J.E. and Williams, R.N. (1985) 'Temporality in human action: An alternative to historicism and positivism', *American Psychologist*, vol. 40, November, pp. 1179–88.

Featherstone, M. (1991) *Consumer Culture and Postmodernism*, London, Sage.

Firat, A. (1985) 'Ideology versus science in marketing', in 'Changing the course of marketing, alternative paradigms for widening marketing theory', *Research in Marketing*, supplement 2, pp. 135–46.

Firat, A. and Venkatesh, A. (1995a) 'Liberatory postmodernism and the re-enchantment of consumption', *Journal of Consumer Research*, vol. 22, no. 3, pp. 239–67.

—— (1995b) 'Postmodern perspectives on consumption, in R. Belk, N. Dholakia and A. Venkatesh (eds) *Consumption and Marketing, Macro Dimensions*, South-Western College Publishing, Cincinatti, pp. 234–65.

Firat, A., Dholakia, N. and Venkatesh, A. (1995) 'Marketing in a postmodern world', *European Journal of Marketing*, vol. 29, no. 1, pp. 40–56.

Fiske, J.C. (1982) *Introduction to Communication Studies*, London, Methuen.

Forester, J. (1992) 'Critical ethnography: On fieldwork in a Habermasian way', Chapter 3 in M. Alvesson and H. Willmott (eds) *Critical Management Studies*, London, Sage, pp. 46–64.

Foucault, M. (1977) *Discipline and Punish: The birth of the prison*, trans. A. Sheridan, New York, Pantheon.

Foxall, G. (1995) 'Science and interpretation in consumer research: a radical behaviourist perspective', *European Journal of Marketing*, vol. 29, no. 9, pp. 3–99.

Fry, D. and Fry, V.L. (1986) 'A semiotic model for the study of mass communication', in M. McLaughlin (ed.) *Communication Yearbook 9*, Beverly Hills, Sage, pp. 443–61.

Furusten, S. (1999) *Popular Management Books: How they are made and what they mean for organisations*, London, Routledge.

Garfinkel, H. (1967) *Studies in Ethnomethodology*, Englewood Cliffs, NJ, Prentice-Hall.

Geertz, C. (1973) *The Interpretation of Cultures*, London, Fontana Press.

Gergen, K. and Gergen, M. (1988) 'Narrative and the self as relationship', *Advances in Experimental Social Psychology*, vol. 21, pp. 17–56.

Gramsci, A. (1971) *Selections from the Prison Notebooks*, New York, International.

Grayson, K. (1997) 'Narrative theory and consumer research: theoretical and methodological perspectives', *Advances in Consumer Research*, vol. 24, pp. 67–70.

Greenley, G.E. (1988) 'Managerial perceptions of marketing planning', *Journal of Management Studies*, vol. 25, no. 6, pp. 575–601.

Gronhaug, K. (2000) 'The sociological basis of marketing', in M.J. Baker (ed.) *Marketing Theory: A student text*, London, Thompson Business Press.

Gummeson, E. (2000) *Qualitative Methods in Management Research*, London, Sage.

Gurswitch, A. (1974) *Phenomenology and Theory of Science*, Evanson, Northwestern University Press.

Habermas, J. (1970) 'Knowledge and interest', in D. Emmett and A. Macintyre (eds) *Sociological Theory and Philosophical Analysis*, London, Macmillan.

Hackley, C. (1998) 'Mission statements as corporate communications: The consequences of social constructionism', *Corporate Communications: An International Journal*, vol. 3, no. 3, pp. 92–8.

—— (1999) 'The communications process and the semiotic boundary', Chapter 9 in P. Kitchen (ed.) *Marketing Communications: Principles and Practice*, London, International Thomson Business Press, pp. 135–55.

—— (2000), 'Silent running: Tacit, discursive and psychological aspects of management in a top UK advertising agency', *British Journal of Management*, vol. 11, no. 3, pp. 239–54.

—— (2001) *Marketing and Social Construction: exploring the rhetorics of marketed consumption*, London, Routledge.

—— (2002) 'The Panoptic role of advertising agencies in the production of consumer culture', *Consumption, Markets and Culture*, vol. 5, no. 3, September, pp. 211–29.

—— (2003) 'We are all customers now: Rhetorical strategy and ideological control in marketing management texts', *Journal of Management Studies* (in press).

Hackley, C. and Kitchen, P.J. (1999) 'Ethical Perspectives on the Postmodern Communications Leviathan', *Journal of Business Ethics*, vol. 20, no. 1, pp. 15–26.

Hammer, M. and Champy, J. (1993) *Re-engineering the corporation: a manifesto for business revolution*, London, Nicholas Brealy.

Hammersly, M. and Atkinson, P. (1983) *Ethnography: Principles and Practice*, London, Routledge.

Harvey, D. (1989) *The Condition of Postmodernity: An Enquiry into the Origins of Cultural Change*, Oxford, Blackwell.

Heidegger, M. (1962) *Being and Time*, Oxford, Basil Blackwell.

Heritage, J. (1984) *Garfinkel and Ethnomethodology*, Cambridge, Polity Press.

Hirschman, E.C. (1986) 'Humanistic inquiry in marketing research, philosophy, method and criteria', *Journal of Marketing Research*, vol. 23, pp. 237–49.

—— (1989) (ed.) *Interpretive Consumer Research*, Provo, UT, Association for Consumer Research.

—— (1990) 'Secular immortality and the American ideology of affluence', *Journal of Consumer Research*, vol. 17, June, pp. 344–59.

—— (1993) 'Ideology in Consumer Research, 1980 and 1990: A Marxist and Feminist Critique', *Journal of Consumer Research*, vol. 19, no. 4, pp. 537–55.

Holbrook, M.B. (1990) 'The role of lyricism in research on consumer emotions: skylark, have you anything to say to me?', *Advances in Consumer Research*, vol. 17, pp. 1–18.

—— (1995) *Consumer Research: Introspective essays on the study of consumption*, London, Sage.

Holbrook, M.B. and Grayson, M.W. (1986) 'The semiology of cinematic consumption: symbolic consumer behaviour in *Out of Africa*', *Journal of Consumer Research*, vol. 13, pp. 374–81.

Holbrook, M.B. and Hirschman, E.C. (1982) 'The experiential aspects of consumption: consumer feelings, fantasies and fun', *Journal of Consumer Research*, vol. 9, pp. 132–40.

—— (1993) *The Semiotics of Consumption: Interpreting Symbolic Consumer Behaviour in Popular Culture and Works of Art*, New York, Mouton de Gruyter.

Holbrook, M.B. and O'Shaughnessy, J. (1988) 'On the scientific status of consumer research and the need for an interpretive approach to studying consumer behaviour', *Journal of Consumer Research*, vol. 15, pp. 398–403.

Horkheimer, M. and Adorno, T.W. (1944) *The Dialectic of Enlightenment*, New York, Continuum.

Husserl, E. (1931) *Ideas*, London, Allen and Unwin.

—— (1970) *Logical Investigations*, London, Routledge and Kegan Paul (first published 1900).

Jankowicz, A.D. (1991) *Business Research Projects for Students*, London, Chapman and Hall.

Keith, R.J. (1960) 'The marketing revolution', *Journal of Marketing*, vol. 24, January, pp. 35–8.

Kelly, G.A. (1955) *The Psychology of Personal Constructs*, New York, Norton.

Kennedy, G. (1963) *The Art of Persuasion in Greece*, London, Routledge and Kegan Paul.

Kerin, R.A. (1996) 'In pursuit of an ideal: the editorial and literary history of the *Journal of Marketing*', *Journal of Marketing*, vol. 60, iss. 1, pp. 1–13.

Knorr Cetina, K.D. and Mulkay, M. (eds) (1983) *Science Observed: Perspectives on the Social Study of Science*, London, Sage.

Kover, A.J., Goldberg, S.M. and James, W.L. (1995) 'Creativity vs Effectiveness? An integrating classification for advertising', *Journal of Advertising Research*, vol. 35, no. 6, pp. 29–41.

Kuhn, T. (1970) *The Structure of Scientific Revolutions*, Chicago, University of Chicago Press.

Kunda, G. (1992) *Engineering Culture: control and commitment in a high-tech corporation*, Philadelphia, PA, Temple University Press.

Larsen, H.H., Mick, D.G. and Alsted, C. (1991) *Marketing and Semiotics: Selected Papers From the Copenhagen Symposium*, Copenhagen, Handelshøjskolens Forlag.

Latour, B. and Woolgar, S. (1979) *Laboratory Life*, London, Sage.

Lavidge, R.J. and Steiner, G.A. (1961) 'A model for predictive measurements of advertising effectiveness', *Journal of Marketing*, vol. 25, October, pp. 59–62.

Leach, E. (1976) *Culture and Communication: the logic by which symbols are connected – an introduction to the use of structuralist analysis in social anthropology*, Cambridge, Cambridge University Press.

Letiche, H. (2002) 'Viagra(ization) or Technoromanticism', *Consumption, Markets and Culture*, vol. 5, no. 3, pp. 247–60.

Lyotard, J.-F. (1984) *The Postmodern Condition: a report on knowledge*, trans. G. Bennington and B. Massumi, Minneapolis, MN, University of Minnesota Press.

Malinowski, B. (1922) *Argonauts of the Western Pacific*, London, Routledge and Kegan Paul.

McCracken, G. (1986) 'Culture and consumption: a theoretical account of the structure and movement of the cultural meaning of consumer goods', *Journal of Consumer Research*, vol. 3, no. 1, pp. 71–84.

Meamber, L. and Venkatesh, A. (1995) 'Discipline and practice: A postmodern critique of marketing as constituted by the work of Philip Kotler', in B. Stern and G.M. Zinkhan (eds) *Enhancing Knowledge Development in Marketing*, vol. 6, pp. 248–53.

Merleau-Ponty, M. (1962a) *Experience and Objective Thought: The problem of the body*, New York, Routledge.

—— (1962b) *Phenomenology of Perception*, London, Routledge.

Metz, C. (1974) *Film Language: A Semiotics of the Cinema*, New York, Oxford University Press.

Mick, D.G. (1986) 'Consumer research and semiotics: exploring the morphology of signs, symbols and significance', *Journal of Consumer Research*, vol. 13, September, pp. 180–97.

—— (1997) 'Semiotics in marketing and consumer research: balderdash, verity, pleas', Chapter 8 in S. Brown and D. Turley (eds) *Consumer Research: Postcards from the Edge*, London, Routledge, pp. 249–62.

Mick, D.G. and Buhl, C. (1992) 'A meaning-based model of advertising experiences', *Journal of Consumer Research*, vol. 19, December, pp. 317–38.

Mills, S. (1997) *Discourse*, London, Routledge.

Morgan, G. (1992) 'Marketing discourse and practice: towards a critical analysis', Chapter 7 in M. Alvesson and H. Willmotts (eds) *Critical Management Studies*, London, Sage, pp. 136–58.

Morgan, G. and Smircich, L. (1980) 'The case for qualitative research', *Academy of Management Review*, vol. 5, pp. 491–500.

Moscovici, S. (1984) 'The phenomenon of social representations', in R.M. Farr and S. Moscovici (eds) *Social Representations*, Cambridge, Cambridge University Press.

Mumby-Croft, R. and Hackley, C. (1997) 'The social construction of market entrepreneurship: A case analysis in the UK fishing industry', *Marketing Education Review*, Fall, vol. 7, no. 3, pp. 87–94.

Munro, R. (1997) 'Connection/Disconnection: Theory and Practice in Organizational Control', *British Journal of Management*, vol. 8, pp. 43–63.

Murray, J.B. and Ozanne, J.L. (1991) 'The critical imagination: emancipatory interests in consumer research', *Journal of Consumer Research*, vol. 18, no. 2, pp. 129–44.

Murray, J.B., Ozanne, J.L. and Shapiro, J.L. (1994) 'Revitalising the critical imagination: unleashing the crouched tiger', *Journal of Consumer Research*, vol. 21, pp. 559–65.

Parker, I. (1992) *Discourse Dynamics: Critical Analysis for Social and Individual Psychology*, London, Routledge.

Patterson, M. and Elliott, R. (2002) 'Negotiating masculinities: advertising and the inversion of the male gaze', *Consumption, Markets and Culture*, vol. 21, no. 3, pp. 231–49.

Peirce, C.S. (1953–66) *Collected Papers*, C. Hartshorne, P. Weiss and A.W. Burks (eds), Cambridge, MA, Harvard University Press.

—— (1986) 'Logic as semiotic: the theory of signs', in R.E. Innis (ed) *Semiotics: An Introductory Reader*, London, Hutchinson.

Peters, T. and Waterman, R. (1982) *In Search of Excellence*, New York, Harper and Row.

Potter, J. and Wetherell, M. (1987), *Discourse and Social Psychology*, London, Sage.

Ritson, M. and Elliott, R. (1999) 'The social uses of advertising: an ethnographic study of adolescent advertising audiences', *Journal of Consumer Research*, vol. 26, no. 3, pp. 260–77.

Ritzer, G. (2000) *The McDonaldization of Society*, New Century Edition, Thousand Oaks, CA, Pine Forge Press, Sage.

Rogers, C. (1945) 'The non-directive method as a technique for social research', *American Journal of Sociology*, vol. 50, pp. 279–83.

Rorty, R. (1982) *Consequences of Pragmatism*, Minneapolis, MN, University of Minnesota Press.

Rust, L. (1993) 'Observations: Parents and their children shopping together', *Journal of Advertising Research*, vol. July/August, pp. 65–70.

Said, E. (1978) *Orientalism*, London, Routledge and Kegan Paul.

Sartre, J.-P. (1943) *Being and Nothingness*, London, Methuen (1958 edition).

—— (1946) *Existentialism and Humanism*, trans. Philip Mairet, London, Methuen (1990 edition).

Saussure, F. de (1915) *Course in General Linguistics*, trans. W. Baskin, London, Fontana (1974 edition).

Schutz, A. (1932) *The Phenomenology of the Social World*, London, Heinemann (1967 edition).

Scott, L. (1990) 'Understanding jingles and needledrop: a rhetorical approach to music in advertising, *Journal of Consumer Research*, vol. 17, pp. 223–36.

—— (1994a) 'Images in advertising: the need for a theory of visual rhetoric', *Journal of Consumer Research*, vol. 21, pp. 252–73.

—— (1994b) 'The bridge from text to mind: Adapting reader-response theory to consumer research', *Journal of Consumer Research*, vol. 21, pp. 461–80.

Sebeok, T. (1991) *A Sign is Just a Sign*, Bloomington and Indianapolis, Indiana University Press.

Shankar, A. (2000) 'Lost in Music? Subjective personal introspection and popular music consumption', *Qualitative Market Research: An International Journal*, vol. 3, no. 1, pp. 27–37.

Shankar, A. and Goulding, C. (2001), 'Interpretive consumer research: two more contributions to theory and practice', *Qualitative Market Research: An International Journal*, vol. 4, no. 1, pp. 7–16.

Shankar, A., Elliott, R. and Goulding, C. (2001) 'Understanding Consumption: contributions from a narrative perspective', *Journal of Marketing Management*, vol. 17, pp. 429–53.

Sherry, J.F. (1991) 'Postmodern alternatives: The interpretive turn in consumer research', in T.S. Robertson and H.H. Kassarjian (eds) *Handbook of Consumer Behaviour*, Englewood-Cliffs, NJ, Prentice-Hall, pp. 548–91.

Sherry, J.F. and Camargo, G. (1987) ' "May Your Life Be Marvellous": English language labelling and the semiotics of Japanese promotion', *Journal of Consumer Research*, vol. 14, September, pp. 174–88.

Sherry, J.F. and Schouten, J.W. (2002) 'A role for poetry in consumer research', *Journal of Consumer Research*, vol. 29, September, pp. 218–34.

Spiggle, S. (1994) 'Analysis and interpretation of qualitative data in consumer research', *Journal of Consumer Research*, vol. 21, December, pp. 491–503.

Spradley, J. (1980) *Participant Observation*, New York, Holt, Rinehart and Winston.

Stern, B.B. (1989) 'Literary criticism and consumer research: overview and illustrative analysis', *Journal of Consumer Research*, vol. 16, pp. 34–46.

—— (1990) 'Literary criticism and the history of marketing thought: A new perspective on "reading" marketing theory', *Journal of the Academy of Marketing Science*, vol. 18, pp. 329–36.

—— (1993) 'Feminist literary criticism and the deconstruction of Ads: A postmodern view of advertising and consumer responses', *Journal of Consumer Research*, vol. 19, pp. 556–66.

Stern, B.B. and Schroeder, J. (1994), 'Interpretative methodology from art and literary criticism: A humanistic approach to advertising imagery', *European Journal of Marketing*, vol. 28, no. 8.

Stern, B.B., Thompson, C. and Arnould, E. (1998) 'Narrative analysis of marketing relationship: the consumer's perspective', *Psychology and Marketing*, vol. 15, no. 3, pp. 195–214.

Stubbs, M. (1983) *Discourse Analysis: The Sociolinguistic Analysis of Natural Language*, Oxford, Basil Blackwell.

Szmigin, I. and Carrigan, M. (2001) 'Time, consumption and the older consumer: an interpretive study of the cognitively young', *Psychology and Marketing*, vol. 18, no. 10, pp. 1091–116.

Tanaka, K. (1994) *Advertising Language: a pragmatic approach to advertisements in Britain and Japan*, London, Routledge.

Thomas, J. (1993) *Doing Critical Ethnography*, Newbury Park, CA, Sage.

Thompson, C.J., Locander, W.B. and Pollio, H.R. (1989) 'Putting consumer experience back into consumer research: The philosophy and method of existential phenomenology', *Journal of Consumer Research*, vol. 17, pp. 133–47.

—— (1990) 'The lived meaning of free choice: An existential–phenomenological description of everyday consumer experiences of contemporary married women', *Journal of Consumer Research*, vol. 17, December, pp. 346–61.

Thompson, C.J., Pollio, H.R. and Locander, W.B. (1994) 'The spoken and the unspoken: A hermeneutic approach to understanding the cultural viewpoints that underlie consumers' expressed meanings', *Journal of Consumer Research*, vol. 21, December, pp. 431–53.

Tonks, D. (2002) 'Marketing as cooking: The return of the sophists', *Journal of Marketing Management*, vol. 18, pp. 803–22.

Umiker-Sebeok, J. (ed.) (1987) *Marketing Signs: New Directions in the Study of Signs for Sale*, Berlin, Mouton.

Umiker-Sebeok, J., Cossette, C. and Bachand, D. (1988) 'Selected bibliography on the semiotics of marketing', *Semiotic Enquiry*, vol. 8, no. 3, pp. 415–23.

Vakratsas, D. and Ambler, T. (1999) 'How advertising works: What do we really know?', *Journal of Marketing*, vol. 63, January, pp. 26–43.

Van Mannen, J. (ed.) (1995) *Representation in Ethnography*, Thousand Oaks, CA, Sage.

Watson, T.J. (1994) *In Search of Management: Culture, chaos and control in managerial work*, London, Routledge.

Wernick, A. (1991) *Promotional Culture: Advertising, Ideology and Symbolic Expression*, London, Newbury Park, Sage.

Williamson, J. (1978) *Decoding Advertisements: Ideology and Meaning in Advertisements*, London, Marion Boyars.

Woolgar, S. (1981) 'Interests and explanation in the social studies of science', *Social Studies of Science*, vol. 11, pp. 365–94.

—— (1988) *Science: the Very Idea*, Chichester, Ellis Horwood, London, Tavistock.

—— (1989) 'The ideology of representation and the role of the agent', in H. Lawson and L. Appignanesi (eds) *Dismantling Truth: Reality in the Post-Modern World*, London, Weidenfield and Nicolson.

Wright, S. (ed.) (1994) *Anthropology of Organisations*, London, Routledge.

Zeman, J.J. (1977) 'Peirce's theory of signs', in T. Sebeok (ed.) *A Perfusion of Signs*, Bloomington, IN, Indiana University Press, pp. 22–39.

Index